Johann Friedrich Agricola published his *Introduction to the Art of Singing* in Germany in 1757. It brought to a German readership the 1723 treatise of the Italian singing teacher and castrato, Tosi, to which Agricola added his own running commentary. The *Introduction* was recognized as invaluable not only for teachers and their pupils but also for advanced singers and professionals. Charles Burney, for example, described it as "the best book on the subject in German," and hailed the author as "the best singing master in Germany." This present edition, translated with introduction and annotations by the celebrated singer Julianne Baird, makes Agricola's work available for the first time in English. Tosi's work was the first basic treatise on singing: it codified important aesthetic principles and gave practical directions for the singers of his time. Agricola, a pupil of J. S. Bach, addressed the style of singing at the court of Frederick the Great and brought Tosi's work up to date. His commentaries are so extensive that the *Introduction* stands on its own as an important document in the history of performance practice.

CAMBRIDGE MUSICAL TEXTS
AND MONOGRAPHS

Introduction to the Art of Singing
by Johann Friedrich Agricola

CAMBRIDGE MUSICAL TEXTS AND MONOGRAPHS

General Editors: John Butt and Laurence Dreyfus

The series Cambridge Musical Texts and Monographs has as its centers of interest the history of performance and the history of instruments. It includes annotated translations of important historical documents, authentic historical texts on music, and monographs on various aspects of historical performance.

Published titles

Rebecca Harris-Warrick (trans. and ed.)   *Principles of the Harpsichord by Monsieur de Saint Lambert*

Ian Woodfield   *The Early History of the Viol*

Robin Stowell   *Violin Technique and Performance Practice in the late Eighteenth and early Nineteenth Centuries*

Vincent J. Panetta (trans. and ed.)   *Treatise on Harpsichord Tuning by Jean Denis*

John Butt   *Bach Interpretation: Articulation Marks in Primary Sources of J. S. Bach*

Grant O'Brien   *Ruckers: A Harpsichord and Virginal Building Tradition*

Christopher Page (trans. and ed.)   *Summa musice: A Thirteenth-Century Manual for Singers*

Ardal Powell (trans. and ed.)   *The Virtuoso Flute Player by Johann George Tromlitz*

Keith Polk   *German Instrumental Music in the Late Middle Ages*

Beth Bullard (trans. and ed.)   *Musica getutscht: A Treatise on Musical Instruments by Sebastian Virdung*

David Rowland   *A History of Pianoforte Pedalling*

John Butt   *Music Education and the Art of Performance in the German Baroque*

William E. Hettrick (trans. and ed.)   *The "Musica instrumentalis deudsch" of Martin Agricola*

Rebecca Harris-Warrick and Carol Marsh   *Musical Theatre at the Court of Louis XIV: Le Mariage de la Grosse Cathos*

Stewart Pollens   *The Early Pianoforte*

Introduction to the Art of Singing by Johann Friedrich Agricola

Translated and edited by

JULIANNE C. BAIRD

Rutgers University

CAMBRIDGE
UNIVERSITY PRESS

Published by the Press Syndicate of the University of Cambridge
The Pitt Building, Trumpington Street, Cambridge CB2 1RP
40 West 20th Street, New York, NY 10011–4211, USA
10 Stamford Road, Oakleigh, Melbourne 3166, Australia

© Cambridge University Press 1995

First published 1995

Printed in Great Britain at the University Press, Cambridge

A catalogue record for this book is available from the British Library

Library of Congress cataloguing in publication data

Tosi, Pier Francesco, ca. 1653–1732.
[Opinioni de' cantori antichi e moderni. English]
Introduction to the art of singing / by Johann Friedrich Agricola; translated and edited by Julianne C. Baird.
    p.   cm. – (Cambridge musical texts and monographs)
Translation of: Anleitung zur Singkunst: aus dem italiänischen des Herrn Peter Franz Tosi / mit Erläuterungen und Zusätzen von Johann Friedrich Agricola (Berlin: G. L. Winter, 1757).
Includes bibliographical references (p.) and index.
ISBN 0 521 45428 X (hardback)
1. Singing. 2. Performance practice (Music) – 17th century. 3. Performance practice (Music) – 18th century. I. Agricola, Johann Friedrich, 1720–1774. II. Baird, Julianne. III. Title. IV. Title: Anleitung zur Singkunst. V. Series.
MT892.T6713 1995
783'.043–dc20   94–11416 CIP

ISBN 0 521 45428 X hardback

Contents

Acknowledgments   *page* ix

Introduction: Agricola's treatise   1

INTRODUCTION TO THE ART OF SINGING   39

Translator's preface   40

Foreword of the author   43
Introduction of the author   45
  1 Observations for the use of the singing teacher   51
  2 Concerning appoggiaturas   88
  3 Concerning trills   126
  4 Concerning divisions   151
  5 Concerning recitative   171
  6 Remarks intended especially for the music student 183
  7 Concerning arias   188
  8 Concerning cadenzas   205
  9 Remarks for the use of the professional singer   216
10 Concerning improvised variations of melodies   232

Notes   239
Bibliography   280
Index   288

Acknowledgments

I wish to express my heartfelt thanks to all who assisted and supported me in this project: George Houle, my advisor and mentor, for his encouragement; William Mahrt and Leonard Ratner, my readers, who together with Dr. Houle corrected my drafts; Eleanor Beers, who untiringly aided in checking and re-checking the translation; Gary Harney, who prepared the musical examples; Laurence Dreyfus, whose suggestions for improvement were invaluable; Hildegard Schnüttgen, Head Reference Librarian, Maag Library, who rendered bibliographic assistance; T. A. Copeland, who suggested stylistic improvements; and especially L. Y. Lange, English Department, Youngstown State University, who served as research, translation, and style consultant from beginning of the project to the end. All errors are my own responsibility. Also I wish to thank my mother for being my "house advisor" and coming to my aid to solve countless problems over the four years it took to complete this work; and my family, Terry, Jessica, and Luke, for their long-suffering patience, support, and help.

I owe a special debt of gratitude to Rutgers University, Camden, for financial assistance in the Henry Rutgers Fellow grant and the Board of Trustees Award; and to Wilbert Jerome, Chair of the Music Department, for inspiration, impetus, and careful scheduling.

Introduction: Agricola's treatise

On 16 April 1755, an advertisement appeared in Marpurg's *Historisch-kritische Beyträge*[1] requesting subscriptions for a book on the art of singing (*Die Kunst zu singen*) that Johann Freidrich Agricola intended to publish. The book appeared two years later, in 1757. It was called *Anleitung zur Singkunst* and consisted of a translation of Pier Francesco Tosi's 1723 Italian treatise[2] *Opinioni de' cantori antichi e moderni* (reflecting the *bel canto* style), with a running commentary by Agricola. Agricola's *Anleitung* soon came to be recognized as invaluable not only for teachers and beginning students, but also for advanced students and professional singers. Charles Burney, for example, described it as "the best book on the subject in German,"[3] and hailed its author as "the best singing master in Germany."[4] The present volume makes Agricola's work available for the first time in English.

By 1757 the work of Tosi (a famous castrato as well as a singing teacher) was already considered out of date in a musical world of rapidly changing styles and tastes. Nevertheless, Tosi had made an important contribution in writing the first basic treatise on singing in the modern sense. He codified important aesthetic principles and gave practical directions for the singers of his time. He defended the ancient style against the moderns, who had lost interest in counterpoint, favoring fast mechanical divisions and interminable virtuosic cadenzas.

Beyond making Tosi's *Opinioni* available, Agricola's chief contribution to the art of singing consists in his commentaries bringing Tosi "up to date," especially in the elaborate discussions of ornamentation, which reflect the tastes and aesthetics of the court of Frederick the Great in Berlin, and in the musical examples to illustrate both his own and Tosi's teachings. It may appear strange to publish a translation of

1

a translation,[5] especially since an English translation of Tosi already exists, but Agricola's commentaries and emendations to Tosi are so extensive that, in fact, the *Anleitung* stands on its own as an important document in the history of performance practice.

The first really useful book on singing to appear in German, the *Anleitung* addressed a serious lack in the musical life of Agricola's countrymen. Treatises published earlier,[6] to use his own words, were not only "incomplete (if one can for a moment ignore their mistakes) in that they contain only the basic rudiments of music – the names of the notes, their values, a few essential ornaments, and few exercises for practice – but they neglect even to mention that which is indispensable to the development of a good singer."[7] Agricola had not been alone in his concern about the dearth of treatises on singing and the deplorable state of musical training in Germany. Because of Graun's complaints about the level of the musical training of the boy chorus that provided singers for the opera chorus, Frederick II in 1746 issued a *Cabinetsordre* directed at bettering the musical education of children in schools: "Having received many complaints of the decline in the art of singing, and the neglect of it in our gymnasiums and schools, His Majesty commands that the young people in all public schools and gymnasiums shall be exercised more diligently therein, and to that end shall have singing lessons three times a week."[8]

Agricola greatly expanded the scope of Tosi's original treatise and tailored it to a wider German audience. Despite his perception that at times Tosi's language was whimsical, awkward or difficult, he maintained an appreciative and respectful attitude towards his author almost always translating him as faithfully as possible; but whereas Tosi wrote primarily for the castrato, Agricola addressed his remarks to both male and female singers, developing and refining Tosi's advice with explanations and musical examples, and yet often taking issue with Tosi's thinking. Traditionally, Italian opera singers, especially the highly paid and respected castrati of Tosi's day, were trained in the art of impromptu ornamentation and expected to override the composer in matters of ornamentation. Thus, the ongoing Italian–German dichotomy of improvisatory freedom versus prescribed composition is here reflected in whether the singer is expected to improvise his ornamentation for the da capo according to Tosi's precepts or whether this was to be written out by the composer according to the philosophy of Frederick and his court composers. Whereas Tosi adamantly supports the singer's right and duty to improvise the ornamentation, Agricola defended the composer's right to notate ornamentation and thereby limit the singer's freedom of improvisation. Agricola was in sympathy with Tosi's hated moderns, especially with respect to having the composer or the singer craft beforehand the supposedly improvised da capo ornamentation; with respect to the rejection of the Guidonian solmization in favor of simpler solmization methods; and with respect to the style of the cadenza. Also, in the spirit of the Enlightenment, Agricola provided copious scientific conjecture on matters of the physiology of the human voice, while Tosi dealt not at all with vocal science, but only with vocal art.

Agricola wished to disseminate the Italian *bel canto* style in his native country, since Italian singers were so fashionable at most of the courts of Europe. At the Berlin court, where Agricola was employed, excellent German singers were forced to go outside Germany to find work; and, in fact, almost all of the German singers mentioned in Agricola's Translator's Preface had made their names in countries other than Germany. Also, certain German composers such as Handel and Hasse had been able to achieve both international status and the long-lasting respect of their German colleagues by assimilating the Italian traditions. German singers and composers who chose to remain at home faced great inequities of employment availability and salary, for a native singer might expect to receive only a small fraction of the astonishing fees paid to Italian singers at most of the European courts. An anonymous critic bitterly complained to Johann Mattheson: "When will we give up our blind worship of foreigners and learn to judge our own countrymen fairly! If we sought the best voices in our schools ... and then gave these students a livelihood while they studied with good teachers; if, when they had learned to sing, we paid them decent salaries – I wager that Germany would produce more fine musicians of both sexes than any other country in the world ... Because of such circumstances, our best performers leave the country in shocking numbers, while wretched Italians are accorded great honor."[9] Although Italian influence on German musical pedagogy had been felt since the seventeenth century in works by Christoph Bernhard and Michael Praetorius, Agricola makes available an updated and far more expansive document on the Italian pedagogical style than any of his predecessors.

AGRICOLA'S LIFE AND ACHIEVEMENT

Johann Friedrich Agricola was born on 4 January 1720, in the village of Dobitschen in the Altenburg countryside, son of Johann Christoph Agricola (princely Kammeragent) and Maria Magdalena Agricola (née Maneke). At his family's encouragement, he began instruction in music at the age of five, especially in keyboard and organ, under Johann Paul Martini.[10]

On 29 May 1738, Agricola matriculated at the University of Leipzig as a student of jurisprudence, history, and philosophy. While a student in Leipzig, he heard the greatly renowned Dresden orchestra in performances of two of Hasse's Passion cantatas and, more importantly, he received instruction in keyboard playing from Johann Sebastian Bach, for whom he served as a copyist and harpsichordist for the church cantatas. Inspired by the Dresden orchestra and encouraged by this master's confidence in him, Agricola resolved to devote himself to his interest in music.

Agricola moved to Berlin in 1741, where he quickly established a reputation for excellence in organ playing. Here he took lessons in composition with Quantz, and studied the works of Handel and Telemann. Also, Agricola was befriended in the early Berlin years by Carl Philipp Emanuel Bach (with whom he collaborated in writing the necrology [1754] of his teacher J. S. Bach). In 1751, the monarch Frederick II, a passionate lover of music, employed Agricola as a well-paid *Hofcomponist* (court composer) in his Royal Berlin Opera.[11]

An aspiring composer and an accomplished flutist himself, Frederick, upon ascendancy to the throne in 1740, lost no time in implementing his ambitious plans for a national opera in Berlin. While building the impressive opera house, which opened in 1742, Frederick sent envoys to France and Italy to hold auditions and hire the best performers. Believing that different nations excelled in individual aspects of the fine arts, for his Royal Opera Frederick hired exclusively German composers (though most of them had had training abroad); exclusively French dancers; and mostly Italian singers.[12] Frederick held a low opinion of Italian music for the opera but because he employed mostly Italian singers and acknowledged the greater ease for singing proffered by the Italian language, he mandated that the opera libretti be in Italian (many by Metastasio) and set to music by German composers.[13] A happy result, of course, was the creation of employment in their native land for such German composers and instrumentalists at Quantz, C. P. E. Bach, Karl Heinrich Graun, and Agricola. Agricola's own operas were performed alongside those of Graun and Hasse and he worked regularly with well-regarded artists including Carl Friedrich Christian Fasch (harpsichordist and composer), Johann Gottlieb Graun (composer and violinist and brother of the Capellmeister Karl Heinrich Graun), and other chief musicians in Frederick's orchestras. Frederick sought the most skilled practitioners available and paid them well. In this sense Agricola had a favorable environment in which to work.

On the other hand, Frederick's artistic control – which, out of his concern for "good taste," he exercised over his "troops" – limited the creativity of all his composers, and was suffocating to a genius such as C. P. E. Bach. Burney remarks of Frederick's legendary authoritarianism: "in the opera house, as in the field, his majesty is such a rigid disciplinarian, that if a mistake is made in a single movement or evolution, he immediately marks, and rebukes the offender; and if any of his Italian troops dare to deviate from strict discipline, by adding, altering or diminishing a single passage in the parts they have to perform, an order is sent, *de par le Roi*, for them to adhere strictly to the notes written by the composer, at their peril."[14] Frederick often brusquely ordered changes in the arias or recitatives of his composers, chiefly those of Agricola and Graun. Frederick sought to "protect" their music from "tasteless"[15] ornamentation by his troops of Italian singers. In one instance, after a series of unsuccessful corrections aimed at pleasing the King, Graun, to his embarrassment, was forced to substitute an aria by Hasse. Agricola, too, fell victim to Frederick's cruel scrutiny. Once, having viewed the rehearsals for Agricola's opera *Amor e Psiche* (1767), the King gave his attendant Pöllnitz written instructions: "You will tell Agricola that he must change all of Coli's arias – they are worthless – as well as those of Romani, along with the recitatives, which are deplorable from one end to the other."[16] After Frederick gave Agricola the duties, but *not* the title, of Capellmeister when Graun died in 1759, the King even more openly and harshly criticized Agricola's operas. Frederick firmly controlled his composers in the interest of taste and cared little how he humiliated them.

Artistic excellence in music, especially in ornamentation, and the concept of "good taste" occupied treatise writers of the Berlin circle throughout the eighteenth century. Under Frederick's influence, they rejected the Italian principle that the very essence of ornamentation, always a significant aspect of music, lies in the artistic interpretation and expression of the individual performer. Quantz, Agricola, Marpurg, and C. P. E. Bach examine, explain, and regulate almost every possible aspect of the ornamental style which constituted this "taste." Frederick Neumann says that the new ornamental fashions "crystallized in ... the 'Berlin School.' The word 'crystallized' is singularly evocative of what happened here: the hardening of a fluid mass into solid and rigid shapes."[17] Among these treatises, Agricola's *Anleitung* best illustrates the tension between the free Italian spirit of creativity versus the regimentation advocated by the Berlin school, and this is particularly evident in his chapter dealing with the appoggiatura.

Under Frederick, Agricola suffered both professionally and personally. In 1751, Agricola's marriage to one of Frederick's Italian *prime donne*, Benedetta Emilia Molteni, broke one of the King's cardinal rules – that female singers or dancers not marry – and angered the monarch, prompting him to severely cut their joint salary. More stultifying than this personal distress was the fact that Frederick despised and discouraged Agricola's beloved church music.[18] (Frederick believed that composing church music tainted the taste of a composer and ruined him for composing in the theatrical style. Despite the King's disapproval, however, Agricola composed numerous pieces for the church, some published during his lifetime.) Even worse, he had to endure Frederick's biting criticism of his operatic compositions and the withholding of the titular promotion to Capellmeister. Frederick's disregard for Agricola and his wife was later manifested in the heartless dismissal of Benedetta Emilia Agricola without pension upon her husband's death. Eugene Helm[19] views Agricola's career as one that was nurtured and fostered by Frederick, only to be later "blighted" and stultified by him.

Frederick's tyranny may have caused Agricola to omit the following paragraph (found in Galliard) from his Tosi translation, for fear that the King would take umbrage: "My long and repeated Travels have given me an Opportunity of being acquainted with most of the Courts of *Europe*, and Examples, more than my Words, should persuade every able Singer to see them also; but without yielding up his Liberty to their Allurements: For Chains, though of Gold are still Chains; and they are not all of that precious Metal ..."[20]

Despite his uneasy relationship with Frederick, Agricola was regarded as a prominent musical personage in his own time and after his death in 1774. Carl Friedrich Cramer in 1786 described him as "one of our most thoughtful musicians" and a "discerning theorist."[21] Agricola's versatility allowed him to function in many capacities. As a tenor singer, his name appears before 1755 with some frequency in the *dramatis personae* of various operas and musical events; and he was considered the "best organ-player in Berlin."[22] As a composer of operas, he developed Frederick's skeletal sketches into compositions; and he composed his own Italian operas for use in the Royal Opera House.

Agricola is, however, most famous for his writings on music. In *Schreiben an Herrn*, a pamphlet written under an Italian pseudonym, he engaged in a biting literary controversy with Marpurg in support of German composers (but not of German as a language for singing).[23] In 1765 at the founding of the *Allgemeine Deutsche Bibliothek*, Agricola was appointed permanent collaborator on musical subjects for the *ADB* – a post he retained until his death. In addition, he wrote notes and comments for Jacob Adlung's *Musica mechanica organoedi*,[24] a major source of information on German eighteenth-century organs. In his most important work, the *Anleitung*, he may be seen working constructively to improve the training of singers and to make performing conditions happier for his fellow-countrymen. Agricola was a musician, composer, theorist, and critic of historic importance in the Berlin court of Frederick II and in Germany at large. In the *Anleitung* he also established himself as the first and foremost German writer of his time on the art of singing.

AGRICOLA'S ADDITIONS TO TOSI'S TEXT

Throughout the *Anleitung zur Singkunst*, Agricola elucidates his careful translation of Tosi's *Opinioni*, not only with short explanatory notes, but also with voluminous original commentaries in which he presents his own opinions and research on theoretical or "scientific" matters, makes observations on taste and refinement in music and gives suggestions for practical training accompanied copiously by musical examples. In the first chapter of the *Anleitung*, of which Tosi's work constitutes about only one-fourth, Agricola expands various of Tosi's subjects most fully: solmization, vocal physiology and phonation, the registers, the appearance of the singer, pitch, and the *messa di voce*.

In his thoroughgoing scholarly fashion, Agricola provides a very detailed analysis of solmization[25] replete with musical examples and charts, to reflect Italian teaching methods accurately even though this complicated system of mutation was falling into disfavor and Agricola himself questions its value. During Tosi's day, an Italian youth would have spent an entire year learning solmization. Under the teacher's tutelage, he performed scales of long notes pronouncing the appropriate syllable, or syllables for each note, learning also how to "mutate," a process that involved changing hexachords when the scale or melody he was singing exceeded the range of a single hexachord. Agricola calls this *Änderungen der Namen der Töne* (the changing of the names of the tones).[26] Besides teaching the student pitches and their names, the three basic hexachords, the modes and their application, and the method of mutating or changing from one hexachord to another, Italian masters believed these exercises in solmization would also strengthen the voice, develop stamina to sustain the long notes, improve the intonation, increase the ability to control a steady pitch, and exercise the student in the formation of four of the five vowels (*ut* being changed to *do* to make it easier to sing) that he would need later when singing with text. Agricola himself feels that intonation is *not* improved by solmization; however, he sees the Italian vowels as helpful to the student in achieving good pronunciation, while the German vowels (*e* as in "get" and *i* as in "hit"), he says, are not helpful but are, in fact, not even "comfortable to sing."[27] Despite efforts by Italian pedagogues and writers to simplify and incorporate the seven-note major–minor scale system into the practice of solmization, Italian singers were still required to become familiar with the cumbersome process of mutation well into the late eighteenth century, as the following 1780 comment of Hiller reveals: "In the Italian schools, they solomize [sic] alone for over one year; i.e., they sing with letters and the Guidian [sic] syllables."[28] In Germany a controversy over this issue had been going on much earlier with Profe and Burmeister but the debate heated up early in the eighteenth century and by 1757 (the date of Agricola's *Anleitung*) several systems existed to replace the antiquated Guidonian format. Mattheson in *Das Neu-eröffnete Orchestre* (1713) had indicated a preference for the newer French and Italian styles of secular music together with a new pedagogical style that involved a simplified system of solmization. On the other hand, Buttstedt[29] (Agricola's chief source for his explanation of the modes) had defended the traditional method of teaching solmization. Although the *Anleitung* provides what Marpurg considered one of the clearest and best organized presentations of the Guidonian system,[30]

Agricola's motive, however, is that of the careful historian and not that of the advocate. Indeed he questions (*Anleitung*, p. 7) whether the results of the study of mutation were worth the time and expense.

In the earliest and most extensive treatment of vocal physiology and phonation in the history of German vocal treatises, Agricola, in his note (o),[31] first presents a theory of sound not unlike modern theory, and then he attempts to explain vocal physiology, voice production, the registers (the head voice and the chest voice), and related matters. Although he passes over important problems and some of his work is confused (that which is based on erroneous received tradition), his thoroughness in other matters is impressive. He goes back to the ancients, Galen and Aristotle, researching the theory through eighteenth-century thinkers such as Dodart, Krüger and Heuermann, and finally summarizing the most recent and most reliable scientific work on the vocal cords by Ferrein, a contemporary French scientist.[32] Without trying to resolve discrepancies, he recognizes Ferrein's theories at the end of his discussion, and seems inclined to accept them, while cautiously awaiting the verdict of the other scientists. Wichmann praises Agricola's work as the first German vocal research to have examined the connection between breathing and laryngeal function. Even though he did not succeed entirely, one must be impressed, Wichmann says, by the results of his (by today's standards) primitive research method.[33] To Agricola's credit, he presents himself as a practical musician rather than as a scientist. He does not claim that an understanding of the anatomical details, etc. will greatly improve the singer's performance[34] but (in the spirit of the Enlightenment and in the interest of scholarly definitiveness) he presents an objective research summary on vocal physiology and function without adding anything new himself. His work on physiology and phonation is a historical curiosity peripheral to performance[35] and can be passed over without further comment.

Closely related to the physical structure and phonation is the matter of the registers, another basic subject Agricola treats in chapter 1. In literature on the human voice one sees even today much confusion on vocal registration. In untrained voices a sharp "register break" can be easily identified by a change in tone quality and pitch as the voice moves up the scale, as, for example, in the contrast between the natural male chest voice and the head voice, and in a similar phenomenon in the female voice. It is now commonly accepted that register changes occur in the larynx and not in the head or chest.[36] Tosi himself recognizes two major voice classifications: the *voce di petto* and the *voce di testa*. To make the matter more clear for any reader who might be confused or need to be able to identify the falsetto range in actual practice, Tosi gives a formula for discovering the falsetto in one who can disguise it: the singer, he explains, will be able to sound the *i* with more strength and less fatigue than the *a* in the high notes. In modern terminology, this probably means that for the *i* vowel the singer will find it easier to sing a high note using the "light mechanism." Agricola's treatment of the head and chest voice is not exclusively concerned with the castrato, as Tosi's largely was, but rather attempts to explore the phenomenon in all singers. Drawn first from Galen, then from Ferrein, his explanations are naturally at variance with each other. Though he identifies the questions he leaves them unresolved.

Many of Agricola's perceptions, particularly when they come from empirical evidence and his own experience, are still recognized as valid, however. He understands, for example, as modern science understands,[37] that the term "head voice" is used figuratively and thinks that the Italians confuse (or combine) the head voice with the falsetto. He says that the chest voice, which has more unforced tones than the head voice, is capable of falsetto tones at the lower end of the register just as the head voice is capable of falsetto tones at the upper end of the register. Like modern teachers and performers, both Tosi and Agricola recognize the desirability of a unification of the registers.[38] Tosi directs the student to attain smoothness in the high notes by singing them more softly as he proceeds up the scale; to avoid nasal quality in the head voice and throatiness in the chest voice; to protect his voice by avoiding the sustained forced chest voice in the upper register; and to attain evenness of sound.[39] Agricola urges the student to strive to produce the tone intermediate between the head and the chest voice – the lowest tone of the head voice and the highest tone of the chest voice – with both kinds of voice, one to be used in ascending the scale and the other in descending.[40] But beyond these directions, he gives no systematic method for accomplishing these skills. This task was also undertaken by Mancini[41] and Hiller.[42]

Agricola is widely recognized as an authority on the variation in Europe of pitch levels (which caused hardships for singers)[43] and despite the fact that Sauveur[44] as early as 1700 had advocated a standard pitch, his well-intentioned recommendation had not been adopted even in Agricola's day.[45] Tosi recommends that the singer be trained in the pitch of Lombardy in order to avoid future difficulties that higher pitched instruments might cause him.[46]

Agricola recognizes, however, that merely transposing the arias to a higher or lower key is not the answer. First, since keys have their own unique "colors" or "moods," the aria itself, having been carefully set to a key appropriate to its mood and sense, would suffer in the transposition to another key. Secondly, this transposition into a higher or lower key often involves a great number of sharps or flats, making performance difficult for the instrumentalist. Thirdly, singers also encounter difficulties because "many a passage, or a sustained note, or a certain word or a particular note can be uncomfortable in one tuning and comfortable in another." Difficulties may occur if a piece lingers around the natural break in the voice.[47] It is also well known by singers that it is not always possible to achieve the same happy *tessitura* with transposition.

Agricola also explains the *messa di voce*, another important pedagogical and expressive feature treated by Tosi in his first chapter on Italian singing. Extensive practice of this device was emphasized by the famous voice teacher Porpora[48] and his followers throughout the eighteenth and nineteenth centuries.

The phrase *messa di voce* (placing of the voice) refers to "the singing or playing of a long note so that it begins quietly, swells to full volume, and then diminishes to the original quiet tone."[49] Probably the first writer to actually use the term, Tosi defines the *messa di voce* similarly as "beginning the tone very gently and softly and letting it swell little by little to the loudest forte and thereafter recede with the same artistry from loud to soft." He rebukes singers of his day who, in their rejection of "old-fashioned" style, were neglecting to practice it but he recommends that it be "used sparingly and only on bright vowels."[50] Except for staccato notes or notes demanding vigorous expression, Agricola, on the other hand, recommends that any note of substantial length be "begun softly, then gradually strengthened, or made to swell, and then ended piano."[51] Agricola's ambivalence about German equivalents in the translation of Tosi is seen in the terms he uses: *Schwellung* (swelling), *lange schwellende Aushaltung* (long swelled sustaining)[52] *eine lange Aushaltung* (a long sustaining), and *Herausziehen der Stimme* (drawing forth of the voice). The latter phrase seems to be related to the French term *son filé* (spun-out tone), "presumably because the note is evenly drawn forth from the throat like the thread from the distaff of a spinning wheel."[53]

In his second chapter, Tosi treats the *appoggiatura* – a single ornamental note usually creating a dissonance with the bass. It is often
described as both one of the simplest and yet one of the most complicated of ornaments. The fact that it consists usually of only one note
(except in the case of the compound appoggiatura and the termination) makes it simple; the complications arise because of the rhetorical
implications that these small ornaments can create and the question of
the prerogative of notation versus that of extempore performance.
Mid- and late eighteenth-century composers are generally more precise in notating appoggiaturas for instruments and less precise for
voices even if they are to be played in unison. But in the Berlin School
composers notated precise note values for appoggiaturas in the vocal
part in order to prevent an unplanned consonance or dissonance
(introduced extemporaneously by the singer) from sabotaging the
composer's carefully crafted rhetorical effect or text painting.[54]

Tosi expresses strong frustration with composers who notate these
ornaments and Italian singers who allow them to do so. In particular,
he attacks German composers who advocate exact rhythmic notation.
However, out of deference to Italian singers' expectations of improvisa-
tional freedom, some operatic composers, such as Mozart, while indicating the appoggiaturas, did so with only the most general of rhythmic
values (usually eighth notes), at the same time offering far more precise
rhythmic information for the accompanying unison instruments.

Agricola's annotations to Tosi's observations on the appoggiatura
reflect the "modern" philosophy of the Enlightenment, which sought
logical explanations and scientific justification in questions of art. He
adheres to the taste of the Berlin School in the regularization of the
nomenclature of ornaments, in their manner of notation, and in their
rhythmic performance. Less rigid than C. P. E. Bach but more exacting than Quantz (his sources), Agricola was himself qualified to write
on the matter by virtue of his theoretical knowledge and his expertise
as a keyboard player and singer. He applies this knowledge with particular thoroughness to the singer's art and requirements, at times
even creating his own terminology.

The major difference between Tosi and Agricola, both singers and
also composers, is their position on the freedom of the performer to
improvise his own ornaments. Tosi's belief, pervasive throughout his
writing,[55] is that the singer ought to have enough understanding of
good taste and training in composition and performance to be able to
introduce extemporaneously not only his own appoggiaturas (the easi-

est of all the ornaments), but also other more difficult ornaments. In diametric opposition to this philosophy, Frederick II exercised strict control to insure that even the Italian singers not deviate in the slightest from the written musical text of the German composers, a view that Agricola's writing reflects. Agricola even alludes to notational signs whose sole purpose was to *prevent* the Italian singer from performing an extempore appoggiatura. By the 1750s, a number of Italian composers had joined the German composers in notating the appoggiatura with exact note values. But despite the repeated pleas by German theorists such as Agricola and C. P. E. Bach that composers specify the exact notation of the time value of the appoggiaturas, Italian notational practice continued to be inexact throughout the eighteenth century. In 1789 Türk was still complaining about the lack of uniformity: "Why all composers do not make use of this more certain method of notation is something I do not understand."[56]

Writers of the Berlin School classify appoggiaturas into two types: variable (long) and invariable (short). The variable appoggiaturas were notated by the Berlin writers in exact note values and the invariable with sixteenth or thirty-second notes; whereas in the older Italian style, all appoggiaturas were indicated by eighth notes.[57] For Agricola the appoggiatura must be short (1) if it precedes triplets, (2) if it fills in descending thirds, or (3) if the intention is chiefly to increase the liveliness and the brilliance of the melody,[58] as, for example, when dissonances occur before consonances. Bach identifies[59] and Agricola reiterates three purposes fulfilled by the appoggiatura: (1) better connecting the melody, (2) adding to the movement of an empty melody, and (3) enriching and varying the harmony. Agricola appends a fourth purpose: adding "liveliness and brilliance."[60]

In contrast with the earlier practices of Tosi, the Berlin writers regularized the performance of appoggiaturas, both by making them on the beat and by indicating their exact rhythmic value. Though a few instances of off-the-beat performance were allowed by Quantz, as for example, between falling thirds, the appoggiaturas were usually notated with exact rhythmic value, as advocated by Bach, and performed on the beat, though Bach himself reveals that the rule was frequently broken. Bach, Agricola and other writers maintain that in duple meter the appoggiatura must receive half the value of the main note and in triple meter two-thirds its value; and that if a rest follows or if the main note is tied to another note, the appoggiatura may even occupy the entire time of the main note.

Agricola's rules for the length and placement of appoggiaturas are quite complicated. His practice of piling up two appoggiaturas – the first written as a grace note and the second as a main note – is at odds with Tosi's rule that no appoggiatura may precede another appoggiatura and causes consternation among later writers such as Hiller. Always the careful scholar, Agricola reports on the controversy engaged in by Bach and Quantz on appoggiaturas between descending thirds, the *couler des tierces* of the French style. Whereas Quantz favors the use of this device and recommends that its time value be taken from the time of the previous note, Bach condemns it,[61] disapproving of the confusion that the ambiguous notation created for performers. While Agricola adopts the on-beat rule for most appoggiaturas, in this instance he remains neutral, justifying this exception by his rule that the appoggiatura can serve the purpose of connecting and filling out the melody. The time value of the performance of an appoggiatura before three sixteenth notes was a source of disagreement among several writers of the Berlin school. While Marpurg thought that the figure should be performed as four equal sixteenth notes, Agricola feels that the figure should be rendered very quickly, but on the beat, creating a Lombardic snap.[62]

The *messa di voce crescente*, like the apoggiatura, is a one note dissonant ornament encompassing a half or whole step, and is accordingly introduced by Tosi in the appoggiatura chapter.[63] It consists of a long-sustained note gradually sharpened in pitch, ending on the main note a semitone higher than its starting point. It is distinguished from the simple *messa di voce*[64] consisting of a long note that is gradually swelled and diminished while remaining on the same pitch. Whereas Agricola notes that the *messa di voce crescente* is performed imperceptibly and smoothly without interruption or impulse of the breath until the top note has been reached,[65] Hiller adds that the ornament may both ascend and descend and that the interval must be a minor half step. He recommends the ornament only to the mature singer.

Agricola and Bach both insist that the appoggiatura not interfere with the purity of the voice-leading and that parallels be avoided,[66] and they assign to appoggiaturas a louder dynamic stress than the surrounding notes, but allow the performer to determine the degree of relative loudness. Thus, the appoggiatura, which is normally a dissonance, should be regulated by the same rules that are valid for dissonances: namely, that they be played or sung louder than the consonances.

The compound apoggiatura (*Anschlag*) consists of two small notes which precede a main note (straddling its pitch), with the first pitched a second or larger interval below the main note, and the second pitched a second above the main note.

Quantz urges that singers practice the compound appoggiatura to achieve the high tones.[67] He allows the two notes of the ornament to encompass the interval of a third, while other writers occasionally allow the interval created by the two notes of the compound appoggiaturas to exceed a third. Agricola points out that compound appoggiaturas of larger intervals such as fourths, fifths, sixths, and sevenths are more appropriate for instruments than for voices.[68] The smaller notes should be performed more softly than the main note they precede. The compound appoggiatura may occur before the beat or on the beat and can undergo only two further rhythmic permutations, according to Agricola, but other writers of the time distinguished four different rhythms. In one of its rhythmic forms, the first note of the compound appoggiatura is dotted and the second softer than the first. Agricola suggests, as did Bach, that the dotted compound appoggiatura be generally reserved for slow pieces of an expressive and gentle sentiment. The slower and more expressive the piece, the longer the dotted note is held. Agricola favors execution on the beat and precise notation of the rhythm in small notes.

The Berlin School is the first to distinguish between the even and the dotted slide and to regularize this distinction by the notation. The following statement by Agricola was mystifying to his contemporaries: "The composer often incorporates those [slides] that precede strong beats into the rhythm with regular written-out notes. It is perhaps their three-note configuration, in which two preceding short notes and a longer one are followed by a dot, that has given rise to the so-called Lombardian Taste, which is preferred."[69] Confused by this passage, Türk wrote: "Agricola's remark will probably be intelligible only to a few."[70] He believed that Agricola wanted to restrict to the weak beats those slides which fill a leap. Frederick Neumann has observed, however, that this was not at all Agricola's intention: "This interpretation, which reveals the anapestic character of the slide in question, is fully in line with Agricola's concept of *anschlagende* and *durchgehende Tactglieder* and his wording that the slide itself falls within the weak *Tactglied*." (Actually, when Agricola uses the term *durchgehende Tactglieder*, he simply means that the slide is incorporated before the strong beat.) Neumann believes that Agricola's remarks on the anapest were made because at that time in singing the *cercar della nota* (gliding into a note) is a "spontaneous gesture of the sensitive throat." Neumann warns that "to perform purely connective ornaments immutably accented on the beat is pedantic enough for the keyboard, but runs counter to the very essence of the vocal impulse."[71]

Agricola's thorough and exacting analysis of the appoggiatura, its functions, rhythms and locations, served as a model for German theorists and singers through the end of the century.

Tosi recognizes that the trill[72] (ch. 3) is one of the most important, yet difficult ornaments for many singers.[73] A conservatory student in Tosi's time might have been expected to devote as much as an hour a day to the practice of the trill. It served the practical function of signalling the end of the cadenza and was considered one of the few substitutions for an improvised cadenza, should ingenuity and wit fail the singer.[74] Yet Tosi fails to provide the singer with practice advice or musical exercises for this skill and written-out exercises for perfecting the trill in eighteenth-century vocal treatises are rare. Mancini felt that the singing teacher must "study nature," search the vocal literature for passages, insist on practice, and exercise extreme patience.[75]

It remained for German writers such as Agricola, Mattheson, and Hiller to remedy this deficiency. With his usual thoroughness, Agricola attempts to dispel the shroud of mystery surrounding the trill. He not only gives a specific exercise for the development and achievement of the trill, but he also provides a system of checks by which the teacher and student can determine whether the trill is being properly executed.[76]

Agricola treats Tosi's eight types of trills: the (1) *grösserer Triller (trillo maggiore)*,[77] trill of a whole step;[78] the (2) *kleinerer Triller (trillo minore)*, trill of a half step; the (3) *halber Triller (mezzotrillo)*, half trill; the (4) *höher gezogener Triller (trillo cresciuto)*, rising trill; and the (5) *tiefer werdender Triller (trillo calato)*, falling trill;[79] the (6) *langsamer Triller (trillo lento)*, slow trill; the (7) *verdoppelter Triller (trillo raddoppiato)*,[80] which involves inserting a few different tones in the middle of a longer trill; and the (8) *Mordent (trillo mordente)*, a very short and fast trill that is effective in divisions and after an appoggiatura.[81] Of these only the rising trill, falling trill, and slow trill were obsolete in Tosi's time; the rest were prominent in current performance practice. Beyond Tosi's list of acceptable trills, Agricola introduces another ornament, the *Trillerketten* or *Kette von Trillern* (chain of trills), in which the trill ascends or descends consecutively from one tone of the scale to the next. Agricola is aware that his *Kette von Trillern* (Tosi's rejected *catena di trilli*) and Tosi's "ascending and descending" trills are different ornaments – a matter that Galliard (p. 45) overlooks. Agricola insists that each trill of an ascending chain have "its own clear termination." In this he differs from other German writers, like Mattheson, who believed that no termination should exist and that chains of trills should sound like one extended trill. In the absence of musical examples from Tosi, one issue that has vexed musicologists is the question of whether Tosi's basic trill – the *trillo maggiore*, from which "all others are derived" – should begin with the upper auxiliary or with the main note itself. Neumann makes a convincing argument for the latter, not only because Tosi describes the main note as having "greater forcefulness" (*più padronanza*),[82] but also because of the awkwardness that an auxiliary-begun trill would create for the chain of trills.

A good trill is described by Tosi[83] as *eguale* (equal), *battuto* (beaten),[84] *granito* (distinct), *facile* (flexible), and *moderamente veloce* (moderately quick). Translators and critics of Tosi are not in total agreement *even on the language* of Tosi's description. "Mr. J. A.," his anonymous Dutch translator,[85] and Agricola both ignore the comma that Tosi places between the two adjectives *eguale* and *battuto*, combining the two concepts to mean "equally beaten." Agricola's rendition is "*gleich schlagenden, deutlichen, leichten, und mässig geschwinden*".[86] Galliard (p. 42) ignores the term *battuto* altogether, translating the passage as "equal, distinctly mark'd, easy, and moderately quick." Tosi's terms are, however, separate and must be considered separately.

The term *eguale* refers simply to the volume level of the two notes of the trill in relation to one another. When the two notes of the trill are not sounded equally, the resultant defective trill is often described by eighteenth-century authors as "lame."[87] Agricola would have the student avoid this limping trill by having him or her practice in two stages: first, beginning with the main, or lower, note until mastery has been achieved; and then beginning with the auxiliary, or upper, note of the trill.[88]

The word *battuto* refers to the vocal technique involving the up-and-down movement of the entire larynx itself used in producing the trill[89] – the "light motion of the throat" that occurs simultaneously with the "sustaining of the breath" in executing the trill.[90] When this "beating" movement of the larynx is not present or cannot be maintained, the trill of two notes collapses into a smaller interval or makes a bleating sound on one note. In reference to this *battuto* quality of the trill, Charles Burney describes trills of opera singers of his time as "open" or "not sufficiently open."[91] Italian writers like Tosi and Mancini use the terms *caprino* (goat-bleat trill) and *cavallino* (horse whinney) to describe the defective trill resulting from an improperly beaten trill.[92] Agricola's term is *Bockstriller*. He provides a valid test for ascertaining whether the two-note trill is being produced properly, so that the bleating sound or *Bockstriller* may be avoided. He recommends touching the fingers to the throat to determine whether the larynx is moving sufficiently to make a trill of two notes. Only a vibration and not a distinct movement is felt if the *Bockstriller* is being produced. *Granire*, from which Tosi derives *granito*, means "to play [or sing] distinctly"[93] or with articulation. Agricola's equivalent of *granito*, *deutlich*, means "clear or distinct."

Tosi's *facile* quality applies to flexibility in the trill. Most writers of the eighteenth century favored a moderately fast (Tosi's *moderamente veloce*) speed for the trill.[94] They believed that flexibility or nimbleness depended on a facile trill. Charles Burney's description of the English soprano Cecilia Davies' technique suggests the preferred speed of the trill: "Her shake [is] excellent, open, distinct, and neither sluggish like the French *cadence*, nor so quick as to become a flutter."[95] The fluttery quality of the trill produced by many late twentieth-century singers would not have been a desired trait by earlier standards. Tosi rejects the *trillo lento* (slow trill) for any use by an accomplished singer but seems to approve of one which increases in speed. None of the Tosi translators regards the very slow trill with any favor. Agricola – who, like Quantz, feels that the expression of the Affect [passion] and emotional character of the piece are factors in determining the speed of the trill – sanctions the use of a somewhat slower trill for an especially sad expression but warns that the "extremely slow trill of some Frenchmen"[96] is too extreme. Quantz[97] had suggested a faster trill for a more lively expression, and Agricola applies the same principle in reverse.[98]

German writers also recognized the size and the acoustics of the performing space as significant factors in determining how fast the trill should be executed. Agricola believes that the singer should have enough mastery of his technique to be able to adjust the speed of the trill to the performance place[99] – which is, of course, no mean feat, given the difficulties attendant on the execution of a good trill in the first place. Yet a third factor in determining the speed of the trill is the voice range of the singer, on which Agricola refers the reader to Quantz who feared that some would censure "subtleties of this sort as useless."[100] Agricola accepts the theory of adjustable speed for the trill, and maintains that the lower the voice the slower the trill and vice versa. Mattheson indicates that the "faster" trill, with both pitches clearly audible, was the normal speed of the regular Italian trill.[101]

In his advice on how to execute the trill, Agricola directs the student to begin the exercise with the dotted main note. This is followed by the upper auxiliary note, which, according to Tosi, must be equal in volume to the first note and connected to it.[102] Agricola insists that the exercise be performed slowly at first, with the [short] auxiliary equal in volume to the main note. Only the very first note of the exercise should receive an impulse of the breath;[103] the rest remains very connected without any new impulse. Agricola's trill exercise perhaps derives from the early seventeenth-century Italian *ribattuta di gola* (restriking of the throat), which functioned both as a stylistic ornament and as a vocal exercise for the acquisition of the *gruppo*[104] and the *trillo*. The *ribattuta* was used by Caccini[105] as a pedagogical device for teaching these ornaments to his family members but it is also mentioned by later authors such as Mattheson.[106] C. P. E. Bach uses the *ribattuta* as a keyboard ornament with no reference to its vocal roots. In his trill-teaching exercise Agricola further insists that the student begin the practice exercise both with the main note *and* with the upper auxiliary to prepare the singer for a trill of either type in performance. Both of the trills that Agricola designates as being *without* appoggiatura begin nonetheless on the note *above*. In a trill *with* an appoggiatura, he directs that the upper note be "somewhat sustained" or held out. If a given musical situation should forbid the appoggiatura, none could be introduced as a prelude to the trill. The oscillation, he says, should be continued the entire length of the trill and the termination performed *in the same tempo* as the oscillations and slurred to them.

Agricola provides detailed instructions for the shorter half trill. Like other German writers he translates Tosi's term *mezzotrillo* as *Pralltriller* (short or half trill), an onomatopoeic word suggesting that the trill must "crackle" in its execution. According to Agricola, it receives an emphasis on the auxiliary and a "snap of the last auxiliary tone of the trill, which must be tossed off, so to speak, with the greatest precision and speed; whereby at the same time occurs a certain special tensing and a flick of the opening of the windpipe ..."[107] He urges the reader to try the ornament at the keyboard, where, according to Bach, the *Pralltriller* is produced by the abrupt removal of a finger from the key: "the upper joint of the finger is sharply doubled and drawn off and away from the key as quickly as possible."[108] Agricola directs that the *Pralltriller* occur only before a falling second, whether this interval is created by an appoggiatura or by a written-out main note. Like Bach, he specifies that a short trill, if it occurs on a rather long note, does not occupy the duration of the long note, as all other trills *must* do. Because the turn and the short trill have many of the same musical features in common, Agricola points out their differences: the last two notes of the turn are *not* connected to the following note (whereas in the Berlin trill their connection is an immutable rule); the termination (last two notes) of the turn may be performed at various speeds; and thus only the first two notes of the turn must be in quick succession, while all notes of the trill must be so.[109]

In *Der critische Musicus* of 1749 Marpurg uses a single ornamental symbol to indicate four different double trills.[110] But after Agricola's attack on the imprecision of this in his pamphlet of 1749,[111] Marpurg[112] later amended the more unusual forms of his double trill and fell into conformity with Agricola and other Berlin writers. In Agricola's *Anleitung* the two forms of the double trill are each represented by a different sign. The rarely used double trill from above can occur in instances when the penultimate note of a cadence has made "a leap of a third from the seventh to the fifth above the bass," according to Agricola.[113] The double trill from below was used most often in an improvised cadenza with the first two notes on occasion repeated several times while increasing in speed. Agricola also allows this kind of trill before a fermata. He prefers to begin the double trill on, rather than before, the beat. Marpurg, whose examples of the four types of double trills clearly indicate a pre-beat rendition, was subsequently also persuaded to adopt performance on the beat.

Agricola also presented helpful suggestions for the mordent trill. To Tosi, this trill is an extremely brief ornament particularly effective when introduced into divisions. Agricola believes that, like most Italians, Tosi is confusing the mordent trill with the *Pralltriller*, or short trill, which, like the mordent, consists of only a few notes and is often introduced in the divisions. Hoping to clarify this obscured issue, Agricola gives the two usual patterns encountered in eighteenth-century ornamentation tables for the mordent proper.[114] He notes that the greatest application of the mordent trill in music is for those keyboard instruments wherein the tone cannot be increased in volume. Like the *Pralltriller*, it should be executed with the greatest of speed. Agricola also approves the performance of the mordent with the raised lower note, a practice that persists even now in late twentieth-century performance.

Agricola concludes his comments on the trill with a description of the vibrato[115] as similar to the effect created in string instruments by "rocking the fingertip back and forth on the same note, making the tone neither higher or lower." He lists it among the essential ornaments "that no good performer, be he singer or instrumentalist, can do without."[116]

Tosi's treatment (ch. 4) of the *passaggi* (divisions) reveals his strong preference for the pathetic style of the ancients, popular between 1690 and 1710, and his distaste for the modern style (1710–20), characterized by fast passages and quasi-instrumental virtuosity.[117] Although he recommends that the young singer learn about improvisation by listening to the best performers, he offers no practical methodology for improvising the divisions, a very large part of the singer's art in the eighteenth century.[118]

Tosi describes the "whole beauty" of divisions as *perfettamente intonato* (perfectly in tune), *battuto* (beaten), *granito* (distinct), *eguale* (equal), *rotto* (broken), and *veloce* (fast).[119] Although Agricola had previously translated the term *battuto* (beaten) as *geschlagen* (beaten) when applied to trills, in this chapter on divisions he uses the word *gestossen* (detached) to describe the same vocal technique. As in the trill, divisions involve the motion of the entire larynx essential to agility of the voice. *Rotto* Agricola translates as *articuliret* (distinct). Simply explained, *battuto* is the clue to the singer for the specific technique he is to use; *rotto* and *granito* are the resultant effect heard by the listener. *Eguale* refers to the even volume level of the notes within the division.

Writers and musicians of the Berlin court classified the divisions in various ways. Quantz sees them as extempore variations and gives many models for fashioning them.[120] C. P. E. Bach was concerned that the performer capture the Affect and *move* the listener regardless of the speed of the divisions.[121] For Marpurg, divisions consist of all improvised embellishments of a melody except for the essential ornaments (i.e. trill, turn, mordent, appoggiatura, etc.).[122] Italian and German vocal treatise writers such as Mancini and Hiller (as well as Mestastasio and Burney) agree that the divisions serve mainly the purpose of demonstrating the technical accomplishments and flexibility of the singer.

Since the singers at the Berlin opera were under strict orders from Frederick the Great not to deviate from the written notes of the composer, Agricola provides no methods for teaching improvisation in the divisions.[123] Instead, he provides one of the most comprehensive eighteenth-century discourses on breathing as well as one of the clearest descriptions of Tosi's two types of articulations of divisions – *sci.volato* (slurred) and *battuto* (detached) – and the most effective method by which to sing them.[124]

Because slurred divisions were permitted far less often than detached divisions in eighteenth-century music, Agricola enumerates the slurred divisions individually. While Tosi allows only a descending or ascending four-note group to be slurred,[125] Agricola extends this slurring to an ascending scale of an octave or more and recommends a middle ground between slurring and detaching for certain very fast triplet divisions, as in the example where "several consecutive notes on the same pitch occur in moderate tempo, above which there is a slur sign and under the slur sign there are dots." For this kind of special effect – a kind of pulsation of vocal intensity – Agricola suggests that "one must neither separate nor detach the notes, but rather execute each one with a slight impulse from the chest."[126] This kind of special effect is rather common in the vocal literature of the era.[127]

In addition to these acceptable divisions, Tosi and Agricola also discuss the *sgagateata* and the *strascino*. The word *sgagateata* (lit., cackling) is a pejorative term, which, according to Agricola, was in current use in Italy to describe the glottal articulation involving the extremely light and fast movement of the voice that is achieved by allowing "the air to push against the palate much as one does in a rather quiet laugh." The *sgagateata* or "glottal articulation" (to use the modern term) was regarded by Agricola as a fault because it causes technical problems for the singer and is too soft for most acoustical situations. Nevertheless, he concedes that this glottal articulation can be useful or acceptable because "they [the singers] can produce the divisions somewhat more easily and faster"; because "there is almost no other way to execute many reiterations of the same tone very rapidly"; and because this type of technique was employed (albeit without its customary lack of strength) by one of the most famous eighteenth-century singers, Faustina Bordoni Hasse, whom Agricola, cryptically, does not identify by name, but who, he says, "availed herself of none other than the [glottal] techniques described above."[128] Burney (quoting Quantz) described Faustina as distinguished for

a flexible throat for divisions, with so beautiful and quick a shake that she could put it in motion upon short notice, just when she would. The passages might be smooth, or by leaps, or consisting of iterations of the same tone, their execution was equally easy to her as to any instrument whatever. She was doubtless the first who introduced, with success, a swift repetition of the same tone.[129]

Although Faustina used this type of "glottal articulation," her voice was frequently described as penetrating and strong. Agricola, who had heard her, reports that the sound of her voice when executing these divisions was "almost as full and strong, if possible, as the sound of the natural chest voice in others."[130] Although Tosi also admired Faustina's singing, he disparages this glottal technique for the reiteration of one tone.[131]

Lo strascino (the drag, to use Galliard's term) is a type of heavily slurred articulation similar to the modern *glissando*. The term (translated by Agricola and other German writers as *das Ziehen*) is used by Tosi not only to denote an extremely slurred manner of singing but also to indicate a special ornament consisting of a slowly descending glissando scalar passage, considered especially effective in the pathetic style. He sees the *strascino* as a sort of rubato over a steady beat.[132] The drag seems to be distinguishable from the slur by its excessively legato character and by its slowness, as Agricola himself explains.[133] Hiller distinguishes between the slur and the drag in this manner: the slur "consists in there being no gap or pause in passing from one note to another, and no unpleasant slipping or dragging through smaller intervals ... Each succeeding note must follow so lightly and firmly as not to scoop or show false intermediary sounds";[134] the drag implies a chromatic passage: "when divisions proceed chromatically, slurring is the only means of performance. Should one wish to choose another name [for the chromatic division], the term dragging (*ziehen*) can be used."[135] Johann Sebastian Bach made a musical pun on *ziehen* by his chromatic setting of the word in the *St. John Passion* soprano aria "Ich folge dir gleichfalls."

Perhaps the most valuable service that Agricola provides in the chapter on divisions is to explain when and how to take the breath, for few treatises of this period even mention breathing, much less provide the useful directions afforded by Agricola. The breath is taken subtly and without noise in inhalation, during rests or after a long note, after strong beats and especially after the down-beat when possible. Having missed his proper breathing place in a division, the singer, Agricola suggests, may unobtrusively breathe during a down-beat note (i.e. omit the note) if it is tied.[136] Faustina, for example, as Burney reports, "had the art of sustaining a note longer, in the opinion of the public, than any other singer, *by taking her breath imperceptibly* [italics mine]."[137] Perhaps the most discussed rule of breathing for singers and wind players in eighteenth-century sources concerns the cadenza, which was to be confined to such a length that it could be executed in one breath. This rule served first, to limit the length of the cadenza, in order to forestall an overly long and self-indulgent tasteless improvisation; and secondly, to spur the singer to develop fully his breath capacity, or at the very least, the ability to disguise artfully the taking of the breath. This skill became a criterion for the comparison of singers and even ultimately gave rise to such extraordinary games as the famous contest between Farinello and the trumpeter.[138]

Agricola's comments about the habits of eighteenth-century singers indicate that the rule limiting the breath was seriously observed by these singers; and that, breath capacity for the cadenza being a major test of vocal ability, the singers used whatever devices they could to get as large a breath as possible and to take that breath at the last moment possible so as to produce the longest possible cadenza. In order to make their breath last as long as possible, they sometimes changed the underlay of the text, or delayed the placement of the syllables – practices that Agricola rejects as errors. He suggests that breathing in the middle of the word and thus interrupting the sentence is not as serious as either changing the text underlay or repositioning the syllables.[139]

On account of the discomfort caused to the singer, Tosi prohibits the Italian *e, i, o,* and *u* for the divisions, allowing only the *a,* open *e,* and open *o.* This had been anticipated over a century before by Maffei, who prohibits the *u* because it sounds like howling, and the closed *e* because it produces sounds similar to those produced by small animals. This prohibition, of course, entailed severe restraints for the librettist in his choice of words for those arias with divisions. Agricola permits divisions in the German language on the same vowels (*a,* open *e,* and open *o*) as in Italian,[140] as well as "on diphthongs that begin with a bright or open vowel – especially the *e* and *a,* as long as the first vowel is held to the end of the division, at which point the second is pronounced."[141]

While clear enunciation entails crisp (*scharf*) pronunciation of the consonants, Agricola warns the singer to be careful not to make double consonants where none exist. Although this crisp pronunciation is not especially pleasant at too close a distance and sounds somewhat affected, at a distance it is quite effective.[142] Agricola credits Faustina with having effective and vigorous diction. To educate the reader in methods of clear enunciation, Agricola draws our attention to a French treatise of 1755 by Jean Antoine Bérard, in which the author (he seems erroneously to think) has made a great effort to clarify the correct pronunciation by the "change or addition of some letters that are not a part of the written word." Bérard really gives a list of incorrect, albeit common faults in pronunciation, which Agricola, it seems, has unfortunately mistaken for a list of *suggested* pronunciations! Bérard's preceding paragraph makes his intention clear: "Here is a list of faults that I have had occasion to notice all of the time; some of them are so bad that they don't even seem plausible [*vraisemblables*]; meanwhile would that they would become less common."[143]

Tosi classifies the *recitativo* or recitative (ch. 5) into three types: church, chamber, and theater. The freedom from strict time,[144] which Tosi allows only for the church recitative, Agricola allows also for all sorts of recitatives, including the *recitativo accompagnato*.[145] Even when illustrating the church recitative, Agricola provides examples of ornamentation with texts in *Italian* (the common language of theatrical or chamber recitative).

Although Tosi mentions the appoggiatura only in passing and this in connection with the church recitative, where many appoggiaturas are required, it was surely the most frequently employed ornament in all styles of recitative.[146] Agricola recognizes its value and provides musical examples.[147]

Agricola favors the appoggiatura of the fourth at feminine cadence endings, and adding an appoggiatura or gentle short trill to fill in the falling third.[148] Appoggiaturas in the recitative, like those in the aria, were usually indicated by composers in the Berlin School.

Much of Agricola's attention is devoted to ornaments for the recitative other than the appoggiatura, such as the mordent, the double trill (*Doppeltriller*), and the trilled turn (*prallender Doppelschlag*).[149] He gives musical examples of small tasteful ornaments that are appropriate for church or chamber recitative or that are permitted only if the Affect [passion] is particularly strong. He illustrates the double trill, and a trill which is performed in connection with a long-sustained and crescendoing appoggiatura[150] together with two types of mordents: the mordent proper (*das eigentlich Mordent*) and a mordent with an appoggiatura from below that may be introduced in the same places.

The composer's indication of the placement of cadential chords in the recitative was often at odds with performance practice (i.e. when they were actually played). Tosi is one of the first eighteenth-century writers to shed light on this discrepancy by his description of the *cadenza tronca* or telescoped cadence, in which the continuo and the vocal parts overlap at the ends of phrases of recitative despite notation indicating that the chords come after.[151] Some composers notate these differences in chord placement while others leave the matter to the performers. Galliard (p. 194) illustrates the telescoping of harmonies so that the continuo and vocal parts overlap. The truncated cadence is appropriate when the dialogue needs to move quickly, as, for example, when one singer responds to another; or when an *attacca* (close connection) to the ensuing aria is needed. Tosi advocates it sparingly, suggesting that out of one hundred cadences, ten of the telescoped variety are sufficient.[152] For Agricola the *cadenza tronca* (which he translates as *abgebrochene Cadenz* [broken-off cadence]) is one whose harmony finishes in an uncertain or inconclusive manner. The only difference between Agricola's notation for the truncated cadence (κ) and his notation for the final cadence (λ) is in the harmony implied by the different bass notes.[153]

The *recitativo accompagnato* (Agricola's *Accompagnement*), or recitative with obbligato instruments, usually employed for soliloquies, was widely used by the Berlin circle. Because its purpose was to move the passions, the recitativo accompagnato lent itself excellently to the aims of *Empfindsamkeit*[154] (lit., sensitivity), an important principle of musical aesthetics at the Berlin court. This style enabled the individual singer (usually in soliloquy) to express his deepest thoughts, reflections, and emotions, at the same time providing an opportunity for the orchestra to mirror, foreshadow, or comment on those same emotions. Among the devices frequently used in the *recitativo accompagnato* were the melodic sigh (descending interval of a half step) and a trembling instrumental effect created by reiterated sixteenth notes.[155] Hasse and Graun, the primary operatic composers performed at Berlin, excelled at this style, which is illustrated for example, by recitatives from Graun's oratorio *Der Tod Jesu*.

Tosi's division of the *aria* (ch. 7) into chamber, church, and theatrical styles is valid for his contemporaries such as Alessandro Scarlatti, Bononcini, Gasparini, and Stradella. The second decade of his century, however, saw these distinctions become irrelevant with the emergence of the more simple, major-key, homophonic style exemplified by Pergolesi, Vinci, and Hasse. In general, these new arias of Vinci and Hasse, composers popular at the Berlin court, were longer than the traditional arias and offered more possibilities for cadenzas (sometimes four or five fermatas were indicated).[156] Tosi's primary objections to this "modern"-style aria were the too-frequent opportunities for cadenza; the orchestral doublings of the vocal part;[157] the effulgent style of the cadenzas; the tendency toward major-key arias and *arie di bravura*; and the consequent neglect of the pathetic and expressive styles.[158] His argument that the repetition of the text occasioned by the tripartite (ABA) structure weakens the expression of the words prompts Agricola to lay the burden for this effect on the librettist, whom he urges to "sacrifice, if necessary, a few poetic embellishments in the arias and choruses, which, after all, consist of only a few lines," and to enjoy almost unlimited freedom in the recitatives, which forbid "him little or nothing except a few quite inappropriate verse forms."[159]

Agricola held in high esteem the libretti of Metastasio, which were often set at the Berlin opera. In the early part of his career the poet made use of a wide variety of forms, but limited himself in his mature years to quatrains of seven-syllable lines. Metastasio believed that the arias in eighteenth-century opera served the function of the chorus in the ancient Greek drama, commenting and reflecting on character and plot. This reflective and metaphorically allusive quality of his poetry was the justification used by supporters of Metastasio in defending the poet from Gluckian reforms.[160] The qualities which characterize the sound of the poetry of Metastasio's arias include liquid consonants; and, at the end of the first stanza, the appearance of a word containing the *a* vowel (such as "mar") – considered the essential vowel for the cadenza or divisions. Whereas Tosi allows three vowels, *a*, open *o*, and open *e*,[161] Metastasio indicates that he was being limited by singers and audiences of the mid-century to only two, (*a* and open *e*). Lamenting the current predilection for "tickling the ears" with excessive divisions (on the vowels *a* and open *e*), he complains that not only are good dramas being banished from the theater but that words, "if not the whole alphabet," stand at risk. In his work on Metastasio, Burney also complains that by the end of the century only the *a* vowel was acceptable for divisions: "at present, Italian composers assign them only to A; on which more labour is bestowed by the Maestro, and attention by the audience, than on all the poetry and sentiments of the singers."[162]

The controversy between ancients and moderns regarding the notation of improvised ornamentation mostly centered on the *da capo* arias. Tosi cautions the singer against writing out the divisions in the arias even as a pedagogical means to become more comfortable with the improvisations that he was expected to provide in the last two sections of the da capo aria, namely the B and A sections.[163] Yet evidence from some eighteenth-century sources indicate that this was precisely what *was* done. Angus Heriot narrates an incident in which Caffarelli was incapable of performing in Naples because he had lost his written-out cadenzas.[164] The German soprano Mara, the prima donna most beloved by Frederick the Great, indicates in an autobiographical note that she ornamented an *aria di bravura* in the opera *Gli Argonauti* by Gazzaniga, which she sang in Venice in 1790. Since this aria was so well suited for variations, she had it copied out with four empty staves above the voice part, on which she wrote out four different ornamented versions. By memorizing the different versions and employing them on subsequent nights during the run of the opera, Mara was able to give the impression of improvisation, which, she boasted, secured her triumph that season in Venice over her rival Brigida Banti, who sang all of her arias "by rote as she had learned them." According to Mara, her own performance brought the same people to the theater night after night, because "one could hear something new every evening."[165]

Mara's aim was to give the impression of extempore improvisation of the aria, but Agricola felt it necessary for the composer to write out the ornamentation in order to protect himself if a bad, i.e. "dead-brained," singer, were to be involved. He asks, "Would it not do more honor to the singer and give more pleasure to the listener for the composer to make a careful effort to indicate how the plain melody of the aria could most skillfully be decorated with extempore variations?"[166]

Tosi's conservative attitudes are nowhere in greater evidence than in his remarks on the *cadenza* (ch. 8). Opposed to the notion that the movement of the bass should be held hostage, at times falling silent, to accommodate the singer in his "ill-conceived" graces, Tosi rejects the "modern" cadenza, which consisted of scales, trills, and other vocal acrobatics over the static harmony of the seventh or six-four chord.[167] Tosi uses only one term, *cadenza*, making no differentiation between its usage as cadence or cadenza.[168] He believes that only the *last* of the three cadences (one at the end of each section of the tri-partite da capo aria) allows a "modest liberty [of improvising] to the singer," and further that, since this cadence must proceed over the bass without offense to the time,[169] the student should seek to reintroduce these special cadenzas and to learn from the ancients their skill of stealing a little time for ornamentation on the final cadence.[170]

Agricola, presenting a carefully wrought essay on the cadenza, updates Tosi in accordance with the mid-century definitions of performance practice, differentiating between the cadence (*Schluss*) and the "modern" *cadenza* of his day. In his short history of the cadenza, Agricola recognizes a number of phases leading up to the development of the cadenza style in which the bass stopped completely.[171] Agricola informs us that the cadenzas that do not delay the rhythmic movement still had some use and validity in 1756. They were sometimes used not only for the cadence at the end of the first section (A section) of a da capo aria, but also at an internal cadence point occurring shortly before the final cadence of the piece as a preparation for the final cadenza.[172]

Tosi distinguishes only two types of melodic cadences, with the melodic patterns 3–2–1 (EDC) and 8–7–8 (CBC) and specifies that if there are other voices or instruments (i.e. obbligato instruments), the singer must abide by the exact notes written for him by the composer and may not partake of the freedom which a continuo aria would afford him in refashioning the melodic shape of the cadence. Agricola, argues, however, that neither of the cadence types to which Tosi objects is any longer preferred, the preferred the now being CDC, and that his rule of abiding by the exactly prescribed notes is necessary only if there is merely *one* instrumental part accompanying the voice. If there are *two* parts, such as violin parts, Agricola continues, the singer is once again free to choose (as he is in the continuo aria), since one of the two parts is going to double his part anyway.[173]

Tosi criticizes the popular cadence type whose melodic line falls a fifth in the *soprano* voice,[174] but Agricola permits octaves which function as unisons in this sort of "bass cadence" since they are intentional. Like Tosi, he objects to filling them in with a running passage because the impact of the leap, and thus the composer's intention, is thereby ruined.[175]

The "good" cadenza should occur, says Tosi, only at the last of the three cadential points of a da capo aria; should be truly improvised (thus not pre-fabricated); should be sung over a continually moving bass; and should be in the style of the aria. More practically, Agricola's rules are that the cadenza not be overly long; that the cadenza be related to the main Affect of the aria, even to the point of using thematic material from the aria presented in a skillful weaving together of "broken phrases"; that cadenzas be varied; that the cadenza not be rushed through; that, while some chromaticism is possible, the cadenza not stray too far into distant keys; that it have an element of surprise, which can be accomplished by introducing notes outside the range of the aria; and that it be made in one breath. This last rule was approved by most writers and was followed rather faithfully. Exceptions existed, of course, and the singers undoubtedly used their ingenuity to devise types of figures and devices by which the breath could be concealed.[176] In the chapter on divisions Agricola satirizes such antics.[177]

The cadenza, especially in a fiery piece, was often used as a vehicle for the singer to demonstrate certain notes of his range that were not permissible in the aria.[178] Presumably the limits of human physical nature, however, kept the ornament to tasteful and reasonable proportions. Hiller, who borrowed extensively from Tosi and Agricola, is refreshingly honest as to the actual practice: "This rule [of not breathing in the cadenza] cannot be kept without exception simply because the very different strengths and weaknesses of the chest and other random circumstances allow sometimes more, sometimes less, and at times all too little expansion."[179]

One of Tosi's chief concerns is variety: he urges that the da capo ornamentation be varied at every performance. In Italy the audiences often included many of the same people who returned night after night not only for socializing, but also for the sake of the contest-like conditions fostered by the judging of the singer and his inventiveness in comparison to other singers. The circus atmosphere which prevailed in opera houses – in which card playing, dining, conversation, etc., were all carried on during the performance in private boxes – spurred the singers on to greater and greater risk-taking and extravagances, if only for the purpose of turning the audience's errant attention back to themselves. Hired private partisan cliques contributed to the general adversarial atmosphere of the competition. Since the practice of improvisation does not seem to have prevailed in Berlin –

where opera was performed only twice weekly, where the traditions of competition and contest were not as strongly ingrained, and where the ornamentation was carefully controlled by the composer and the monarch – Agricola makes little reference to performance conditions requiring such virtuosic variation. Yet Agricola is also concerned, like Tosi, that the singer not construct cadenzas that sound overly repetitive because the singer has availed himself of too few musical ideas[180] and suggests that different figures should be interchanged to avoid the problem.[181] But despite Agricola's suggestions, it was only in the late eighteenth century that composers of cadenzas regularly began to avail themselves of thematic material. Conversely, Quantz is concerned with the tedium of too *many* different figures.[182] To Agricola's rules, Hiller adds a number of varied musical examples for tasks such as ascending and descending.[183] Agricola insists that the cadenza must always be related to the main Affect of the aria and if possible should include some of the most beautiful individual phrases or periods from the aria.[184]

Agricola's statement that he would rather hear *no* cadenza than one which is "bad" or "rushed through" implies that if even if the cadenza were not to be improvised, it should at least *sound* improvised, the singer maintaining a delicate balance between his breath capacity and the series of slight delays needed to create the impression of improvisation. Improvisation is a burden, he says, "for those who are poor in invention." He suggests using a series of *abgebrochene Sätze* (broken phrases) to achieve the improvisatory spirit.[185] Agricola implies (contrary to the normal Berlin practice of composer-specified ornamentation) that the singer in the cadenza bears some of the responsibility for the creation if not improvisation of his own cadenzas.

Agricola counsels moderation in the use of chromaticism in the composition of the cadenza, preferring it, nonetheless, in the cadenza of a pathetic or flattering aria.[186] This use of notes outside the scale, if not excessive, was regarded as an essential element of surprise in the cadenza. This element of surprise was achieved in the cadenza by the singer's revelation of the special qualities of his voice, whether range, flexibility, accuracy, or dynamic control. Special effects improvised in the passage work – such as those achieved by figures comprising runs, jumps, triplets, chains of trills, etc. – were sought after by the singer to make what Mattheson called his "farewell bow." Agricola suggests that the unexpected introduction of notes outside the range of the aria was an especially effective way to surprise the listener.

Double cadenzas consist of either two voices or a voice and an instrument. They are less restrictive than the solo cadenza in that they do not have to be performed in one breath (although breaths must be concealed) and in that the meter (which is totally free in the solo cadenza) must be maintained during the imitation of those figures that the other singer must perform. They are more restrictive in that they should be composed beforehand. Agricola advises performers to adhere faithfully to what the composer has written. He recommends listening to other good singers, reading Quantz's treatise carefully,[187] and following the dictates of good taste.

Tosi (chs. 7, 8, and 9) was one of the first writers to discuss *tempo rubato*,[188] which he considered critical to good taste: "Whoever does not know how to stretch out the notes [*rubare il tempo*] can certainly neither compose nor accompany himself and remains deprived of the best taste and the finest insight."[189] His references to it in chapter 7 demonstrate that the device was regarded as a common and effective way for the singer to vary the da capo of the aria, particularly in the pathetic style. Tosi praises a contemporary, Francesco Antonio Pistocchi, for teaching "all of the embellishments of the art without going against the observance of time."[190] Tosi, like other discriminating musicians, considered (in ch. 8) the appropriate application of *tempo rubato* to be a critical aspect of the singer's good taste and expressivity.[191] One of Burney's few criticisms of Faustina is that, compared with her execution of lively pieces, her performance of adagio arias – where great sorrow is expressed such as "might require dragging, sliding, or notes of syncopation, and *tempo rubato*" – was not so successful.[192]

Tosi's *tempo rubato* refers to a rhythmic displacement that does not disturb the underlying tempo and that consists in the borrowing of time rather than the stealing of it.[193] The feature was usually found in the pathetic or adagio aria and in the improvised cadence. A singer's improvisatory skill might be measured by his use of the *rubato* in the rhythmic alterations of his da capo divisions and by his ability to keep steady rhythm in the bass while accompanying himself at the keyboard. Self-accompaniment was required to satisfy the nobility[194] and the singer was measured against other singers by his skill in this.[195]

Tosi differentiates two types of *tempo rubato* – the first in which the time is gained in order to be lost again (rushing followed by lingering) and the second (which he prefers), in which the time is lost in order to be regained (lingering followed by catching up). Agricola finds this explanation puzzling and thinks the *tempo rubato* had been made "too much of."[196]

For Bach, *tempo rubato* consists in presenting an irregular number of notes, as, for example, five sixteenth notes in the time of one quarter note, or seven eighth notes in the time of a half note – all performed with great sensitivity, freedom, and flexibility. Bach's *Sechs Sonaten ... mit veränderten Reprisen* provide the performer with an extremely precise and fairly complicated polyrhythmic *tempo rubato*, which may be exchanged, he states, for a freer interpretation (perhaps closer to the Italian concept) with notes left out, etc. According to Bach, the notation simply provides a point of departure and once the player has mastered the concept, he need no longer remain bound to it.

Berlin writers, including Quantz and C. P. E. Bach, retain the Italian terminology *tempo rubato*, or more simply, *rubato*. Agricola and Marpurg translate the term by a variety of more specific German words showing the subtle interpretations of the practice, thereby revealing their need to solidify and crystallize the free and subtle fashion of the Italian practice into a regular, precise, and predictable one. In his translation Agricola uses two terms – *das Verziehen der Noten*, which means literally "a delaying or distortion[197] of the notes" and *Zeitraub* (lit., time robbery) – for the stealing of the time.[198] Marpurg uses the term *tempo rubato* only to refer to anticipation: "This is what the Italians call various ways of anticipating notes."[199] By 1763 Marpurg's own understanding of the Italian concept had become more complete, since he states that "the Italians tend to group under the single term *tempo rubato* that which we call *Tonverziehung* [delaying the notes] and *Tonverbeissung* [a hocket effect]."[200] The former involves sustaining or anticipating a note without affecting the harmony and includes all melodic *Rückungen* (syncopations) and all types of tied syncopations. The latter, *Tonverbeissung*, involves letting the weak beat sound and making a rest on the strong beat and using two notes of the same pitch.

Marpurg and Bach categorized and illustrated in great detail the various modifications of the rhythm by which they understood the *tempo rubato* of the Italian writers, who left no notated examples. Marpurg in particular gives an impressive variety of possibilities replete with musical examples for the *tempo rubato*;[201] Agricola provides only a pair of musical examples and a description.[202] Agricola's two examples of this feature are apparently taken from Marpurg's *Anleitung* of 1755, where they are described respectively as "anticipation" (*Vorausnehmen*) and "suspension" (*Aufhalten*).[203]

The fact that Agricola chose to use the word *verzogen* (distorted) instead of Marpurg's "anticipation" reveals his greater understanding of the irregularity and freedom associated with Italian performance practice. Agricola also does not prescribe any specific amount of time to be robbed: "Distorting the note values (*rubare il tempo*) actually means to take away from a prescribed note some of its value and add it to the next one or vice versa ... And this [freedom] may be applied to various kinds of notes, figures, and rhythms (meters)."[204] He cautions that the notes which are to receive this *rubato* not be so wrenched or pulled out of shape from their original value that the melody thereby becomes unclear or unintelligible. Like Leopold Mozart, he believes that the best means of learning *tempo rubato* is by demonstration.

RECEPTION OF THE *ANLEITUNG*

Since vocal music was considered much more important than instrumental music in the mid eighteenth century, it is probable that the *Anleitung* was at that time accorded a position of greater importance than even the books of Agricola's distinguished colleagues, Quantz and C. P. E. Bach. Orders for subscriptions had been plentiful. Telemann, for example, had ordered thirty copies of the *Anleitung* when subscription copies were advertised. The *Anleitung* was received with great enthusiasm and glowing reviews. Contemporary critics were grateful for Agricola's clear explanation of Guidonian solmization, one of them characterizing it as "the clearest most organized program for the understanding of the old six-syllable mutation system that has ever existed";[205] for his thorough and useful explanation of the principles and methods of improvising ornaments and varying the melody; and even for his section on the physiology of the voice. "The translator has provided," notes one reviewer, "a most complete and useful discussion of the improvised ornaments and the variations of the melody along with other useful explanations."[206] The extent of Agricola's original thinking and influence in his lifetime and after his death is revealed in the direct borrowings from his writings by Hiller, Türk, Marpurg, and others, as noted above. Less directly, his influence can perhaps also be seen in similarities in thinking and in such mechanical matters as chapter organization. This is true especially in Türk's *Klavierschule*, ch. 3, on the appoggiatura, which relies heavily on

Agricola; and in Hiller's *Anleitung* (1780) in discussions of the trill, appoggiatura and divisions, which also depend substantially on Agricola. Updating Agricola by providing specific directions and musical examples of how these ornaments should be performed pertinent to his own day, Hiller, the only other notable writer of a German singing treatise in the era of Agricola, used and modernized the *Anleitung* and supplanted Agricola as the foremost German writer in the eighteenth-century tradition of singing and as an authority on ornamentation.

But there are other reasons to explain the fact that even during his life and for many decades after his death in 1774, Agricola's reputation came to be somewhat eclipsed and his original work forgotten and ignored, or devalued so that he became known as little more than a translator of Tosi, and even believed erroneously in the twentieth century to be a poor one at that. In his 1933 study of the Italian *bel canto*, Bernhard Ulrich, for example, mentions Agricola as Tosi's translator only to dismiss him for his outdated language, and his many errors in translation,[207] without taking into consideration Agricola's own useful notes and detailed explanations, some of which are very useful in illuminating the *bel canto* tradition and Tosi.

A chief factor in the diminished reputation of Agricola was his somewhat misguided or misunderstood controversy with Gluck. In the preface to his *Alceste* (1769),[208] in which he disparaged the style and practices of contemporary opera, Gluck pledged to return music to its true function as a means of expression for poetry and fables unencumbered by superfluous embellishment. He repudiated the conventions represented by Hasse and Metastasio: formal plots of love and power; stiff contrived characters in the service of a sort of operatic "book of conduct" for the moral edification of princes; the formal and restrictive plan of the music, with alternating recitatives and arias and elaborate action-delaying ritornellos; and the license allowed singers to improvise overly elaborate ornamentations. Gluck's reform is the strongest reaction against the degeneration of embellishment, which was also vigorously opposed by Hasse among many others including Tosi and Agricola, though not so sweepingly or harshly.

In his review of *Alceste*,[209] Agricola (who does not make his identity known) responds that poetry that in itself does not produce a good effect without music is contemptible, to be sure, while music without the benefit of words can express imprecisely and only by suggestion; thus, music needs poetry to clarify its intentions. Music, he contends, does not rob poetry of its charm. To Gluck's statement that he opposed making the singer involved in a heated discussion wait until the end of a boring ritornello in order to be able to speak again, Agricola replied that the ritornello must evoke the same heat in its tones as the words of the poetry, continuing and intensifying it. In these issues both seem to agree to the aesthetic principle that form must be appropriate to content. On various such issues, Gluck, Agricola, Tosi and others were substantially in agreement, at least theoretically – even though the musical realization of their ideas produced quite different results[210] – but Gluck, many believed, went too far. Agricola was not the only force against Gluck's extremism. Composers, for example Rossini and others of the so-called "Neapolitan school," also dissented and singers themselves were a mighty force against him.

The current polemical style was pigheaded, petty, and charged with gratuitous acrimony. In his reviews and polemical writings Agricola held his own in the fashion of the times. Thus, it is not surprising that his critics, even after his death, meted out judgment in kind. Cramer identified the reviewer,[211] calling him a pedant and suggesting that his mental powers were failing. This assessment of Agricola was carried into the future. In his work on Mozart, Otto Jahn refers to Agricola's review in similar terms as revealing his lack of understanding, his pedantry and triviality.[212] Wucherpfennig sees him as a child of his time, petty and not generous enough to free himself from the current prejudices. Time and changing tastes went against Agricola and Gluck's elegant music became quite influential for later composers.[213] Thus Agricola's criticisms of Gluck and Cramer's statements about the review continued, in an atmosphere favorable to Gluck, to be cited against him by music historians, throwing him in an unfavorable light, which may have caused his writings to be dismissed without a careful reading.

Throughout the nineteenth century and until recently, very little attention was paid to Agricola's best contributions to singing theory and performance; he was relegated mainly to the role of Tosi's translator and (with M. Jakob Adlung) author of the book on organs. On the other hand, he seems to have been something of an influence on, or an impetus for, the work of Manuel Garcia,[214] famous for his invention of the laryngoscope (1854). Garcia's first important work, *Mémoire sur la voix humaine* (Paris, 1840), presents his theories on the registers and timbres of the singer's voice in its various classifications; this work served as foundation for his *Traité complet sur l'Art du Chant*, Part I (1841).[215] In his preface to the latter, Garcia's references to the works of Tosi, Agricola, Mancini, and others suggest that he has studied these works and found them vague or incomplete. (In this preface he also emphasizes the importance of vocal physiology to the actual practice and performance of the singer.) In 1856 appeared his *Nouveau Traité Sommaire sur L'Art du Chant*, based on the 1841 edition. In this book Garcia treats at length many matters presented by Tosi and enlarged upon by Agricola: vocal apparatus and physiology, registers, blending of the registers, diet habits, choice of vowels, the *bocca ridente* and the conduct of singers. His *Mémoire sur la voix humaine* is now recognized as the precursor and basis of all following scientific studies of the human voice mechanism and his *Traité complet sur l'Art du Chant* was for decades the standard work on singing, superseding the works of Tosi, Agricola, Hiller, and all earlier writers on the subject.

Late in the nineteenth century, Hugo Goldschmidt mentions Agricola as a source on solmization, passages, and trills,[216] but not until thirty years later was a serious attempt made to rescue him from oblivion. In his German dissertation on the life and works of Agricola, Hermann Wucherpfennig recognizes his substantial achievements in the musical world of his era, citing evidence of the high prestige Agricola enjoyed as composer, singer, and instrumentalist (pp. 11–35). On the other hand, except for the sections on ornamentation, Wucherpfennig does not share the general enthusiasm (p. 45) with which the eighteenth century greeted the *Anleitung*, though he praises Tosi's work as the most thorough and comprehensive in the history of singing treatises and compliments him for "words worth heeding ... still meaningful today" (pp. 48, 62). Justifiably, Wucherpfennig focuses criticism on Agricola's somewhat unclear and undiscriminating presentation of older and newer theories on various aspects of vocal physiology (pp. 48–57), a field that, from the present writer's perspective, is only of peripheral interest to the performing artist.

The late twentieth-century resurgence of interest in historically informed performance of eighteenth-century music has been aided by the ready availability of facsimiles, reprints, and translations of instrumental treatises such as those of Quantz and C. P. E. Bach. Similar materials to aid the singer have been slower to become available. Although Mancini, Porpora, and Tosi have been easily accessible through English translations for some time, a number of other writers such as Hiller and Agricola existed only in reprint in the original language until recently.

In the 1960s Agricola began to assume his proper place in music both for his value as an historical figure and for his assistance to the contemporary singer. The year 1966 saw the appearance of Erwin R. Jacobi's new German edition of the *Anleitung*, with Preface and Appendix in both German and English, accompanied by the original Italian text of Tosi. These were used as the basis of the present translation. In the same year also appeared Kurt Wichmann's introduction and running commentary to the Jacobi edition as well as *Der Ziergesang*,[217] a work on ornamentation in singing and the development of the appoggiatura, in which he repeatedly refers to the contributions of Tosi and Agricola.

For modern singers the value of Agricola lies chiefly in his trill exercise (both in the musical example and in the detailed description of how to achieve it), his description of the variety of types of articulations of passages, his discussion of the singers of his day, his essay on the cadenza, and his discussion of enunciation and solmization. Robert Donington has praised the Italian–German alliance represented by Tosi and Agricola as "invaluable for singers,"[218] and Eugene Helm considers the *Anleitung* a "landmark in the teaching of singing."[219]

Since Agricola's value to the modern singer of eighteenth-century music is considerable, the present author is pleased to offer the *Anleitung* here in English translation.

INTRODUCTION

TO

THE ART OF SINGING

Translated from the Italian of

PIER FRANCESCO TOSI,

Member of the Philharmonic Academy

with

Commentaries and Additions

by

JOHANN FRIEDRICH AGRICOLA

Royal Prussian Court Composer

Berlin: Printed by George Ludewig Winter
1757

Translator's Preface

I doubt if there exists anywhere a book that presents more clearly and completely for the prospective singer most of what he must know and practice; that provides for the more advanced singer various special benefits [i.e. refinements] as yet unknown to him, despite his having collected a quantity of bravos, often in public assembly; and finally, that would sharply criticize the faults of those many virtuosi who think themselves so perfect in the art of singing – in short, a book that gives such complete advice on that art as *Opinioni de' Cantori antichi e moderni, o sieno Osservazioni sopra il canto figurato* [Opinions regarding ancient and modern singers; or Observations on the florid song] by *Pier Francesco Tosi,*[1] *of the Accademia Filarmonica.*[2] In this happy conviction, I take special delight in translating into German this book, now rare even in Italy, and presenting it to my most worthy countrymen.

I could well have taken herein the opportunity to rebuke the Germans generally in that, for most of them, their country does not yet provide those opportunities available to the Italians to bring the art of singing to the high level of perfection[3] that it enjoyed in Italy during the time of the author I am translating. On the other hand, I could have belittled the contributions of our Italian neighbors to the art of singing, or at least have tried to divide the credit between Italy and her neighbors. Since each of my fellow citizens should keep in mind two objectives – [first] to seek out the good in the realm of truth and beauty and [secondly] to adopt it from wherever and whatever country he finds it, no matter how opposed he might be to that country – I hope, therefore, that the gentle reader is inclined to forgive me if I engage in no controversy concerning national taste or national preference.[4] Our purpose is rather to try to make use of the insights, experiences, and examples of all skillful people, regardless of the nation to which they belong.

40

The author of this book, which I hope to make generally useful through this translation, was by birth an Italian; by profession a singer, and indeed one of those destined by art or by cruelty to retain his high voice his entire life.[5] He visited most of the European courts; that he did not remain long at any court nor find any special place in music history makes it easy to believe that by nature his voice was not the most beautiful. A friend of mine assured me that he had known him in Dresden in 1719, and in London in 1727.[6] Because he lacked the advantages of a charming voice pleasing to all listeners, he sought to compensate by a thorough understanding of music itself. That he was not unskilled, even in composition, is proved by some of his extant cantatas, one of which I myself possess. His own writing on the art of singing will, however, be the best witness of how deeply he researched this, his chief work.

Insofar as I possibly could, I have tried to follow exactly the author's thoughts; but I have taken the liberty of incorporating here and there my own remarks and clarifications – particularly in those chapters on the methods of making the voice skillful in singing and in those which deal with essential ornaments of song – because the author, it seems to me, has not explained them fully enough.

I have introduced a rather extensive examination of the manner of production and the classifications of the human voice. Both the student and the teacher must be experts in the voice, but in the beginning, the latter more than the former. One will readily take me at my word that I am not a scientist by profession, when he sees that I have at times availed myself of knowledge of the general principles of physics and anatomy, especially those parts involved in speaking and singing – as found in the best authorities: **Krüger**,[7] **Dodart**,[8] and **Ferrein**[9] – and to avoid error, at times using their very words. One can no more expect a singer to be totally expert in anatomy than he can expect a scientist to know the secrets of the art of singing from the ground up. I have tried to reconcile the principles of the scientist with the experience of music experts and singers. Should I have erred somewhere therein, I earnestly beg the great scientists and anatomists to correct me. Perhaps the art of singing will provide for some of you, Gentlemen, a pleasant diversion. For your part, may you contribute something to make our pleasures mutually more complete. Through my treatise I am giving you the opportunity to do so. Let us therefore work together for the common pleasure. If you do it by means of examination and comparison, I will do it by questions and answers. Finally we will unite in a common purpose.

Here I would especially like to give public thanks to Messrs. **Quantz**[10] and **C. P. E. Bach**[11] for the assistance that both of their excellent writings have afforded me in adapting many of my precepts to theirs.

Concerning the style of writing of the original – in which the author [Tosi], as he himself acknowledges, was no scholar, but neither does he belong to the worst of his nation in previous times – I would not need to make excuses, I hope, were I not afraid that in certain awkward places in the original I have been led into greater awkwardness. After all, I do not pretend to be a writer.

A contrast in the size of the print will differentiate what originates with the author from what originates with the translator.[12]

I shall be happy if my efforts have not been in vain; if the Germans, my countrymen, are inspired anew to prove indeed that our fatherland can be just as rich in good voices and singers as any other region under heaven.

But who could doubt this truth since out of our nation (not even taking into account the olden times) we have already produced a **Bümmler**,[13] a **Grünewald**,[14] a **Riemschneider**,[15] a **Hurlebusch**,[16] a **Raaf**[17]; as well as a **Kayserinn**,[18] a **Reuterinn**,[19] a **Hessin**,[20] a **Simonettin**,[21] a **Pürkerin**,[22] etc. (I could never name here all the great male and female singers), some of whom have also had the opportunity, and most deservedly, of winning the admiration not only of our southerly neighbors [Italy], but also of more distant lands.

But above all, should I not have incorporated into this small list of excellent German singers two of the most famous Capellmeisters of the German nation? ... No. Because their well-deserved fame in singing will almost overshadow the even greater service [in composing] they have rendered to their nation as well as to others, and it is that, without even mentioning their singing, that will preserve them immortally in our memory.[23]

I beg the indulgence of my dear reader.

Berlin
written on 2 May 1757

Foreword of the Author

Worthy reader,

Love is a passion in which the power of Reason does not always show its strength. If you are a singer, you are my rival. And if the modern pleases you the most, I on the contrary, declare myself for the ancient way. If, however, the extraordinary passion, which both of us entertain for the most beloved, the most beautiful music, sometimes clouds our power of judgment, we should then, at least during our lucid hours, both be equally generous: you, in that you forgive the errors that I write; I, in that I overlook the mistakes which you practice. If, to your credit, you are a scholar, know then, that to my shame, I am not. Should you not believe this, read on.

Introduction of the Author

1.[1] Various are the opinions of the ancient historians concerning the origin of Music. **Pliny** believes that **Amphion** was the inventor; the Greeks maintain that it was **Dionysius**. **Polybius** attributes it to the **Arcadians**; and **Suidas** and **Boethius** give all the glory of the invention to **Pythagoras**, asserting that he, from the sound of three blacksmiths' hammers of different weights, discovered the diatonic scale; to which **Timotheus the Milesian** later added the chromatic; and **Olympicus**, or **Olympus**, the enharmonic. One reads in the sacred writings, however, that **Jubal** of the line of Cain was the **father of those who play on stringed and piped instruments**, both apparently capable of producing different harmonic tones – from which one sees that Music appeared shortly after the creation of the world.

2. So as to be sure of not erring in her precepts, she accepted many laws of Mathematics; and, after various instructions from it concerning lines, numbers, and relationships, Music thus received the pleasant name of Daughter of Mathematics, in order that she might merit thereby the title of a science.

3. One might assume that over the course of thousands of years, Music has always been the tender delight of the human race, but for the fact that the Lacedaemonians took such excessive delight in it that it seemed necessary to ban the above-mentioned Milesian from that Republic, so that the subjects would not neglect their domestic, state, and military activities.

4. But it seems to me impossible that Music has ever made such a great display of her charms as in the last centuries, when she appeared with the most noble and stirring majesty to the great soul of Palestrina[2] (a), to whom she bequeathed a divine originality to serve as

45

an everlasting example to posterity. In truth (thanks to the eminent souls of the great masters of our times), Music is preferred, on account of the sweetness of her harmony, to the other fine arts [lit., beautiful sciences] her sisters, who give her rightful pre-eminence.

(a) Otherwise known as Praenestinus (Joh. Peter Aloysius), who shortly after the time of the Council of Trent, introduced into music – which stood in danger (at that time) of being banned from church – a more clear, more understandable, and more appropriate manner of composition for the furthering of worship.

5. The extremely powerful, and at the same time, sweet impression that Music, above all other arts, makes upon the heart is almost sufficient evidence to incline one to believe that she is a part of the blessedness of eternal life (b).

(b) Since exact proof of the above-mentioned thoughts of the author would digress all too far from our main purpose, which is to give an introduction to the art of singing, we will thus wisely refrain from doing so.

6. Having noted the advantages of Music, we now turn our attention to the good singers, specifically in order to note their merits since the obstacles which attend them are great. A singer must have the basic intelligence capable of surmounting with ease the most difficult compositions but at the same time of singing them securely at sight. He must also have an excellent voice and use it inventively, for he will not deserve the name of a virtuoso, if he is lacking in a prompt variation – a difficulty that is not found in the other fine arts.

7. May I point out that poets, painters, sculptors, builders, and composers of music themselves, prior to exhibiting their works in public, ultimately have all the time they need for correcting and polishing them; but for the singer who errs there is no remedy: his error is irreparable.

8. How great must be the concentration of one who is obliged not to err in producing the improvisations of his own invention and how great the preparation necessary to control the voice in this most difficult of arts, while making it skillful in constant variation. This difficulty is more easily imagined that described. I must candidly confess that whenever I am forced to reflect on the inadequacy of many teachers, on the endless errors that they allow to creep in (rendering ineffectual their students' dedication and study), I am increasingly amazed that among so many musicians of the first rank who have undertaken to write – some in order to disclose the proper rules of

harmony and from them the rules of counterpoint, others to facilitate the organist in the playing of the figured bass – not one (so far as I know) has ever attempted anything more than publishing the primary rules of the art of singing well (which are already generally known), while omitting the most necessary rules. The situation is not remedied by the excuse that the composers are responsible solely for composition and the instrumentalists who accompany should not become involved with that which properly concerns the singer – although I know a few who are perfectly capable of disabusing any who hold this notion. In his *Istituzioni armoniche* (pt. 3, ch. 46 [sic]), the incomparable Zarlino had hardly begun to inveigh against those who in his day sang with defects, when he broke off; and I would like to believe that had he continued, those precepts – despite their age of almost two centuries – would nonetheless serve the more refined taste of our times.[3] Deserving of even greater blame is the negligence of many famous singers who, the more their insights are raised, the less they can justify their silence even under the pretext of modesty, which ceases to be a virtue when it subverts the common good. Encouraged thus, not by empty ambition for fame, but by the need for this work, I have determined, but not without reluctance, to be the first to publish to the world these, my few modest observations, which (if I am fortunate) will enlighten the **singing teacher**, the **music student**, and the **actual singer**.

9. First, I shall try to clarify the duties of a teacher in instructing a beginner in the art of singing well; secondly, I shall speak of those appropriate to the more advanced; and finally, I shall endeavor in greater detail to make easy for the competent singer the path whereby he may arrive at greater excellence. Difficult and perhaps foolhardy is the undertaking; but should its results fall short of my intentions, I shall at least have prompted the scholars of this beautiful science to elucidate it more fully and correctly.

10. Should someone reproach me for publishing things which are already commonly known to all teachers, perhaps he deceives himself because among these observations are many that, never having heard of them elsewhere, I must consider my own; and as such, it seems that they could not be known universally. May they succeed in gaining the approval of people with insight and taste.

11. It is quite superfluous for me to say that verbal instructions in themselves are of no greater use to singers than to shield them from errors, since everyone knows that no printed matter [but practice

alone] is capable of eliminating them in actual performance. The results of this undertaking will either encourage me to make new discoveries to the benefit of the profession, or I will be shamed (but not dissuaded) and suffer it with equanimity if my fellow masters publish my ignorance, with their names under their titles, so that I may both better myself and thank them.

12. But though my intention be to demonstrate a number of modern abuses and defects that have spread through the realm of singing, so that (unless they cannot be) they may be corrected, I would hope that those who – through feebleness of talent or through negligence of study – could not or would not improve themselves do not imagine that I was depicting them in their imperfections. I solemnly pledge that if I have too zealously attacked the errors, that I nonetheless have respect for the persons who perpetrate them. A Spanish proverb teaches me **that poison pens often turn on their writers themselves**.

Azia te accusas quando murmuras.[4]

Christianity dictates even more to the believer. I speak in general, and if at times I focus on a few specific errors, [the reader] should know that I have no other model in mind but my own work, wherein alas I have ample material worthy of criticism without having to look for it elsewhere.

CHAPTER 1

Observations for the use of the singing teacher;

in which is included an essay by the translator concerning the nature
and use of the human voice

CHAPTER 2

Concerning appoggiaturas;

Wherein appoggiaturas, terminations, compound appoggiaturas, and
slides are discussed

CHAPTER 3

Concerning trills;

Containing, besides the various types thereof, also descriptions of the
various small essential graces, namely the mordents, the turns, etc.

CHAPTER 4

Concerning divisions;

Including a discussion not only of the execution of some special musical figures but also of their articulation and expression

CHAPTER 5

Concerning recitative;

Including something about the manner of performance of church
music

CHAPTER 6

Remarks intended especially for the music student

CHAPTER 7

Concerning arias

CHAPTER 8

Concerning cadenzas

CHAPTER 9

Remarks for the use of the professional singer

CHAPTER 10

Concerning improvised variations of melodies

CHAPTER ONE

OBSERVATIONS FOR THE USE OF THE SINGING TEACHER[1]

1. Musical mistakes insinuate themselves so easily into youthful minds and it is often so difficult to find anyone to correct them as they arise, that ideally only the very best singers should undertake the task of teaching, because they, better than any others, know the way to success and, with perceptive insights, are able to guide the student in developing his talent from the beginning stages to perfection. But since among the best singers of today, unfortunately, not one can be found (unless I am mistaken) who does not detest the idea [of teaching], we must reserve them for those refinements of the art that immediately enchant the soul.

2. Therefore, until such time as the student can sight-read without faltering, instruction in the basics, it would seem, must be entrusted to an average [lit. middle-level][2] singer. This person must be of impeccable character, industrious, well practiced, and without nose or throat defects *(difetti di naso e di gola)* in singing. He must have agility of voice, some inkling of good taste, the ability to make his thoughts easily understood by others, completely accurate intonation, and the patience to tolerate the trying difficulties of the most tiresome employment (a).

(a) He must, of course, **be able to sing himself** if he wants to teach others to sing. It will benefit him as well as his students if he can accompany at the keyboard so as to help them master more easily for themselves accurate intonation and hear at the same time, not only the bass line, but also the attendant correct harmony.[3] At the present time, many German singing teachers lack the first skill; and many Italian so-called singing teachers, the latter. Concerning the above-mentioned nose and throat defects (which will be more clearly explained below) and the lack of agility in the voice, one might argue that a teacher should be able to hear and correct them in others

51

while not being able to avoid them in himself. This is true. But would the students not be unconsciously led astray by his bad example? And would he not perhaps be ashamed, while reprimanding his students for a fault, to have it revealed in himself?

3. Before he begins to instruct, let the teacher with these necessary qualifications first read the four verses of Virgil, *Sic vos non vobis* (You work thus not for yourselves, etc.),[4] for they seem to be (though they are not) composed expressly for him; and having carefully considered them, let him examine his own dedication. As a common Italian proverb has it: **It is vexing to one who is thirsty to bring wine to others when he may not drink himself.**[5] If the present time is advantageous for the singer, it is only right that it should not be adverse for the one who teaches singing.[6]

4. At the outset, let the teacher listen with a disinterested ear [i.e. without considering his own monetary gain] to determine whether the aspiring student actually has the voice and the aptitude for singing; so that the teacher does not have to give God a strict accounting because he has cheated both the parents by the poor investment of their money and the child by wasting his time, which could better have been spent in some other profession. I do not mention this without good reason [lit., speak idly]. The singing teachers of former times (b) differentiated between the rich man, who wanted to learn singing to grace his nobility, and the poor, who sought to earn his living by it. They supported themselves [lit. made their livings] by teaching the former; the latter they taught out of love of mankind [i.e. charity] when they discovered, instead of wealth, the ability to become [an important] man. Very few modern teachers reject students if they pay, and little do they care that their voracious greed undermines their colleagues and ruins the profession (c).

(b) When the author refers to the ancient and the modern voice teachers, singers, and composers, it should be noted that he wrote this in the year 1723. This note will be of more importance in what follows.[7]

(c) Even when they taught the rich man only to earn money, they assumed without exception the strict duty of teaching him with the same diligence, care, and faithfulness as they taught him who wanted to make music his main occupation. How unpardonable is the prejudice of many a music teacher that it is not necessary to disclose to an amateur, especially of the upper class, all of the secrets of the art: that it does not matter whether a lady sings in rhythm or not. Even if the gentlemen who speak in this fashion are not trying to cover their ignorance or laziness, they betray their spiteful jealousy. How

52

ridiculous they become! The amateurs who learn music just for their own pleasure are certainly not those who seek to deprive these gentlemen of their bread. Were we not hindered by this common prejudice, would we not perhaps have more genuine connoisseurs, if not more generous patrons, of music?

5. Gentlemen teachers, Italy no longer hears the excellent voices of times past, particularly among women, and to the shame of the guilty, I will explain why: ignorance does not permit the parents to perceive the ugliness of their daughters' voices, and poverty makes them believe that singing and wealth are one and the same, and that nothing more than a pretty face is needed to learn how to sing...**Can you teach her?...**

6. Yes, perhaps you could teach them what to them is singing... Modesty allows me to speak no further.[8]

7. If the teacher is compassionate, he will never counsel the student to submit to being robbed of a part of his humanity, perhaps to the detriment of his soul.[9]

8. From the very first lesson to the last, the teacher should remind himself that he is responsible for everything that he has neglected to teach and for all the mistakes left uncorrected.

9. He should be fairly strict; he should be feared without being hated. I know, of course, that it is not easy to find the balance between severity and gentleness; but I also know that both extremes are harmful, since excessive severity causes obstinacy and too much leniency, contempt.

10. Since it is easy to find this information elsewhere, I will not discuss notes and their value, time and its divisions and tempo, the rests, the accidentals, and other basic fundamentals.

11. Besides the C clef, the teacher should teach his student the other clefs, especially the F and the G clefs, so that he may not experience what often happens to some singers who, in *a capella* compositions, are unable to distinguish the **mi** from the **fa** without the organ because they are not versed in the G clef,[10] so that occasionally in the holy house of the Lord one hears such discordances that their shame is matched only by the shame of those singers who, old and gray, are still unable to find the pitches. I should be lacking in integrity if I did not say that whoever fails to teach such essential rules is either negligent or ignorant.[11]

12. Next teach him to solmize those scales in which flats occur, so that he can find the **mi,** particularly in pieces in four flats, and in

those in which the fifth flat is often required as an accidental on the sixth above the bass. (d) Those of insufficient study who believe that all notes marked with a flat are called **fa** should realize that the matter is not so simple. Were this true, it would indeed be superfluous to have six names for the notes if five of them were the same. The French have seven syllables to name the notes and thereby save their students the trouble of remembering to change the names in the ascending and descending scales.[12] We Italians have only these: **ut** (e), **re, mi, fa, sol, la**; and these suffice to read in all keys (f).

(d) Here the author means the sixth above the tonic in the transposed Dorian scale, or, to be more specific, what today is called B♭ minor[13] proper when no G♭ is marked [in the key signature]. In Tosi's time, many composers still had the habit, when they composed in B♭ minor (or, to use the old terminology, in the Aeolian mode transposed up a minor second), of not providing the sixth above the tonic with a flat sign. Even in other similar keys, such as F minor and D minor, for example, the flat sign was omitted. The author erroneously indicates here, although it does not apply to our modern B♭ minor, that the fifth flat usually occurs accidentally; on the contrary, it is the natural sign which is the more common accidental.

(e) For ease of enunciation in singing, the Italians have changed **ut** to **do.**

(f) It is true that these syllables might have sufficed for **Tosi** and the **other Italians** and for those Germans who were inordinately in love with olden times. However, whether the effort of their pupils in learning to correctly place these syllables merited the expense incurred before the apprentices achieved skill therein (one which assured the teacher secure income for a whole year without their having learned anything other than to designate seven notes with six names) were for the purses of the learners a total loss – that is another question. No one reading Mattheson's **Neu-eröffnetes Orchestre,**[14] and his **Orchester-Kanzeley**[15] in the second volume of his **Critica Musica** [p. 186], will doubt a decision [made] to the disadvantage of the **solmizers** [Utremifasollaristen].[16] For the sake of music history and so that these paragraphs of Tosi above are better understood, I will describe here the entire solfege system in more detail.

In the eleventh century there lived a Benedictine monk named **Guido of Arezzo,**[17] who strove zealously towards the betterment of music in his time. He not only instituted our current system of the five-line staff but he also organized the twenty-two diatonic tones customary at that time (which already included the flat sign) into seven **hexachords,** or intervals of six consecutive whole and half steps. In actuality there were only **three** different **hexachords**, but their repetition within the gamut[18] produced **seven.** The **first** of these hexachords began with **G**, the second with **c**, and the third with **f**, etc. Thus they were the following: the first (spelled in our current manner) contained **G A B c d e**; the second, **c d e f g a**; the third, **f g a b c′ d′**; the fourth, **g a b c′ d′ e′**; the fifth, **c′ d′ e′ f′ g′ a′**; the sixth, **f′ g′ a′ b′ c″ d″**; and the seventh, **g′ a′ b′ c″ d″ e″**. He provided each note of these **hexachords** with its own name. For this he borrowed six syllables from each line of the first stanza of a contemporary song, in which St. John the Baptist,[19] called in the Bible a **voice crying in the wilderness,** was invoked for singers as an intercessor against hoarseness. It started thus:

> *UT queant laxis REsonare fibris*
> *MIra gestorum FAmuli tuorum,*
> *SOLve polluti LAbii reatum Sancte Johannes.*[20]

Consequently, the three principal **hexachords** are called:

ut	re	mi	fa	sol	la,
G	**A**	**B**	**c**	**d**	**e**

ut	re	mi	fa	sol	la,
c	**d**	**e**	**f**	**g**	**a**

ut	re	mi	fa	sol	la,
f	**g**	**a**	**b♭**	**c′**	**d′**

One syllable name was always lacking, therefore, to complete the octave. It is unclear whether Guido tried to compensate for this deficiency in the newly invented hexachord system by designating **mi**, and **fa** for the recurring half-steps **e–f**, **b–c**, **a–b♭**, or whether the necessary differentiation among the three [sets of] half steps and the other diatonic whole steps inspired him to use **hexachords** instead of **septachords** (group of seven notes) for the division of his tonal system. In any case, the half steps were called **mi–fa** in the ascending scales as well as when generally referred to. The hexachord beginning with **G** was called **hard**; that beginning with **c**, **natural**; and that which had **f** as the lowest note and **b♭** instead of **b♮** was called the **soft hexachord** – in summary, the **hard**, the **natural**, and the **soft**. The two beautiful Latin verses:

C naturam dat: F, b molle tibi signat.
G per ♮ durum dicas cantare modernum.

(The [hexachord on] C is designated the natural: that on F signifies the soft. That on G designated by the natural sign means to sing in the modern style.)

were intended to inculcate this lesson better into the memory.

To illustrate this even more clearly, I have included a chart, which, as taken from Otto Gibelius, may be found in the third part of Mizler's **[Neu eröffnete] musikalische Bibliothek.**[21] The first perpendicular column (reading from top to bottom) gives the old alphabetic designations for the pitches; the second column, the new. The rest of the seven perpendicular columns designate the pitches of the hexachord by syllables. The Roman numerals above the columns refer to the hexachords themselves.[22]

		I	II	III	IV	V	VI	VII
ee	e̿							la
dd	d̿						la	sol
cc	c̿						sol	fa
hh	h̄							mi
bb	b̄						fa	
aa	ā					la	mi	re
g	ḡ					sol	re	ut
f	f̄					fa	ut	
e	ē				la	mi		
d	d̄			la	sol	re		
c	c̄			sol	fa	ut		
h	h				mi			
b	b			fa				
a	a		la	mi	re			
G	g		sol	re	ut			
F	f		fa	ut				
E	e	la	mi					
D	d	sol	re					
C	c	fa	ut					
♮	H	mi						
A	A	re						
Γ	G	ut						

In order to correctly identify the half steps of the mode when singing more than six consecutive notes, a singer must repeatedly change from one hexachord to another and name the half steps according to the system of the new hexachord. For example, to ascend stepwise from **c** to **e″**, he should start with the proper syllable of the **second** hexachord in the above chart and ascend to **G** with the indicated syllables. On the **a**, which is the **note below the lower note of the half step**, he should change to the **fourth** hexachord and continue to sing the syllables until the end. Continuing upwards, he should change again on the pitch below the half step (namely on the **d**) to the **fifth** hexachord, continue to the **seventh**, and conclude by calling the **e″ la**. In descending stepwise from **e″** to **c**, he should begin with **la** in the **seventh** hexachord and sing down through **b♮**; then he should change on the **a′** to the **fifth** hexachord and sing to the end. To descend farther, he should change on the **e′** to the **fourth** hexachord, and thereupon, on the **a** to the **second**, etc. In the **soft mode**, he should ascend, beginning with the lowest note of the **third** hexachord, changing to the **fifth**, and later to the **sixth**. To descend, namely from **d″** down to the **c′**, he should start with the highest note of the **sixth** hexachord for the first three syllables and then should change on the **a′** to the **fifth** hexachord and so on until the end. To descend even further, he should change on the **d′** to the **third** hexachord, etc.

Mutation is the name given to the substitution of one syllable name for another. In proper German, it is called the **changing of the names of the tones** and is accomplished, in ascending, with the syllable **re**; and, in descending, with the syllable **la**.

In the **natural** and the **hard modes**, which conform exactly to one another, **mutation** occurs, in **ascending**, on every **D** where **sol** is changed into **re**, and on every **A** where the **la** is changed into **re**. In **descending**, on every **E** the **mi** is changed into **la**; and on every **A**, the **re** into **la**.

In the **soft modes**, in ascending, mutation occurs always on the **D** and **G**. On the pitch **D**, la changes into **re** and at **G**, **sol** changes into **re**. In descending, this occurs on the **A** and on the **D**. The former is called **la** instead of **mi**, and the latter is called **la** instead of **re**. Perhaps a musical example will illustrate this more clearly:

The hard and natural modes in ascending.

D

ut   re   mi   fa   sol   mi   fa   sol   la

changes to
re

The natural and hard modes in descending.

A

la   sol   fa   mi   re   sol   fa   mi   re   ut

changes to
la

E

la   sol   fa   mi   sol   fa   mi   re   ut

changes to
la

Ascending soft modes:

D

ut   re   mi   fa   sol   la   mi   fa   sol   la

changes to
re

G

ut   re   mi   fa   sol   mi   fa   sol   la

changes to
re

Descending soft modes:

A

la   sol   fa   mi   sol   fa   mi   re   ut

changes to
la

D

la sol fa mi re sol fa mi re ut

changes to
la

I will once again reproduce these scales in various keys indicating how one solmizes ascending and descending. The + sign above the note indicates the mutation.

I. The natural and soft modes in soprano and alto clefs.

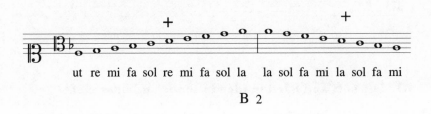

ut re mi fa sol re mi fa sol la la sol fa mi la sol fa mi

B 2

If one ascends:

re ut   fa re mi fa sol la la sol fa la

If one descends:

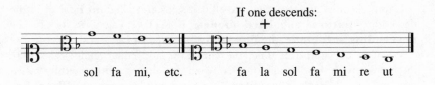

sol fa mi, etc.   fa la sol fa mi re ut

59

II. The natural and soft modes in the tenor and bass clefs.

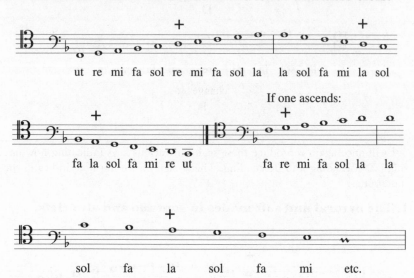

ut re mi fa sol re mi fa sol la   la sol fa mi la sol

If one ascends:

fa la sol fa mi re ut   fa re mi fa sol la   la

sol   fa   la   sol   fa   mi   etc.

III. The soft and hard modes in tenor and bass clefs.

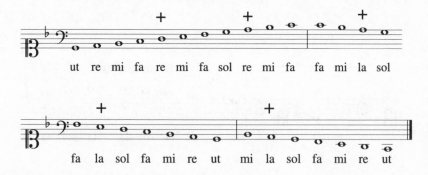

ut re mi fa re mi fa sol re mi fa   fa mi la sol

fa la sol fa mi re ut   mi la sol fa mi re ut

In this fashion, all these modes can be easily transposed into all the other clefs.

It thus becomes apparent that not all half steps are called **mi fa** since in the descending **natural** and **hard modes**, F to E is called **fa la**. In the **descending soft mode**, the B♭ to A is also called **fa la**.

When in the course of time, the chromatic and enharmonic scales were interwoven with the diatonic, that is, when the pitches represented by raised keys on our modern keyboards and indicated with **sharps** and **flats** were introduced, then the already numerous difficulties greatly increased. When one of the old diatonic modes was transposed a step or more higher or lower,

60

its pitches after transposition were named with the same syllables as the original modes, and a [single] syllable as a result of the transposition could be applied [lit., belong to] all notes. For example, in a transposition of the so-called **sixth** or **Ionian mode** (our present-day **C major**), both the transposed [tonic] note and the original one are called **ut**.

Ionian mode.   **Some of its transpositions**

in D major:

ut re mi fa sol re mi fa   ut re mi fa sol re mi fa

in E flat major: in E major:

ut re mi fa sol re mi fa   ut re mi fa sol re mi fa

in A major: in B flat major:

ut re mi fa sol re mi fa   ut re mi fa sol re mi fa

and likewise the rest.

The same is true of minor scales. For example, when transposing the so-called **fifth** or **Aeolian** mode (our present-day **A minor**), the tonic note is always called **re**.

Aeolian mode.

Some of its transpositions

The other modes are handled in the same manner. Since the half-steps always occurred in different places in all of the old **diatonic modes**, one can easily imagine the fear that the students had to overcome in naming all the notes correctly.

The already laborious mutation would have been made even more difficult were the accidental sharps and flats to have been designated by **mi fa** or **fa la**. However, in these circumstances the rules became less rigid [lit. one began to yield] and permitted that, in **a great many semitones, caused by accidentals, no mutation might be made, though this might be accomplished by the raising or lowering of the voice alone.** (See **Critica Musica, II,** page 186[23].) But if certain circumstances exempt the half step from being called **mi fa** or **fa la**, what point is served by the entire complicated [system] whose purpose it is [to correctly identify the half steps]?

A few modern Italians still retain the old and exact solmizing,[24] as I have described above, for those modes containing **sharps** as well as **flats**. For convenience, others give the same names to the notes of the scales that have been marked with **sharps** as they would to those notes found on the lines and spaces of the so-called natural modes but observe only the so-called soft modes. The latter they teach thus:

With one flat.

do re mi fa re mi fa sol re mi fa sol la la sol fa mi

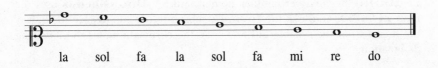

la sol fa la sol fa mi re do

With two flats.

do re mi fa sol re mi fa re mi fa sol la la sol fa la

sol fa mi la sol fa mi re do

and so on and so forth as already demonstrated above in the transpositions of the **Ionian scale**. Why bother with half the trouble of solfeging, when they and their students could be spared the entire bother?

The frequent repetition of the above mentioned syllables can be defended, although not solmization itself, in that they prepare the way more comfortably for good pronunciation in singing than did the German names of the notes. This justification seems not entirely unreasonable to me. We recognize [lit. it is true] that schools of singing are not schools for learning to read. But speaking and singing are also two very different things. That which is easily pronounced in speaking cannot be enunciated as easily in singing if the voice is to continually maintain a good sound. With each vowel the mouth takes on

63

a different position. While the **Guidonian**[25] syllables contain all the vowels, the **German** nomenclature includes only two, neither of which is among the most comfortable to sing. In any case, good preparatory exercises for enunciation in singing are, at least, not harmful. The effort spent upon the six syllabic mutations, however, is always wasted since it neither accomplishes its purpose, nor solves the intonation problems of those with a poor ear, as could be demonstrated by incontestable examples. Were a singer to wish to avoid naming the notes by the names commonly used in Germany, he could adopt the invention of **Erycius Puteanus**,[26] a learned Dutchman, who in the sixteenth century boldly added to the six **Guidonian** syllables a seventh syllable, **si**, to designate the B♮ (designations that the **French** still use)—and not give preference to the others?

The **Dutch** call the notes by the following syllables: **bo ce di go lo ma ni**. **Hitzler** invented yet another nomenclature.[27] **Otto Gibelius** uses the term **ni** for B♮; and, like the **Italians**, substitutes **do** for **ut**. He took away the final **l** from the syllable **sol** and gave the chromatic notes the following designation:

$$\begin{cases} \text{di,} & \text{ri,} & \text{ma,} & \text{fi,} & \text{si,} & \text{lo,} & \text{na} \\ \text{cis,} & \text{dis,} & \text{eis,} & \text{fis,} & \text{gis,} & \text{as,} & \text{b.} \end{cases}$$

Mersenne[28] uses the term **bi** for B♮; and **Mairus** invented seven new syllables: **va** or **ta, ra, ma, fa, sa, la, za**. **Calvisius**[29] was one of the first to object to the unnecessary complications of **Guidonian** solmization.

Incidentally, if one runs [his finger] horizontally (from left to right) across the boxes for each note name, in the table on p. 11 [p.00] above, he will find the common **Italian** designations (without singing) for these notes and simultaneously discover the reason for their designations. For in **Italy** the **C** is called **c sol fa ut**; the **D, d la sol re**; the **E, e la mi**; the **F, f fa ut**; the **G, g sol re ut**; the **A, a la mi re**, the **B♭, b fa** and the **B♮ b mi**. Thus, all syllables that specify each note of the various hexachords are pronounced. The **Italians** designate the **chromatic pitches** more precisely than the **Germans**, by attaching to each note marked with a **sharp** the word **diesis**; and to each note marked with a **flat**, the word **be molle**. C♯, thus, is called **C sol fa ut diesis**; and D♭ is called **D la sol re be molle**. This nomenclature is obviously very cumbersome. The **French** shorten it by using, for example, *ut dièze, ré b-mol*, etc.

Should one not marvel that there are still in our times such vehement champions of **Guidonian** solmization as those who formerly, in many a quarrel over the use of this system,

> with animosity, tossed
> their glasses of wine [lit. Pontac][30]
> into each other's faces!

In closing, I will summarize for the benefit of the singing teacher the main points of this discussion of solmization in the following rule: he may call the notes whatever he wishes, so long as he assigns to each one its own comfortably singable name. **He must correctly indicate for his students the half steps of each scale and make sure that these same half steps are neither too narrow nor too wide, too low nor too high.** Singers who have been brought up in the **Italian** solmization still lack this true intonation. But our **Tosi** will now further elucidate.

13. The teacher should make sure, when the student sings the note names, that the pitches are produced precisely in tune. If his ear is not good, he should undertake neither to teach nor to sing, since the defect of a voice that rises and falls like the ebb and tide is utterly unbearable. The teacher should pay much attention to this, for a singer who does not sing in tune certainly loses all his other good qualities. Except in a few singers, I can truly say that modern intonation is very bad.

14. Also, in solfeging (g), he should have the student try gradually to attain the high notes, so that he may attain, by means of practice, as wide a range as possible. But he should take care that the higher the notes are, the more softly they are produced, in order to prevent shrieking.

(g) The term **solfeging** (or **solmizing**, as we call it) literally means, for the **Italians**, to sing the names of the notes with the **Guidonian** syllables. It can also mean singing all the notes of a piece on a single vowel, without syllables or words. Pieces intended for this practice are called *solfeggi*.

15. He must have him intone the half steps according to the exact rules. Since the difference between the major and minor half steps cannot be demonstrated on the organ and harpsichord if they do not have split keys, many people are not aware of the major and minor semitones (h). A **whole tone**, the upper and lower limits of which are a whole step apart, may be divided into **nine** almost imperceptible parts, which the **Greeks** (if I am not mistaken) call **commas**, that is, very small parts; and the **Italians**, *come*. **Five** of these constitute the **major** semitone and the other **four** the **minor semitone**. Others believe, however, that there are only **seven commas**, the larger number of which make up the **former** [i.e. the major]; and the smaller number, the **latter** [the minor]. My weak understanding does not find this opinion sound, since the ear would have no difficulty in distinguishing the seventh part of the whole step, whereas it has a great deal of difficulty in distinguishing the ninth part. In singing that

is accompanied by either of the instruments mentioned above [organ and harpsichord], this knowledge is irrelevant; but since the time that composers instituted the custom of accompanying, in every opera, a number of arias with string instruments alone (i), an understanding of this matter has become very necessary; for if a soprano, for example, sings **D♯** at the same pitch as **E♭**, a good ear will hear that it is out of tune, since the latter pitch should be somewhat higher than the former. For more information, one should read various authors who have dealt with the subject (k) or consult the most famous violinists (l). In the middle voices it is not as easy to perceive the difference, even though it would seem that everything that can be divided can also be distinguished. I will deal with the matter of these two half steps further in the chapter on the appoggiaturas and demonstrate that one cannot be confused with the other.[31]

(h) In some of the old organs and keyboards, the keys of the upper rank of the keyboard were divided, so that one part of the key made the pipes or strings sound a lower pitch and the other a somewhat higher one. These were called **split keys**. Generally, there were two of them in each octave: the key between the **G** and **A** and that between the **D** and the **E**. The former differentiated between the **G♯** and the **A♭**, and the latter between the **D♯** and the **E♭**. Today the split keys have been abolished on account of the difficulties they caused with keyboard instruments, and more conformity is sought by means of **temperament** or **tempered tuning**.

(i) Nowadays this is not so common a custom as it was in **Tosi's** lifetime, thirty or more years ago, but it has not completely disappeared.

(k) Among these are such writers on temperament and the interval system, as for example, Telemann[32] in Mizler's **[Neu-eröffnete] musikalische Bibliothek**, vol. III, pp. 713ff.; Sorge, **[Ausführliche und deutliche Anweisung zur] Rational-rechnung**;[33] and other famous writers. Since there are even more intervals in use nowadays, singers should take pains to sing even the smallest differences in intervals as accurately and carefully as possible. Otherwise, how can they succeed in performing many of Telemann's vocal pieces?

(l) Also flutists. See, for example, Quantz's **Versuch einer Anweisung die Flöte traversière zu spielen**, pp. 35, 37, 243, and 244.

16. The teacher should teach his students to sing all of the leaps within the scale with perfectly pure intonation, confidently, and skillfully (m) and have him apply himself, even excessively, to this most important lesson if he wishes him to produce the notes accurately in a short period of time.

(m) I would like to draw attention to an ugly fault common today that has been adopted by a great number of **Italian** singers. It must have arisen when some famous singer or other, due to a bad condition of his throat, was unable to avoid it – which fault some may even regard as beautiful, though I cannot imagine why. With a leap, even a small one, they sing, before they get to the higher note, one or even two or three lower notes. These are indistinct and may even be sung with a harsh aspiration. They even introduce ad nauseam this *cercar la nota* (searching for the note) to interval leaps larger than a third – which was not common practice among the ancients. It is much easier to demonstrate this fault than to describe it with words or notes. In listening to many singers, one will soon notice and be convinced of the unpleasantness accompanying this error. Thus **Tosi** is quite right to insist that the teacher drill the student **excessively** in the exercise on leaps.[34]

17. If the teacher himself cannot compose, he should obtain good practice exercises[35] in various styles, which proceed gradually from the easy to the difficult, in accordance with the increasing ability of the student. But even the more difficult exercises should always be natural and tasteful in order to stimulate the student to study with pleasure and learn without boredom.

18. One of the principal concerns of the master is the **voice** of the student itself, which – be it chest voice (*voce di petto*) or head voice (*voce di testa*) – should always be pure and clear, without (as one says) going through the nose or getting stuck in the throat.[36] These are the two worst defects in a singer and, once entrenched, are impossible to correct.

19. Many an instructor of solfege, through lack of experience, will have the student sustain long whole notes with a forced chest voice in the high range, so that the throat becomes daily more and more inflamed, and even if the student does not altogether lose his health,[37] he loses the soprano range.

20. Many teachers have their students sing in the alto range, either because they do not know how to help them find the falsetto, or in order to avoid the bother of looking for it.

21. The diligent instructor, knowing that a soprano without falsetto is confined to the narrow compass of a few notes, will not only try to help him find it but will also try in every way possible to unite it indistinguishably with the natural voice. Unless this unification is perfect, the voice has an uneven sound, or (as the **Italians** say) consists of various registers (n) and consequently loses its beauty. The province of the natural, or chest, voice usually ends at the fourth space or the fifth line of the staff[38] (where that of the falsetto begins) not only for the

67

ascent to higher notes but also for the descent into the natural voice. It is at this juncture that the greatest difficulty is encountered in making the notes sound even. The teacher should fully realize the importance of correcting this defect, which ruins the student if ignored. In female sopranos, one sometimes hears a voice produced totally in the chest register; with regard to males, however, it is unusual that they keep the chest voice after puberty. Whoever wants to discover the falsetto in one in which it is disguised should notice that in falsetto, the vowel **i** is sung in the high notes with more ease and strength than is the vowel **a**.

22. The head voice moves easily and is more agile; it has more strength in the high notes than in the low. The trill is more easily achieved in it but is also more in danger of being lost because it [the head voice] lacks the strength to support it (o).

(n) The term **register**, or **voice**, is borrowed from **organ** nomenclature to describe the sound that occurs when some notes are played in one distinct organ register and other notes in another register.

(o) Various issues have been introduced in the above paragraphs noteworthy of attention, but until now I have diligently avoided interrupting the author in order to better present everything in sequence. Perhaps the first question in the reader's mind is this: what are the **chest voice**, the **head voice**, and the **falsetto**?[39] It is clear that in the Italian nomenclature, the term "head voice" is a figurative one, to be interpreted individually. Certain primary basics of physics concerning the origin of sound and the organs of the human throat that are involved in the production of the voice are necessary to answer this question, as the following explains:

(1) Sound arises when air within a body is collected in a small space and compressed. The instant that the resistance of the body is relaxed, the resultant freedom allows the air to expand. This air, which has been forcefully compressed and is now suddenly expanded, occupies a greater space than it had previously occupied before being compressed. It pushes against the surrounding air, which cannot escape so quickly. The new outside air expands yet again and becomes compressed anew. Thus arises a circular[40] motion in the air by which sound travels from one place to another.

(2) If the sound is to continue and not dissipate instantaneously, the movement in the air must be constantly renewed, and, consequently, the particles of air must be continually compressed and expanded. In order to produce a continuous sound in the air, the body must be capable of maintaining it in a constant quivering motion and, thus, must itself be constantly vibrating. No body can vibrate if its parts do not alternately separate from each other and grow closer again. When parts of the body separate more widely from each

other, the body changes shape; and when they come together again, it resumes its former shape. A body that is capable of changing and again resuming its former shape is an **elastic body**. It is impossible for a body that is not elastic to produce a continuing sound in the air. The less elastic or the softer a body is, the less capable it is of producing a continuing sound. The hardest bodies have the greatest elasticity, and the greater their firmness, the more adept they are at producing sound.

(3) A sound is loud when many air particles are vibrating, and soft[41] when only a few are vibrating.

(4) A sound is high when the vibration is fast, and deep when it is slow.

(5) It is not the vibration of the entire elastic body but rather the shaking of its component parts that causes the sound. Both movements, however, are almost always in accord with each other, so that as the vibration of the body becomes faster, its smaller parts also vibrate with greater speed. Similarly, the longer the string of an instrument, the more slowly it vibrates; the shorter it is, the faster, if they are equally stretched. Likewise, a thick string of the same length as a thin one and equally stretched moves more slowly than the thin one. If its diameter is twice as thick as the other, it will sound an octave lower. Thus, a longer and thicker string generally produces a lower sound than a shorter, thinner one. The more a string is stretched, the faster its vibration is; the higher, consequently, is the sound (and vice versa). With two strings of the same length, tautness, and diameter, the depth of the sound is determined by the elasticity of the material used. With two equal strings, one of gold and the other of iron, the gold string will sound a fifth lower than the iron string.

(6) When air moves quickly through a narrow opening, it becomes compressed and afterwards must expand again. As it comes into a vibrating state, a sound arises, since the air is passing quickly through a narrow opening. The sound of all wind instruments, such as organs, trumpets, flutes, etc., is based on this principle.

(7) The **more elastic** the material of the body whose vibration has to produce the sound, the **stronger** the vibration of the air and, consequently, the louder the sound. Indeed, the sound becomes **softer** with the **slightest degree** of reduced **elasticity**.

(8) The **narrower** the opening, the **faster** the vibration of air particles and the **higher** the sound produced. The **wider** the opening, the **slower** the vibration of the air particles and the **lower** the sound (4).[42]

(9) When one sound is compared with another with regard to the speed of vibration of the air particles, it is called a tone.

(10) Not only in the opinion of most ancient and modern scientists but also at first inspection, the human windpipe has the properties of a hollow body

through which a sound is produced. By means of the small opening called the **glottis**, the fast-moving air produces sound as it does in a wind instrument (6). This opening consists (and thus it is movable) of nothing but cartilages, which are connected to each other by means of an elastic membrane. It is thus completely elastic. The cartilages of the lower part are almost completely round. The cartilages of the upper part, or head (**larynx**), however, are different in shape from the others. The small opening of the windpipe, called the **rima glottidis**, is surrounded by two of the upper cartilages and two stiff cords which protrude forward. It is covered by another cartilage, which is attached in the front to a shield-shaped cartilage, free in the back and, consequently, able to open and close. The latter is called the **epiglottis**, or the throat lid. All of these cartilages at the head of the windpipe are connected by means of elastic ligaments. In order that there be enough air for the movement of these cartilages and ligaments, the lung is capable – by means of the channel of the windpipe and the bronchial tubes below it and going into the whole mass of the lungs – not only of drawing in the air from the outside but also of forcing it out with varying degrees of strength.

(11) Because the above-described opening of the windpipe can be expanded and contracted by means of the muscles for the purpose, it can produce high and low pitches (8).

(12) The two sides of the opening of the windpipe stand at the most about [the width of] a line apart or the tenth part of an inch.[43] Despite this tiny opening, the human voice can still comfortably produce twelve whole notes. Thus, when the voice produces a whole step or sings a major second higher or lower, the opening of the windpipe becomes about 1/120th of an inch narrower or wider. Scientists have proven, however, that the voice can further divide a whole step into at least a **hundred** other very small gradations, with the result that a human being capable of producing twelve whole steps can also produce 2,400 different pitches, which a fine ear should be able to distinguish (just as it perceives the change when a string is made shorter by only a hundredth part). Furthermore, it has been proven that, whether or not the ear detects these differences in pitch, the number of notes that the voice is capable of producing would be infinitely great because the opening of the windpipe, like any other line, can be divided into an infinite number of infinitely small parts. This actually occurs when the voice moves gradually from one pitch to another with a continuous sound, since, when the opening of the windpipe contracts, that movement goes through all points of its diameter.[44]

(13) When one tries to produce too deep a note, the opening of the windpipe becomes so large that the air is able to go through quite freely. Consequently it does not begin to vibrate, and thus no sound is produced (l). When one tries to produce too high a note, the opening of the windpipe becomes entirely closed, so that the air finds no way out, and again no sound can be produced.

(14) When a sound has been produced in the windpipe, it escapes partly through the mouth and partly through the nose, after it has been reverberated therein. The greatest beauty of the voice arises from this reverberation of the air that causes the sound. When the nose is pinched shut, the sound is not reflected so that it can return to and go out through the mouth, but it gets lost in the soft parts of the nose. In that case the person is said to **talk through his nose**. Quite the opposite, however, is true. For when a sound moves through the nose, it is actually quite audible, but not if the nose is missing, stuffed up, or pinched shut. The nose, in a word, is a sound chamber. At the same time, the cavities of the mouth and nose also adjust themselves to the various pitches, lengthening for lower notes and shortening for the higher ones, in accordance with the most minute [lit., some remote] musical proportion. The change in the capacity of these cavities occurs thus: as the opening of the windpipe becomes larger, the windpipe itself expands for pitches that demand a greater supply of air. On the other hand, when the opening of the windpipe itself contracts, the rest of it lengthens, becomes stretched, and consequently narrower, as the head of the windpipe rises in the base of the throat, and less air is expended to accommodate the rising pitches. This shortening and lengthening is visible in the rising and falling of the knot on the head of the windpipe (the shield-shaped cartilage [i.e., the so-called Adam's apple]). When the windpipe shortens, the double cavity of the mouth and nose lengthens; when the windpipe lengthens, the same cavity becomes shorter.

(15) In addition to the reverberation of the sound in the cavities of the mouth and nose, another source of beauty in the voice is the smoothness of the windpipe and especially its head. The smoothness is caused during speaking and singing by the extrusion of an oily liquid from a gland in the throat, assisted and maintained by certain muscles.[45]

(16) The foregoing explanation serves only to show how, by means of the windpipe, a human being can produce sounds that are high or low, loud or soft, and distinct or indistinct. If a person is to pronounce and enunciate the words clearly without affecting the pitch or volume of the sound, the palate, the uvula, the tongue, the teeth, and the lips must also assist in countless ways the reverberation in the mouth, by their position or their movement, by the expulsion of the air through the **glottis**, and by their alignment. In singing, these mechanisms for enunciation must operate smoothly in conjunction with those for sound production.

First, in accordance with the above information, which I assumed, but which is now proven by scientists, let us examine the various voice types by range (8). The principal types are **soprano, alto, tenor, bass**; and the most common middle classifications: **low soprano**[46] and low **tenor** (*baritone*). The alto's windpipe opening is larger than a soprano's. The tenor's is larger than an alto's, and the bass's is larger than the tenor's. Since the parts of the human body naturally have exact relationships with one another, it is highly

71

probable that the width or narrowness of the whole windpipe conforms exactly to the width or narrowness of its opening. Experience shows that the main voice classifications can have numerous subgroups. One soprano might have a few extra notes in the high register than a second who has more in the low register than a third, etc. This is also true of other voice types. One person can produce more unforced notes than another in the high or low range; thus, the windpipe opening of a soprano with a larger range of notes is capable of more expansion and contraction than that of a soprano with a smaller range. **Farinello**, in his younger years, sang from **a** to **d'''**.[47] I know a **female singer** who easily sings from **b♭** to **e'''** with equal strength and purity of tone.[48] Mattheson in his **Grundlage einer Ehren-Pforte**, p. 21, reports that **Caspar Forstern the Younger**, once a famous **Danish** Capellmeister, sang from **a'** down to **Contra A** three octaves lower.[49] It is impossible to know whether any forcing may have crept in on the highest and lowest notes of this extraordinary singer. Likewise, **Porpora**, who taught the **Italian** bass **Montagnana** (who was famous in **England** and **Spain**),[50] not too long ago assured me that he [Montagnana] was capable of singing quite naturally from the [great] **E** of the bass up to **a'**. Also, a certain **Saletti**,[51] who had in his power all the tones from **f** up to **b♮''**, not to mention other singers.

Secondly, the high voice of uncastrated men normally lowers around the fourteenth year, as can be gathered from the above material. Most growth takes place at about that time. Consequently, the opening of the windpipe, which is smaller in children than in adults, becomes markedly wider. Because the body then becomes stronger in general, the muscles here gain the strength to make the windpipe permanently wider. Since this change is usually rapid, equilibrium is maintained among the muscles that contract the windpipe and those that expand it. The production of high notes thus becomes difficult because of the countering effect of the muscles that expand the windpipe. On the other hand, the production of low notes is hindered when the muscles involved have insufficient strength. When the voice begins to change, it usually experiences a certain amount of hoarseness, which can last half a year or more. For this reason, even speaking, not to mention singing, becomes difficult. So precise is Nature in observing the established laws of proportion that, in general, the male soprano changes into a tenor, the male alto into a bass, the lower-voiced male soprano into a low tenor (baritone), etc.[52] The voice usually loses a seventh in the upper part of the range, which it regains in its lower part. With most castratos also, a similar type of hoarseness and difficulty with speech manifests itself for a time at puberty. They also grow as strong as other males [during this period of growth] and the voice remains as high as before. The reason for this, it seems to me, is easily found in what has just been said. Because their bodies in general do not reach the full strength [in later growth] that other males attain, in all probability the muscles lack the necessary strength to expand the windpipe sufficiently, and an attempt to do so is futile. In addition, the countering effect of the contracting muscles is too weak, and the voice remains as it was before. Since at this age, females grow and become stronger and have incurred no interference that hinders their muscles from strengthening, how is it according to nature's laws that they retain their high voices? We leave this question to the scientists for further investigation.

Thirdly, we notice that anything that inhibits either the free expulsion of air through the windpipe opening or the reverberation, or flow of air in the mouth and nose, results in a bad sound in the voice. These obstructions can arise either from natural defects – as when the inner opening of the nose is too small, or when there is some other defect in the inner structure of the nose; or when by chance the nose is congested by a cold or by the use of too much snuff with its many oily particles; or else through some illness that adversely affects the nose – or they can arise out of voluntarily acquired faults in singing, such as the unnecessary arching or pulling back of the tongue, which should lie as flat and straight in the mouth as possible; or by an insufficiently open mouth; or by clenched teeth. The so-called singing in the nose is caused by the first two, and singing in the throat (*il cantar di gola*) by the third – and there are many more of these faults. Those caused by natural defects certainly cannot be corrected. To improve those which are accidental or acquired, one need only to remove their causes and correct the position of the various parts of the mouth.

Fourthly, we see, moreover, that not every word and not every letter of the alphabet can be sung with equal comfort. For with all the letters and words with whose production the parts of the mouth assume a position in speaking that impedes the [free] passage of air in some way, the sound of the voice cannot be emitted as well as with those in which the air is not obstructed. Consequently, the former [the impeded letters and words] are less comfortable to sing than the latter [free ones]. Thus, that language is best for singing which contains the fewest words that hinder the free passage of the sound. Consequently, the librettist does the least harm by seeking out the most comfortable sounds of the language.[53]

Finally, let us examine what causes the phenomena of the so-called **chest** and **head voices**. Since the chest voice is generally stronger than the head voice, the opening of the windpipe must be harder and therefore more elastic (2) and (1); it thus requires more air to set it in motion (3). Accordingly, it is probable that in the chest voice, the windpipe itself and its opening are wider than in the head voice. It would logically follow that chest voices can never sing as high as head voices (8). But experience contradicts this. Scientists have proven that, in general, the **glottis** expands to expel more air and contracts to expel less air; that it can expand or contract just enough to accommodate the degree of loudness or softness desired and is capable of making the transition from loud to soft, and vice versa, without changing the pitch itself; and that consequently, the faster vibrations that would occur when a greater volume of air passes more quickly through the opening of the windpipe are counterbalanced by this expansion, so that even though the air passes through with more strength, it neither beats faster nor is higher in pitch. The speed of the air remains the same, whether in crescendoing, when more air presses against the **glottis**, causing it to widen to accommodate the passage of the air at a greater degree of speed than before; or whether in decrescendoing, when less air presses against the **glottis**, causing it to narrow in order to maintain that degree of speed before the decrescendo began.[54] In general, the opening of the windpipe is wider when a note is sung loudly than when it is sung softly. Why should not the whole windpipe and its opening be somewhat wider with the chest voice than with the head voice without causing the voice to become lower, and why should the head voice, like the chest voice, not observe the ratio of expansion and contraction with a larger or smaller amount of air passing through? Human understanding has never been able to determine exactly how one note is miraculously replaced by another in loudness or softness without becoming higher or lower as the natural driving force [of expulsion] sets it in motion. It follows thus that in two male sopranos who have the same range – the first in chest voice and the second in head voice – that the windpipe and the **glottis** of the first must be somewhat larger than that of the second, although the difference is imperceptible to the human eye. The same is true of male altos, tenors, etc. The low notes of the chest voice will always be louder and more forceful than the low notes of the head voice. The singer whose chest voice is predominant, even though he can sing quite high, will prefer the middle notes of his range (*étendue*) for comfort; conversely, one whose head voice is predominant will generally prefer to keep to the higher range. An aria that is comfortable for the head voice in the key of **D** will be more comfortable for the chest voice of the same range in the key of **C**, a step lower. When a chest voice has to linger in the higher register too long, the lungs, which have to take in more air because the opening of the windpipe is contracted, cannot expel as much air as they have taken in; consequently this air remaining in the lungs pushes the chest out violently. Not to mention the long continued contracting of the fibers of the **glottis** and the resultant difficulties. Should the head voice linger too often and too long in the low range, the lungs will demand ever more air than they are capable of taking in at once.

If it is true that more air vibrates in the chest voice, a fast sequence of notes is more difficult to produce in it than in the head voice. At least, it is more troublesome for the chest voice than for the head voice to execute certain divisions with agility [lit., easy speed]. With regard to the opinion that the chest voice is not suited for speed, this is clearly refuted by the great facility of the famous chest voices of certain rather famous older and more recent singers. That some singers are totally incapable of executing fast notes in chest voice is due either to laziness and the lack of necessary practice, or to the stiffness of the **glottis**, which is incapable of causing to vibrate with the required speed the volume of air that the windpipe is capable of holding. This lack of flexibility in the chest voice, if it is otherwise well-trained, may be compensated for, however, in the fast passages, by emphasis, clarity, and sharpness of attack. That which may be clearly heard in the chest voice at some distance necessitates in the head voice a much greater proximity. Even when the fast passages are executed extremely quickly in the head voice, fire can be lacking in the execution. The fast notes seem to be produced somewhat too softly and lifelessly. Notes are slurred when they should be detached. For in all probability, the opening of the windpipe is not elastic enough to give each fast note its due amount of emphasis and sharpness.

It is generally more difficult for one singing in the chest voice to negotiate the trills and other small ornaments because a greater amount of air is in vibration, and because the **glottis** is somewhat harder than it is when singing in the head voice. Nevertheless, if they [chest voice singers] apply the requisite diligence, their trills will generally become more in tune, more even, and clearer than those of the others [head voice singers], such as those who, because of too great facility, can often sink if they are not careful, into faintness or into bleating or into the trill of a third.

In the so-called chest voice, the fibers of the **glottis** are stronger, and the windpipe somewhat wider; consequently, because nature always observes proportion, the lungs also can easily hold more air. Hence one can expect a chest voice to last longer than does the head voice of the same age. Most singers who have the chest voice keep it until old age still in good condition, unless it has been harmed in some way, whereas the head voice at the same age has been lost long before. Experience bears this out. At the age of over seventy, **Gaetano Orsini**[55] still had a beautiful voice, even though it could not be compared with his voice at the age of twenty-five. Some lose a few higher notes with age but, in compensation, gain several lower notes, without losing in the slightest their strength and beauty. **Carestini,** among others, can attest to this by his example.[56]

From the description of the **chest voice**, some of the causes and properties of the so-called **Italian head voice**, described by **Tosi** himself, can be deduced: to be specific, in the head voice the opening of the windpipe is softer and thus less elastic; the windpipe is itself more narrow; and the lungs are not as expandable. But it is not necessary to expound any further on the matter.

Like Tosi himself, the Italians often confuse what one should actually call the falsetto with the name of the head voice. A more detailed description of the **falsetto** is therefore necessary. One who knows something about singing will already have a glimmer of understanding when he hears the term **falsetto** (compare **Fistelstimme**[57] in colloquial German). Most scientists and musicians describe the falsetto notes that occur in every voice in its highest reaches, as well as those in its greatest depth, as **forced tones** and a **falsetto** voice as a **forced voice**. But how are these forced notes produced? Let us first examine the falsetto notes of the upper register. In singing, one knows by the sensation of forcing in the throat that one can produce much higher notes than the ordinary range of the voice. When ascending in the natural voice without forcing, regardless of the range, at some point it seems [to the singer] that no further sound is possible, due to the windpipe's being completely closed and unable to admit further air for producing notes. However, he can produce several higher notes without resorting to artifice – sounds, which, in the absence of some special skill will sound different from the preceding ones, and he will perceive that the air that escapes through the **glottis** vibrates further back in the cavity of the palate. The only explanation for the production of these notes is that the whole head of the windpipe becomes further stretched and pulled up higher and further into the deepest cavity of the palate under the hyoid bone. In this position the **glottis**, stretched yet further begins anew to contract its remaining opening with the increasing ascent, until it [the opening] closes entirely and no further note is produced. By means of this upward stretching of the windpipe, the entire oral cavity is thus shortened further as it accommodates itself to each [rising] pitch. In descending with the falsetto into the lower register, one who is attentive will notice that the head of the windpipe suddenly relaxes [lit., leaves its highly stretched state] and resumes its previous position. However, this process will make it rather difficult to progress from the last note in the high register that the **glottis** can produce in its natural position to the first that comes out in the stretched position, and vice versa – that is, from the lowest falsetto note to the highest in the natural position of the windpipe. Both of these notes are also generally weaker than the others. Special attention must be paid and extra practice given to equalizing these notes if one is to attain a voice in which all the notes are equally strong and beautiful. For some singers, especially those of the female sex, this succeeds quite well. The disposition of their vocal apparatus – the muscles, the membranes of the head of the windpipe, etc. – is so pliant that one can hardly notice the break between the natural and the falsetto voice. **Tosi** is perhaps referring to this when he says that once in a while, one finds female singers whose voices are comprised of pure chest notes. By nature this would be impossible unless their voice range encompassed only a very few notes. The voices of certain female singers, consistently even in strength, beauty, and sound, perhaps misled him. Most singers of the male sex, especially tenors and basses, cannot hide this break in the voice so easily. Some adult male singers have nothing but pure falsetto notes, and these singers are actually called **falsettists**. Their lower notes are generally more out of tune and softer. With such singers, the following can contribute to the attainment of the whole range of a high voice in exclusively falsetto notes (namely, that a tenor can sing a full soprano and a bass a full alto): that they make the effort, from the time in their youth when the high voice is about to change into the deeper one, to continue to force out the high notes in the manner described above; and thus, through practice, to effect a greater capability in the muscles that contract the windpipe than in those which expand it. Physiology demonstrates that this is possible. All singers are capable of adding some falsetto notes to their upper range in the natural voice, even if they do not wish to make a profession of purely falsetto singing.

76

The chest voices, like the head voices, thus have falsetto notes, with the one difference that chest voices generally have more unforced notes than the head voices. The falsetto generally starts in the soprano range with the **g″** and in the tenor with the **a**. Thus, Nature scrupulously maintains a ratio in that the tenor is only a seventh lower than the soprano, with alto and the bass in exactly the same relationship. In the head voice, however, the falsetto tones generally start for sopranos with **d″** or **e″**, and for tenors with **e′** or **f′**. This is perhaps why the **Italians** confuse the **head voice** with the **falsetto**. It is just as difficult to find two people whose voices are completely the same in every aspect as it is to find two people with the same figure. Whereas one has an extra note in the lower range and feels more comfortable there, another may have an extra note in the upper range. And in sound there are innumerable variations, as in the loudness and softness of the voice, etc. – variations as innumerable (although of the minutest possible) as there can be in the parts intended for the production of the voice. The less these changes are understood by the mind [lit., face] [58] and emotions of human beings, the greater is our obligation to honor with deepest humility the omnipotence and wisdom of the Creator.

It is of great advantage in uniting the natural with the falsetto voice in the upper register if one can produce the intermediate note, the highest of the one and the lowest of the other, with both kinds of voice: for example, if a soprano can produce **g″** just as well, as loudly and as purely, with the natural position of the windpipe as with its position in the falsetto. The former is needed in ascending and the latter in descending. This achievement is not possible for everyone, but it is the art and natural advantage of those whose voices sound the same throughout.

There are not so many difficulties in the lower register with falsetto notes. For they [the lower falsetto notes] cannot be produced, as the high falsetto notes are, by raising the head of the windpipe, nor, on the other hand, [can they be produced] by lowering it. Hence there are very few low falsetto notes. Moreover, they are also always weaker than the natural low notes; and the lowering of the lower jaw, accompanied by an inclination of the head – which in this case is almost the sole recourse of those who wish to attain more low notes – place, in another way, obstacles in the path of the free passage of air from the mouth. Consequently, these forced low notes can never maintain the same power and beauty as the natural notes. The falsetto notes in the upper register, on the other hand, are just as strong and beautiful as the natural high notes with many singers who know how to handle them. The **Germans** call those **baritones** (high basses) who try too hard to force out notes lower than are natural for them [by the name of] **straw basses**. However, singers with high voices who wish to sing too low (besides the fact that their low notes are not heard well) are in danger of ruining the entire voice by forcibly stretching the windpipe.

For most voices that are not professional falsettos, singing words in falsetto is uncomfortable, though more so for some than for others.

I have stated previously in (10) that, **according to most ancient and**

modern scientists, the human windpipe possesses most of the characteristics of a wind instrument and produces sound in a similar way, namely, by means of air forced out rapidly through the **glottis**. From **Aristotle**[59] and **Galen**[60] to **Dodart**[61] – who, as is made clear in the **Mémoires de l'Académie Royale des Sciences**, among all the moderns, was most occupied with the investigation of the mechanical origin of the human voice – little doubt of this [theory] has arisen. Many more recent scientists, for example, **Krüger**, **Heuermann**,[62] and others, agree with this opinion, or at least have not contradicted it. However, in 1741, **Ferrein**, a French physician, presented to **l'Académie des Sciences** in Paris a treatise on the origin of the human voice, **De la formation de la voix de l'homme**, in which he made known several recent discoveries, and, after a discussion of these discoveries, contradicted **a part** of the hitherto prevailing opinions on this subject. He observed that, on the lips of the windpipe are located two delicate ligaments or **bands**, which are covered by a fine membrane. These bands are stretched in a horizontal position and fastened at both ends to the anterior and the posterior cartilages of the head of the windpipe but are free in the middle and thus can be stretched to a greater or lesser degree. They consist of unusually elastic stringy fibers. In an adult they are about one-tenth of an inch wide and one inch or one and one-fifth inches [lit., ten or twelve tenths of an inch] long. However, it is easy to assume that these dimensions are not alike in all persons but must differ in some respect with each person.

After the many experiments that **Ferrein** made on the heads of the windpipes of human beings, as well as those of some animals, he found that these bands are the actual organ [lit., tool] of sound. They are made to vibrate, and thus to sound, by the air that is forced through the opening of the windpipe and thus must necessarily touch them (as are, let us say, the strings of a violin [touched] by the stroke of the bow). He was able to observe this vibration clearly through a magnifying glass. He noticed that these bands sound in the same relation to each other as the strings of a musical instrument: that is, that when he placed an object on the middle of each band and then blew through the opening of the windpipe, both of the parts of the bands, thus separated, vibrated and produced the octave higher, and so it was with the other intervals, just as they are determined by the sliding of the bridge of a monochord. The vibrations were much faster with a higher note; and with stronger blowing, which caused a louder sound, they occupied more space. If he placed an object in the middle of only one band and left the other free, the two outer notes of an octave were heard at the same time. Upon shifting the object on the one band, however, he heard other intervals at the same time. When he prevented the vibration of one band, the sound was twice as loud [lit., half as weak] as it was when both bands were free, and so on. Because the two bands correspond so exactly with the strings of an instrument, Ferrein called them *cordes vocales*, or **vocal cords**.

The more he stretched these bands, the higher the note became; the more he relaxed them, the lower they sounded. Whether he widened or narrowed the opening of the windpipe, whether he blew harder or more softly, [the effect was the same]. The cartilages to which the bands are attached – the anterior **shield-shaped cartilage** [thyroid cartilage] and the posterior **watering-can-shaped cartilages** [arytenoid cartilage] – effect the stretching of these bands. As is known from anatomy, the shield-shaped cartilage can move voluntarily **backwards and forwards** and **up and down**, while the watering-can-shaped cartilages move from **front to back**, though not as far as the former. Thus nothing is easier to understand than this: that when the former pulls forwards and the latter push backwards simultaneously, the bands or **vocal cords** must necessarily be more stretched, and, conversely, relaxed. According to **Ferrein's** observations, the space in which these cartilages can separate from their natural silent positions measures **two- or three-tenths** of an inch. The space [between the cartilages] thus encompasses as many degrees of elongation of the **vocal cords** as the range of the human voice is capable of. A person can perceive the movement of the shield-shaped cartilage by placing his finger on his throat while singing.

From all of these observations **Ferrein** concludes **that the higher pitches in speaking and singing originate in a greater stretching of these vocal cords, and the lower pitches in a lesser stretching; and that the air forced from the lungs contributes nothing more to the sound of the voice than this: that it causes the vocal cords to vibrate; thus, that the windpipe is both a string instrument and a wind instrument** – an instrument whose invention has long been desired, but which has not been discovered until recently (despite the fact [lit., not to mention] that it was invented in the beginning at the creation of the world). [In effect] he accuses all other scientists and others of being in error, in that they hold that the opening of the windpipe must be made narrower for higher notes, and wider for lower notes. In his opinion almost the opposite occurs.

In view of the general silence of the other scientists on this point, it is not for us who view the organs of the voice, not as anatomists or physicians, but as singers, to decide whether or not **Ferrein's** discoveries, supported [as they are] by so many experiments, are correct in every respect. Otherwise, there would be little to object to in his conclusions. But assuming that all his conclusions are entirely correct, we can nevertheless draw all the conclusions that we have deduced from the general opinion of most scientists (conclusions with which we must be the most concerned) also from **Ferrein's** observations. In fact, we can thereby corroborate them. In the **first** place, we can explain the causes of the higher and lower voices in their whole range, in that we establish that the higher voices have **thinner** vocal cords, and the lower voices **thicker** ones – since it is known that a thinner cord produces higher notes, and a thicker one lower notes, when the one is as greatly stretched as the other. There is no doubt that the length of the vocal cords corresponds to their width. Since the whole vocal cord, which can produce so many notes, is not even as long as a thumb's breadth, it is indeed very small. In a person in whom the space in which the shield-shaped cartilage and the watering-can-shaped cartilage can make their opposite movements is somewhat wider, the voice has a greater range of notes than in one whose throat space is narrower. **Secondly**, we also see the reason for the voice change in males in puberty. Because at that time all parts of the body begin to become stronger and firmer, the vocal cords and the three attached cartilages will not be excluded [from this process]. The castrato is an exception, in that no part of his body attains full strength, as is perhaps the most noticeable in the vocal organs. Why women's voices do not become lower is a question that we shall leave here, as previously, unanswered. Also, a question that remains unsolved is how it happens that some singers, as they age, gain a few notes in the low register and lose a few in the upper register, while others do not. These changes occur mainly in the years in which the human body begins to decline. As far as the **third** and **fourth** of the previously mentioned conclusions are concerned, **Ferrein's** discovery does not contradict them in the least, since the location of a sounding string and the freedom of vibrating air contribute so greatly to the better or worse sound of the string. **Fifthly**, from **Ferrein's** principles with all the conclusions noted above, we shall also be able to explain chest and head voices if we assume that with the **chest** voice the **vocal cords** are **more elastic** and consequently **harder**, while with the **head voice** they are **less elastic** and consequently **softer**, and therefore that with the chest voice more, and with the head voice less air is required to cause the **vocal cords** to vibrate. Even more clearly will these principles show why the greater volume of air cannot, in itself, make the pitch higher: it is because the highness or lowness of the note depends solely on the degree of stretching of the **vocal cords**; but its loudness or softness depends on the volume of air that touches them. If anyone might object that with all stringed instruments a too heavily bowed string sounds **higher** (if it is not tuned higher), we may concede that with too much air, the three cartilages that tune the cords of the **glottis**, so to speak, are lowered to the extent necessary to keep the desired pitch from becoming higher. However, many singers, especially those with weak voices, sing a little too high when they wish to sing loudly. The cause of their singing sharp may be that the violence they do themselves prevents the vocal cords being sufficiently lowered or conversely, causes them to be overstretched. Concerning the **falsetto**, **Ferrein** chooses not to investigate its mechanical causes other than to say that his general description of the **mechanical causes of the voice** is adequate to explain the weaker notes of the falsetto. This [general description] would suffice were a person able to feel his own throat and notice that, as soon as he enters the falsetto, the shield-shaped cartilage no longer moves forward, but backward and upward, as does the whole head of the windpipe.

23. The teacher should have his students clearly pronounce all vowels so that they are heard for what they are. Some believe that they are singing an **a** and yet an **e** is heard. When not the fault of the teacher, the error may be ascribed to the singers who, barely out of school, take pains to sing in an affected manner because they are too

bashful to open their mouths a little more. Others, perhaps because they open their mouths too wide, make both of the above vowels sound like **o**, so that it becomes impossible to distinguish whether they have said *Balla* or *Bella*, *Sesso* or *Sasso*, *mare* or *more* (p).

(p) Or whether many a German sings **meinarr** and **deinarr** for **meiner** and **deiner**, **lecht** for **licht**, etc. The vowel **i** is difficult for many. They pronounce it either too darkly like **ui** or too brightly like **e**. The teacher must also take care that he break the habit in the pupil of provincial pronunciation errors that have clung to him from his locality. He must hold him to the best and purest pronunciation of which each language is capable. One born in a province of **Germany** where the **o** is pronounced almost like an **au** would be laughed at in other provinces were he to sing **Braut** for **Brod**. Too many Italian singers have very strong provincial dialects, particularly those who are not of the school of **Porpora**, who (besides his far more important accomplishments in singing instruction) is especially insistent on clear and correct pronunciation. He who is somewhat conversant with Italian dialects will easily be able to differentiate the **Bolognese**, **Florentine**, **Milanese**, and the **Brescian**, etc. – each of which has about as many pitfalls in pronunciation as the other. The **Milanese** and their neighbors to the west, when not careful, sing **u** for the vowel **o**, for example. Many **Bolognese**, in a run [lit., fast passage] on [the vowel] **a**, commonly have the unpleasant habit of letting half a dozen other vowels and diphthongs be heard, usually beginning with **u** before they make an ending. **Roman-born** singers, as I have often noticed, usually have the purest and best pronunciation in singing, and this corresponds with the dialect of their country. This does not mean, however, that those of other provinces, if they take the necessary care, cannot attain as good a pronunciation. One can prove the contrary with many good examples. In the various provinces of Upper Germany and in Silesia, but not in Swabia and Bavaria, the generally clearer pronunciation of some diphthongs, especially the **au**, **ei**, and **eu**, makes many words in their dialect far more comfortable to sing than those of Lower Germany. When a Meissner sings the words, **mein Geist ist ganz entzücket; mein Herz ist freudenvoll** (My spirit is enraptured; my heart is full of joy), one cannot find much that would be a hindrance to the free flow of the voice from the mouth. Let someone give these same words to a singer from one of the many Low German provinces, who would pronounce them approximately thus: **möin Jöist ist ianz entzuücket; möin herz ist froidenvoll** – and listen to hear whether the voice would not sound much darker with this kind of pronunciation, if not absolutely frightful. I know that Upper Germans ought to be able better to differentiate the **ei** from the **eu**. Do the Low Germans perhaps not pronounce these diphthongs too darkly? Why not steer the middle course, so that both the singing teacher and the speech teacher are satisfied? Do many Thuringians and Prussians not steer the middle course with regard to the diphthongs mentioned above? This might be a matter for investigation. After further instruction by the author [Tosi], some information on the **pronunciation of consonants** will follow below.

24. One must always have the student sing in a standing position so that the voice will develop with complete freedom (q).

(q) **Mattheson**, who in his younger years was as good a singer as an actor, writes in his **Vollkommener Capellmeister** (p. 98, para. 28)[63] that when one sings sitting down, he can save a bit more air than when standing. It is self-evident that this observation does not apply to beginners.

25. The master should take care that the pupil maintain a noble bearing while singing, so that he will please the listeners with a decorous appearance.

26. He should sternly reprimand the student if he contorts the head or the torso, or if he grimaces with his mouth. The mouth must (if the meaning of the words permits) assume a pleasant smile instead of the serious expression of an official (r).

(r) When one smiles, one pulls the lips apart and toward the sides. Smiling allows the advantage of being able to better cover the teeth, the exaggerated display of which, however white they may be, is not quite decorous. But the main advantage of the wide-open position of the mouth is to permit freer movement of the air and thus the voice. In order that an aspiring singer can observe all this better in himself and better guard against grimacing, he would do well to sing now and then in front of a mirror. Few are the singers who do not have at least one small bodily or facial mannerism. Such mannerisms might be overlooked [without mirror observation]. When watching a singer make faces, it is hard to keep from laughing or expressing disgust – were one only able to hear him sing without having to look at him! It would have been so easy at the beginning to prevent this from becoming a bad habit. Some singers try to facilitate the emission of certain fast notes by the exterior contortion of the mouth and face. This too is unpalatable. The Italians like to say of certain dandies, who pay more attention to an attractive stance of the body than to the art of good singing, *canta bello*, instead of *canta bene*.

27. The teacher should accustom the student to the pitch of **Lombardy**, and not to that of **Rome** (s), not only so that he may acquire and maintain the high notes but also to spare him the difficulties that high-pitched instruments may cause him later on. The forcing caused by overly high singing is just as annoying to the listener as it is to the singer. The teacher should keep this fact well in mind. As age increases, many voices tend to become lower, and many a soprano who, while in school, did not have enough practice in the higher register, now either must sing alto or, if his foolish vanity insists on his

being called a soprano (t), must ask his composers to write no higher than the **c″** (which is the fourth space of the staff) and to avoid any sustaining in that range. If all teachers of the beginning levels would make use of this one rule given above, and if they were capable of helping their pupils unite the natural voice with the falsetto, soprano voices would not nowadays be so rare.

(s) In **Lombardy** and especially in **Venice**, harpsichords and other instruments are tuned very high. Even so, their pitch is only about a half step lower than our common choir or trumpet pitch (the trumpet **c** is approximately a **c#**). In **Rome** the tuning is extremely low, and is comparable to the former French tuning. It is a major third lower than choir pitch, so that the trumpet **c** almost coincides with the **e** of the other instruments. It is a half-step lower than the so-called **A-chamber pitch** that is established in many places in Germany, in which the **a** of the instruments coincides with the **c** of those tuned in the chamber pitch. The **Neapolitans** steer the middle course between these very low and very high tunings. If the **instrumentalists** do not object to standardizing the pitch level, singers certainly will not, since they do not care whether the tuning is low or high, so long as it is consistent in all places. **Sauveur's** recommendation of a **designated fixed pitch** (in his physics treatise [*Système général des intervalles des sons*,[64]] presented to the **Académie Royale des Sciences** of Paris in the year 1700) has not been generally adopted; and since tuning also differs greatly in many places in Germany, singers are continually being caused a great deal of distress because composers must conform to the pitch of various localities. Arias that are conceived at a lower pitch and subsequently performed at a location where the pitch is higher, are ultimately too high; and those arias whose range was determined by a high pitch level, become too low at a lower pitch. **Roman** arias can hardly be sung by **Venetian** singers, and **Venetian** arias are barely singable in **Rome**. The pitch of Roman arias is too high in Venice, and the Venetian [arias] too low in Rome. Simply transposing the arias into higher or lower keys does not solve the problem because the arias would suffer immeasurably since they had been carefully set in a certain key, not to mention the inconvenience often caused to the instrumentalist. Singers who like to sing high prefer a low pitch, of course, and those who like to show off their low notes prefer a high one. The former seem to gain a note for their upper range, and the latter a note for their lower. It might seem that one or one and a half steps would hardly make such a difference to a singer; but in that point in the voice where the natural voice divides from the falsetto, experience often proves the contrary. Many a passage or a sustained note or a certain word on a particular note can be uncomfortable in one tuning and comfortable in another. Under such circumstances, the happiest singers are those in whom the unification of the natural voice and the falsetto does not cause much difficulty and who, in case of necessity, have a few extra notes in their high and low registers.

(t) In **Italy** higher voices are preferred to lower voices. Sopranos always consider themselves to be superior to altos, etc. Unless special preference should cause an exception to be made, sopranos demand the best roles in opera and, consequently, better salaries. In a concert setting with a variety of singers taking part, it is the established custom that the higher voices take precedence over the lower. This is why so many singers force themselves to sing high as long as they can, even if their high notes are poor. The vanity that **Tosi** in passing has condemned here, stems from this.

28. The instructor should teach his student to sustain notes so that the voice neither trembles nor wavers uncertainly.[65] If at the beginning he uses for this purpose two measures of long notes (the so-called **breves**), the improvement will be so much the greater. Otherwise, the desire of most beginners to keep the voice moving and the effort of steadily sustaining the voice cause the pupil to be unable to sustain the voice on one note, and thus he doubtless will acquire the bad habit of wavering back and forth, after the manner of those with the poorest of taste.

29. Along with these lessons, the master should teach the art of the *messa di voce* (u), which consists in beginning the note very gently and softly and letting it swell little by little to the loudest forte and thereafter recede with the same artistry from loud to soft. This beautiful **drawing forth of the voice**[66] (*metter la voce*) unfailingly achieves a beautiful effect in the mouth of a skilled singer when used sparingly and only on bright vowels (x). Nowadays few singers consider it worthy of their taste, either because they prefer the wavering of the voice or in order to distance themselves from the hated old-fashioned taste. It is, however, a patent injustice that they do the nightingale, the inventor and the only source of the *messa di voce*[67] that human ingenuity can imitate. It must then be the case that, among our feathered kind, they have heard some that sang in accordance with the modern style![68]

(u) I know well that the translation of the Italian concept *metter la voce* by the words **Herausziehen der Stimme** (drawing forth of the voice) does not fully express the meaning. A more detailed description is necessary, and Tosi gives that here. The French call it *son filé* [spun-out tone], presumably because the note is evenly drawn forth from the throat like the thread from the distaff of a spinning wheel.

(x) The teacher must try to prevent the student while crescendoing a sustained note from driving his voice so hard that it breaks, or from accentuating a part of the beat such as the second half of the syncopated notes – which in this case is a fault. Practicing the crescendo and decrescendo when sustaining longer notes extends the benefits to singing in general. A basic rule of good taste is that every note regardless of its length should be given a crescendo and decrescendo – which can be compared with the so-called **beautiful lines in bodies and paintings**, as presented by **Hogarth's** book, **Analysis of Beauty**.[69] From the very beginning, then, an aspiring singer becomes conditioned when sustaining all appropriate notes to make the crescendo and decrescendo with the result that it becomes fluent and all the easier . The mouth gradually opens with the crescendo and gradually closes with the decrescendo. The reason for this is self-evident.

However, the singing teacher must be careful not to subject his students to the strain of singing such sustained notes[70] too often and especially for too long a time. He should not assume, judging from the strength of his own chest, that all people are similar, by having all his students practice long sustained notes every day for two consecutive hours. Out of four students, perhaps one will be able to withstand these rigors, whereas the other three will not and might even suffer weakening of their chests, headaches, spitting of blood, and even the partial or complete loss of their voices.

30. The teacher should never weary of having the student solfege as long as he sees the need (y). If he lets him sing too early only on the vowels, he does not understand how to teach.

(y) Which is to say, until the student has learned all the variations of Guido's system of solmization by heart. This, of course, takes quite a bit of time. With a student who is not initiated in the six syllables, it will be time to stop practicing them when he knows the pitches, the notes and their values, and can negotiate leaps in tune. In this way he will be ready much sooner.

31. Hereupon the teacher should have the student practice the three open [lit., bright] vowels, especially the first (z). He should, however, not let him constantly sing on the same vowel, as is the tendency nowadays, so that the student may not be misled by too much single vowel practice into interchanging one vowel with another and so that he may advance more easily to the singing of whole words.

(z) These are as follows: the **a**, the open or bright **e**, and the open [lit., bright] **o**. Germans may add a few bright diphthongs. The **a** is the simplest and the easiest vowel, and its pronunciation causes the least hindrance to the free emission of the voice. To pronounce this vowel, the tongue is depressed and somewhat flat, held straight and firmly behind the teeth. Consequently, the mouth cavity is larger and freer with this vowel than with any of the others. With **o**, and especially the bright or open Italian **o** (which is really somewhere between the German **a** and **o**), the tongue is in almost the same position as for the **a**, the only difference being that the lips are held somewhat closer to each other, making the cavity of the mouth become somewhat smaller. Next after these comes the bright **e** noted above following **a**. In general, the teacher must carefully inculcate the pushing down and flattening of the tongue whenever possible because this position of the tongue can help prevent faults that involve the nose and throat.

32. Once the student, through this practice, shows a marked increase in his ability, the teacher should then make him acquainted with the first ornaments of the art, which are the appoggiaturas (about which I will speak further on), and have him sing these on the vowels.

33. Thereupon he should teach him the art of slurring from one note to another and of dragging the voice smoothly [lit., little by little] in a pleasant manner on the vowels, while proceeding from high to low. Because these skills, so important to elegance in singing, cannot be taught merely by solmizing, they are often utterly neglected by the inexperienced teacher (aa).

(aa) In the chapter on the divisions, the slurring and the *messa di voce* will be discussed in more detail. At this point, I will give the singing teacher only one reminder: he should take care that the notes emitted by the student are well connected to one another and thus legato.[71] Unless the composer indicates the contrary, by means of rests or staccato signs, or unless a breath is needed, the legato [should] occur – which consists of allowing the preceding note to sound until the following begins, so that there is no gap between them. It is common for beginners to make a little space after each note, especially when the next note entails a leap that they are not confident of negotiating accurately. A very bad habit can ensue from this practice, to be avoided right from the beginning. In its place the foundation can be established for one of the greatest charms afforded by singing.

34. If the teacher lets the student sing words before he is able to solfege freely and securely or before he is able to sing the vowels with appoggiaturas, he will ruin him.

Because it is very advantageous for the singer to be able to play the keyboard and to understand the rules of figured bass – not only so that he can accompany himself and thus sing whenever he wants to, without needing an accompanist, but also so that he can fashion the extempore variations with absolute accuracy and certainty – for all who would excel in singing it is thus advisable to try to study the keyboard and the figured bass.

He who aspires to become a good singer must plan early on to maintain his **voice** as long as possible. Irregularities and excesses in life-style can cause the loss of the most beautiful of voices before the loss is even noticed. A good life-style and diet, therefore, are the best means for maintaining the health and the voice as long as possible; thereby necessitating very little medication. Some old German singing teachers are too strict in prescribing a diet for the singer. They can almost count on their fingers the foods that a singer may [lit., may or may not] enjoy. The list of healthful foods in which singer may indulge can be injurious to his purse, especially since it includes pheasant, lark, merlin, trout, etc. Furthermore, many common foods that are not harmful to a healthy person and that one cannot always avoid are on the list to be avoided. Those good old singing teachers did not realize that when one is used to some of the so-called harmful foods, they are harmless, especially if not consumed excessively. A singer (like any other person who wishes to stay healthy) must generally avoid excesses in eating and drinking; if this is his usual pattern, once in a while it will not harm him to eat something very greasy or very salty. It does, however, do harm to the voice to constantly eat those things that make the lungs slimy or caustic or those that cause gluey, viscous phlegm, which would indeed do the voice no good. The old teachers prohibited herring, but it is said that **Farinello** always ate one uncooked anchovy before he sang. They forbade sour foods and foods cooked with lemon; experience teaches over and over again, however, that a spoonful of vinegar or a little lemon juice with zwieback is very useful in preventing or cleansing the throat of mucus, which is most harmful to the voice. On the other hand, many sweet baked goods and other sweets do exactly the opposite. Many such useful references can be found in Mattheson's **Vollkommener Capellmeister** (part 2, ch. 1). Singing right after a meal, or on a full stomach, deprives the lungs of needed free space for air. Some singers who have a demanding engagement in the evening eat very little or nothing at noontime. Matheson tells us that Bimmler, the former Capellmeister from Ansbach and a considerable phonologist, before an evening performance, refused both tea and the noonday meal, drinking only a warm drink with fennel from time to time, as he sang his part easily and gently at the keyboard.

Experienced physicians will provide the best advice for hoarseness and other ailments of the voice stemming from curable physical weaknesses, and also concerning whatever else may serve to cleanse and strengthen the lungs.

CHAPTER TWO

CONCERNING
APPOGGIATURAS

1. Of all the ornaments of singing, none is easier for the master to teach or for the student to learn than the appoggiatura.[1] In addition to its pleasing quality, it alone in the art enjoys the privilege of being heard frequently without becoming tiresome to the listener, so long as it does not exceed the limits of good taste as prescribed by those who understand music.

2. Since the appoggiatura was invented to grace music, the reason why it cannot be used everywhere remains as yet undiscovered. After vainly seeking the answer from the best singers, I have concluded, since musical science must also have its rules [as do the other sciences], that we must do everything in our power to determine them. But assuming that I have not yet succeeded, connoisseurs of the art will at least find I have tried to approach my goal. The following rules come solely from my observation and thus beg greater indulgence in this chapter than in the others.

3. I know from experience that, within the diatonic scale, a singer can ascend and descend by means of the appoggiatura without any difficulty from one **c** to another through all of the five whole and the two half steps that constitute the octave.[2]

4. That one can gradually ascend by half steps on every note marked with an accidental sharp, to the neighboring note, by means of an appoggiatura and return in the same manner.

5. That from any note that is preceded by a natural sign, one may ascend by a half step with an appoggiatura to any other note marked with a flat sign.

6. My ear tells me, on the contrary, that one cannot ascend a half step from **F♯ G♯ A♯ C♯** or from **D♯** by means of the appoggiatura to the next note.[3]

7. That one cannot use the appoggiatura to proceed from a minor third above the bass to the major third, or the reverse.

8. That two consecutive appoggiaturas cannot be used to go by half steps from one whole step to another.

9. That one cannot use the appoggiatura to ascend from any note marked with a flat sign to the half step above it.

10. And, finally, that where the appoggiatura cannot ascend, it also cannot descend.

11. Practical experience cannot provide the reasons for all of these rules. Let us see then whether those who ought to give an account of them can do so.

12. Theory teaches that in the above-mentioned octave consisting of twelve unequal half steps, one must differentiate the larger half steps [the major] from the smaller ones [the minor] and advise the student to consult the tetrachords (a). The most famous authors on this subject are not all in accord, for some maintain that the half steps between **C** and **D** and those between the **F** and the **G** are equal to each other, but others are doubtful.

(a) The author has already explained what a tetrachord is in his note (f) in the previous chapter. Instead of **tetrachord**, it would have been preferable to say **the calculation of the mathematical ratios of notes**. Since **Tosi's** time the issue has been much more carefully examined by many famous men and, though not proven conclusively, has at least been more correctly articulated than before.

13. The ear itself, which is the ultimate judge and best teacher in music (if I understand its rules correctly), tells me that the appoggiatura discriminates so precisely the sizes of the half steps that, in order to recognize the larger half steps, it is necessary only to locate this ornament in any given passage. The fact that it is found so frequently going from **mi** to **fa** (b) indicates that this is a large half step, which is true. But why is it that, while the appoggiatura can so freely ascend this half step, it cannot ascend from this same **fa** to the next adjacent sharped note (c), when this, too, is a half step away? The ear answers that the latter half step is a minor half step. From this, I can conclude that the reason for the limitation of the freedom of the appoggiatura stems, to a large degree, from rules **preventing its stepwise movement from a major half step to a minor one, and vice versa** (d) – always deferring, of course, to the judgment of experts.[4]

(b) For example, from **E** to **F** and from **B** to **C**.

(c) From **F** to **F♯**, and from **C** to **C♯**.

(d) Why is it that an appoggiatura does not please the ear when a small half step is involved? The human voice itself can, as was shown above, produce far smaller subdivisions of a whole step. More than likely, the reason for this is the fact that **F♯** and **C♯** are tones too foreign for the tonality. Composers sometimes use such foreign [chromatic] notes to stimulate the ear. But the heightened expression produced by such chromaticism would be totally weakened were an appoggiatura inserted in front of it. The appoggiatura in this case would defeat its own purpose, as will be further elucidated below.

14. An appoggiatura can be made on a note that is distantly removed if it does not create thereby a deceptive leap (e). He who cannot sing such an interval precisely, cannot sing.

(e) Such **deceptive leaps** occur mainly on notes that are distant from the regular notes of the scale, for example, in **G minor** from **G** to **C♯**.[5]

The reason why an appoggiatura from **g′** to **c♯″** is not good here is the same as that given in note (d) above.

15. Since it is not possible (as I have said) for the singer to ascend by means of an appoggiatura from a larger to a smaller half step, good taste mandates that the singer must first ascend a whole step in order to descend the half step with the appoggiatura (f) or suggests that he approach[6] the higher half step by means of a *messa di voce crescente*[6] which gradually becomes higher in pitch without using an appoggiatura (g).

(f) Thus, usually for the reasons in given in (d) above, no appoggiatura appears at this point. Good taste here rules it unsuitable. For example this phrase:

would be sung thus:

which is better.

(g) Here the voice is allowed to ascend imperceptibly and smoothly through as many small subdivisions of the half step as possible until it reaches the requisite interval of a half step. This is, of course, more easily demonstrated by singing than described in words if one has no prior conception of it. It is self-evident that the voice flows completely without interruption and is sustained without any new impulse of the breath until the prescribed note has been reached.

16. Appoggiaturas become so familiar through regular practice that the student who has been correctly taught them, though just out of school, will laugh at composers who indicate them by notes because they either think this custom fashionable or want to give the impression that they know how to sing better than the singers themselves (h). If their talent is so great, why not also not write out the extempore variations, which are much more difficult and even more important than the appoggiaturas (i)? If they are indicating them so as not to lose the glorious title of **Stylish Virtuosos**,[7] they should at least realize that this one added note requires little trouble and even less work. Poor Italy! Please tell me, do today's singers not know where the appoggiaturas should be placed, without having them pointed out to them? In my time, their own understanding served them therein. Eternal shame on those who first introduced this foreign infantile practice to our nation, which has the reputation of being able to teach other nations most of the fine arts, especially the art of singing! Oh the great weakness of those who follow this example! Oh libelous insult to you, modern singers, who submit to infantile instruction. Those nations on the other side of the Alps deserve to be imitated and highly respected, but only in those things in which they excel (k).

(h) A composer would find it very distressing not to be able to make known within an aria, completely of his own invention, where an appoggiatura could or should be added. A composer who writes out the appoggiaturas cannot be charged with any other greed for fame than this. But how can we in our time – the time of this German translation and annotation – reprimand **Tosi** for quarreling with the moderns, all of whom have grown old, when we ourselves find it necessary to invent warning signs where no appoggiatura should be made and to stop the appoggiatura madness of the newest Italian singers and instrumentalists, who seek to imitate each other in competition?[8] Whom would our author [Tosi] then inveigh against [since his wishes are already being observed]?

(i) Singers having a thorough knowledge of the laws of harmony and endowed with an inventive spirit surely do not need the composer's help in this. But if an aria that is suitable for extempore variations falls into the hands of a bad singer – devoid of any knowledge of harmony, whose imagination is all dried out, and who either does not perceive the reigning passion of the aria or ignores its expression in sacrifice to his mania for variation – would it not do more honor to the singer and give more pleasure to the listener for the composer to make a careful effort to indicate how the plain melody of an aria could most skillfully be decorated with extempore variations? Some of us German singers on the **other side of the mountains** [i.e. the Alps] would prefer, in the event of not being able to invent something clever ourselves, to be guided by the composer or, at least, by the accompanist (if the piece is too difficult or too uncomfortable for us to accompany ourselves while practicing at the keyboard).[9] Even if we want to pretend to be what we are not, it is not necessary to disclose all of our secrets. Nevertheless we shall strive with confidence to perform the written-out variations in an exact and true manner befitting their reigning passion. Those whose own invention and sensitivity makes them capable of performing good variations should not be denied the opportunity regardless of their native homeland.

(k) The practice of indicating most appoggiaturas by means of small notes has remained the custom of most composers until now, despite the complaints of our author.[10] Let us now endeavor to examine rather more completely and carefully the nature and use of appoggiaturas.

The performer's purpose in providing some notes of the melody with appoggiaturas is either (1) **better to connect the melody**, (2) **to fill in the movement of the melody when it seems somewhat empty**, (3) **to enrich the harmony and make it even more diverse**, or, finally, (4) **to impart to the melody more liveliness and brilliance**. At times only one of these reasons necessitates the appoggiatura and at times more apply.

All appoggiaturas are sung at the time when the main note to which they belong should be performed as part of its written value, whether with the bass or any other accompanying parts. **Thus, they belong to the time value**

of the note which they precede and not to the note which they follow; and consequently, whatever time is allotted to the appoggiatura is taken from the main note.[11] The singer, as a result, must abide by the following very important rule: **when a syllable falls on a main note, which itself is notated with an appoggiatura or any other ornament, then it** [the syllable] **must be pronounced on the appoggiatura**.[12]

If the value of a note before which an appoggiatura occurs is very **short**, the appoggiatura likewise should receive the **same duration** and be performed in the same rhythm [as the main note]. They take as little time as possible from the length of the main note, but it is understood that they occur mostly before short notes because their intention is mainly to increase the liveliness and the brilliance of the melody. However, when appoggiaturas in a fast tempo occur as follows in front of four figures of the melody:

these appoggiaturas should not then be performed as sixteenth notes but as thirty-second notes. If the above musical example were performed like the one below, it would violate the intention of the composer in his desire to notate correctly and exactly:

Other appoggiaturas that are **longer** than these have their own specific rules, since they are **not always of the same value** as the note before which they occur. Because of the changeability of their duration, **Bach**, in the **Versuch über die wahre Art das Clavier zu spielen**,[13] calls these appoggiaturas **variable**. The short appoggiaturas he calls by the name **invariable appoggiaturas**. I shall adopt this nomenclature because it is very exact.[14]

The **variable appoggiaturas** ordinarily last half of the time of the main note. I will continue to indicate them by means of the smaller notes according to exact value, thus:

If the main note is dotted, the appoggiatura takes the time of the main note, which itself in turn will receive the value of the dot. For example,

This example   is performed thus:

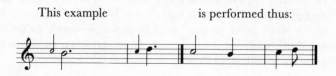

An analogous situation often occurs before notes followed by a rest where, in like manner, the appoggiatura takes the time of the entire main note, but the main note is not sounded until the time of the rest. This rule is not without exception, however, and is suitable only in a melody of flattering[15] Affect[16] [expression]. An example of both:

This is performed as though it were written:

If the main note is tied to an even shorter note, the appoggiatura takes all the time of the main note, which in turn is not sung until the time of the short note. For example:

im - pa - - - -

lento

Se il mio duol se i ma - li, etc.

ti fa - rei ca - der

is sung thus:[17]

im - pa - - -

Se il mio duol se i mali, etc.

ti fa - re - i ca - der

The expression of the Affect [passion] also demands occasionally that the appoggiatura be held longer than half the note value. For example:

o ca - ra o ca - ra.

is performed thus:

If the goal is to better connect the melody, the appoggiatura should be bound in a legato fashion to the following note, so that no space remains between them. Thus, **all appoggiaturas must be slurred to their main note**.

In a trill preceded by an appoggiatura, it is therefore incorrect to rearticulate the first note of the trill after singing the appoggiatura, since the appoggiatura is simply a lengthened first note of the trill. For example:

Incorrect execution,   Correct execution.

If a composer desires the opposite, he should notate the **d″**, not as an appoggiatura, but as a main note.

So that the ornaments that have been added to the melody with the help of the appoggiatura are more apparent and more clearly perceived, **each appoggiatura**, whether long or short, variable or invariable, must **always be more loudly performed** than its **main note which follows**. The discretion of the performer dictates how much louder the appoggiatura is than the main note, although the former must always be somewhat louder than the latter. If the appoggiaturas are long, they should start softer and become louder like all long notes of a melody, and thereafter diminish as they are slurred onto the main note.

Appoggiaturas very often either repeat the previous note:

or they introduce a new one – which most often occurs in the execution of one or more descending leaps of a third (α), but this also happens in other circumstances (β).

Thus **appoggiaturas** either **rise or fall, by step** or **by leap**.

Appoggiaturas that do not repeat the preceding note but introduce a new one occur only from above. The harmonic explanation for this freedom, especially if the appoggiaturas are variable and do not fill out the leap of a third, is the following: they consist of a note from the previous harmony, which holds over as an appoggiatura to the following pitch. They thus have the same effect as dissonances, which most appoggiaturas are, in that they are a hold-over from the previous harmony or a foreshadowing of the consonance to come. Appoggiaturas that fill in leaps of a third, however, do not function in this previously mentioned way but serve only to connect the melody. Because of this, an exception to the strictest rules in the treatment of disso-nance is occasionally allowed. Many a liberty is permitted the written-out main notes of a melody when an appoggiatura occurs. Such freedom exists with the introduction at will of **invariable appoggiaturas**, which serve mainly to increase the brilliance or lustre of a melody. Sometimes these are taken from the previous harmony and sometimes not, as is illustrated by the following examples:

These invariable appoggiaturas occur quite frequently in fast tempo when the main note, which was previously introduced on an weak beat, is repeated on the strong beat, and the following note descends a step. A rest may or may not follow. If this happens, an appoggiatura of a second above is always introduced before the repeated first note.

For example:

When two descending leaps of a third occur consecutively, the appoggiaturas that occur between them are generally invariable. Should a third one occur, it becomes variable.

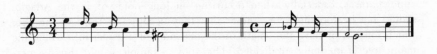

Some famous performers want the appoggiaturas that occur between the descending leaps of a third to be taken from the time of the previous note,[18] in the French manner, giving the appoggiatura a gentle aspiration in order to distinguish it from the termination of the previous note. In all other respects it is treated like another appoggiatura. Consequently, they perform the following example:

as

In doing so, they intend to differentiate the expression of these appoggiaturas from the expression of another commonly written-out figure in which the first note is shorter than the second, and which is particular to the so-called **Lombardian Taste**.

But they acknowledge that in the above figure, the first note must be performed louder and more distinctly [lit., sharper] than if it were an appoggiatura. Other famous performers, however, treat this situation according to the general rule for appoggiaturas, so that the appoggiatura derives its time from the time of the note which follows it.[19] It is their intention that these appoggiaturas, especially when occurring on long notes or in the Adagio, should not be too short, but rather that they occupy one-third of the note which follows, or have the length of the first note of a triplet into which the main note is mentally subdivided. The above example would thus be performed in the following manner:

Appoggiaturas which precede triplets are always invariable.

Variable or long appoggiaturas, which besides serving to connect the melody also enliven the harmony, usually create a dissonance against the bass. This dissonance is usually a fourth, a seventh, or a ninth, when the appoggiaturas descend; and a ninth or second, a seventh, and a fourth when they ascend.

Above all, it is the dissonances which make the harmony more interesting. According to the rules of good taste, dissonant notes, in general, are produced more loudly than consonant notes. This is in part why appoggiaturas are more loudly performed than the main notes, which in these instances are generally consonances.

Because the appoggiatura also serves to fill in emptiness that might occur in the movement [of the melody], a function which can be accomplished as well by consonances, in certain circumstances the variable appoggiaturas themselves consist of consonances.[20] For example[21]:

al - fin   di   vi - ta

de - stin   ti - ran - no.

The consonant appoggiatura is often a note from a six-four chord or an eight-four chord before a root position chord (γ) or a seventh chord (δ), and, once in a while, it is the sixth before a diminished fifth (ε) or the fifth before the sixth (ζ), etc. It can thus be seen, contrary to the previous rule, that a main note, once in a while, can be a dissonance (η) or may become one due to the sustaining of the appoggiatura (ξ). Even so, one must perform the appoggiatura louder and the main note softer.

(γ)   (δ)   (ε)

(ζ)   (η)   (ξ)

The following example, besides illustrating a variety of things, also shows instances where ascending appoggiaturas can have a good effect.

Naturally, **variable** appoggiaturas can occur before notes that are somewhat long, either because of their written value or because of the tempo, and [they can also occur] before notes where a dissonance is allowed. Consequently, they can occur only before **accented notes** at the beginning of the so-called **strong** [lit. good] **pulses**[22] (ɩ), or in a slower tempo before each **beat**[23] (χ).

ge - mer co - si mi pa - re

che non si può sof - frir.

a lui piu degno affetto

Short and invariable appoggiaturas may be introduced before **weak** [lit., bad], or **passing**, **beats** and generally in front of all short notes except in a slow tempo as in the above example and in similar cases. Not all appogggiaturas that occur before strong beats consisting of long notes are long themselves, since in some rare cases short appoggiaturas may occur before long notes. For example:

Appoggiaturas such as these, however, are not quite as short as the invariable ones, but also do not proceed according to the rules for the variable. Thus they are a compromise between the two.

He who has not yet gained from the above examples a sufficient understanding of what is meant by **pulse**, **beat**, **accented** and **passing notes**, should notice that, among the types of **duple metre**, 4/4 time and the true alla breve time [4/2] – which properly has one breve or four half-note beats – have two actual and indeed equal parts per measure, the first beginning with the first [quarter or half note] and the second part with the third quarter or half note. Each quarter note or, in the alla breve metre, each half note constitutes a **beat**, of which the first and the third (which coincide with the beginning of each pulse of the measure) may be designated **strong**, and the second and fourth may be called **passing**. Among the even smaller note values into which the beat may be further subdivided, the odd-numbered notes are called **strong** or **good**; those of even number, **passing** or **bad** notes. For example, the first, third, fifth or seventh quarter note, eighth note, or sixteenth notes are **strong**. The second, fourth, sixth, and eighth of these smaller note values are **passing**. In **2/4** time and in the **divided alla breve metre** [2/2], consisting of two half note beats, for each measure there is only one pulse, but two beats. Here every measure consists of only one part. The **true triple time** signatures [3/4, 3/8] have only one pulse per bar, but three beats, the first of which in this case is **strong**; and the other two, **passing**. **Compound triple time**, such as 6/8 and 12/8, has two pulses; and 12/8 time has four beats, each of which consists of three eighth notes. Smaller notes in uneven time have the same relationship with regard to strong or passing as those in even time.[24]

106

Aside from the above-mentioned four rules, it is not possible to specify with complete exactness the rules that govern the appoggiaturas, the places where they are required, or their duration. An arbitrary factor remains that depends upon the taste and sensitivity of the composer and performer. Composers frequently will indicate as main notes notes that are really appoggiaturas, thus incorporating them into the beat. In other circumstances an appoggiatura, especially in vocal music, can become a main note to accommodate the underlay of the text. This happens for other reasons as well. Moreover, certain musical situations often do as well with an appoggiatura as they do without, and they are dependent on the individual preferences of the performer and the composer, [so long as] no offense is done to good taste. Because of this, and to prevent the performer from the danger of going against the intention of the composer, would it not be better for the composer not only to indicate the most necessary appoggiaturas but also to specify their true values by means of little notes? The performer who has no insight into composition is greatly helped if the composer complies in this. And for the experienced performer they [the little notes] cause no great inconvenience.

I have mentioned above that appoggiaturas may serve to fill in **something seemingly empty** in the movement of the melody. Were it quite empty, the composer is truly in error since, if he possesses good taste, he has already introduced the necessary appoggiaturas and other **essential** ornaments into the design of his melody and imagined their execution within the framework of the whole piece. It is unthinkable that he should not seek to express his thoughts as clearly as possible. One must be able to distinguish whether it is necessary or not to fill in an emptiness and consider that a thing that is beautiful may, by degrees, become even more beautiful.

Various mistakes are made regardless of the care that composers and performers, singers as well as instrumentalists, exercise in the use of the appoggiatura and the other essential embellishments. The most common mistakes are the use of appoggiaturas where none should be and performing them with incorrect note values or expression. To provide guidance for the prevention of these mistakes, I thus add the following:

No appoggiatura should be employed if one or more of the above-mentioned four main reasons is not present or unless these principles are contraindicated.

One may not introduce an appoggiatura on the first note at the beginning of a piece, or a main part thereof, or after a rather long rest, because it is unable to serve the function of connecting or smoothing out the melody, there being no previous note with which to connect it. On the contrary, the harmony that begins anew, or at least after a silence, most certainly cannot be enriched, since the appoggiatura cannot even function as a dissonance. This rule applies as well to the notes which start a small section of a melody after a punctuation mark in musical speech, even when there is no previous rest. Consequently, all the appoggiaturas indicated in the following musical example are superfluous and tasteless.

107

Ca - ro   mio ben,   si,   vi

la - scio;   per - do - na   se   du   bi - tai

The third example above and other similar instances could be excused if the Affect [expression] were intended to convey moving energy. In such instances, instead of an appoggiatura on the syllable *se*, one could introduce either a **compound appoggiatura**[25] or a **slide of three notes**, both of which are more fully described at the end of this chapter.

A strong-beat dissonance on a main note that is intended to stand out would be thwarted and its expression weakened by a consonant appoggiatura. The appoggiatura would be contrary to the intended effect and would achieve the exact opposite result. This rule also applies when the voice enters alone on the strong beat, with the dissonant bass entering only after a rest. Perhaps **Tosi** had this rule in mind in his above discussion of **deceptive leaps**. Another example which illustrates this and the previous rule is given below:

Del   mio de - stin   ti   ran - no tut   -

- to l' orror   io   sento,   tut   -   to l'or   -

Appoggiaturas in front of either of the two half notes set with the syllable *tut* would be very bad. Not only are both notes dissonances, which should be preserved as such, but they also begin a small new section of melody.

Both of these above-mentioned mistakes (which involve introducing an appoggiatura where none should be) have been creeping into Italy for some time. Perhaps some otherwise adept or famous singer once took the opportunity of substituting sighing and moaning where a truly noble and gentle expression was called for. Many contemporary singers of that country now moan through appoggiaturas, even in arias where the listener is to be convinced of their courage in killing some kind of monster. **Tosi's** contemporaries did not do it that way.

If the appoggiaturas are to serve to enrich the harmony and make it more diverse, it is obvious that they may not cause voice leading, which is forbidden by the [rules of] harmony and which would clash with the realization – whether because of their pitch or because of their duration. The rules of harmony thus often determine the placement and duration of the appoggiaturas. When, for example, variable appoggiaturas result in forbidden consecutive parallel octaves (which are very obvious), or in a progression of fifths (prohibited and very noticeable) or in forbidden parallel fifths, or in overly harsh strong-beat dissonances – then one must either refrain from using them or shorten or lengthen their duration, even if this is contrary to the usual rules, and thus correct the errors against the pure [intervals of] harmony. It is customary to grant to the performer well versed in harmonic laws a certain freedom to introduce the usually forbidden parallel octaves caused by **short** appoggiaturas, as well as the even more forbidden parallel fifths. Whoever allows himself such freedom must learn to distinguish a fifth which is only **seen**, from one which is **heard**. He must always keep in mind the underlying voices, which are played at the same time, and be mindful that the freedoms he takes not cause more harm than good.

Other errors can result when long appoggiaturas are substituted for short ones, and short appoggiaturas for long ones, thus altering one figure into another, contrary to the intention of the composer. We have already encountered such a mistake with regard to the short appoggiatura. A similar mistake is caused by placing variable appoggiaturas in front of triplets where only invariable appoggiaturas should occur, so that the figure of a triplet is changed instead into four sixteenth notes. For example:

correct   incorrect

109

This error can also arise when one turns a figure of two eighth notes into triplets by means of the appoggiatura.

correct   incorrect

The brilliance that the composer intended the short appoggiatura to create sounds dull and lame when triplets instead are executed.

It is also a mistake to introduce appoggiaturas into a passage that the composer intends to be performed seriously and in a certain formal manner, especially if the notes of the appoggiatura are staccato. The Affects of brilliance or flattery have no place here. The same is true of staccato notes or other dotted notes that should be performed in a pompous or serious manner. If, however, the intended expression of slow dotted notes is to be flattering, long appoggiaturas are permissible. Paying attention to the meanings of the words of the piece will make this obvious.

The overuse of appoggiaturas, which if used sparingly would have been beautiful, can make a melody either boring because of excessive busy-work that is contrary to the purpose of the appoggiatura, or wild and bizarre because of too much gaiety.

Further embellishment of the melody can occasionally be accomplished by means of yet another grace that follows the appoggiatura and is introduced before the main note. After the fieriness of a wide-ranging grace, appoggiaturas may also serve as the "color in between" before returning again to the very simple. Thus **appoggiaturas may occur before and after other graces**. They can appear before **long** or **short trills**, before **half trills** with **terminations**,[26] before **mordents**, etc. They may also occur immediately after such graces. It seems to me obvious that not every appoggiatura must be followed by one of these graces, nor that every one of these graces must have an appoggiatura before it, nor that every [main] note after this ornament must have an appoggiatura before it. That which specifically concerns these graces will be dealt with in the next chapter. However, to the extent that appoggiaturas are connected with other graces, or may follow them, I will add the following.

In front of appoggiaturas notated as such, no other appoggiatura can be introduced, with the exception of those [appoggiaturas] notated as main notes, before which an appoggiatura traditionally could have been placed. In this

instance an appoggiatura from **above** can be introduced. This happens
mainly on notes over a six-four chord that resolves to a chord in root position.

On the other hand, similar appoggiaturas that are incorporated into the
rhythm and are [approached] from below do not permit an additional appoggiatura.

After a quickly beaten trill – regardless of whether it is short or long, or a
whole or half step – when no appoggiatura is indicated, one may introduce
an appoggiatura from below, especially if this occurs at the close of a phrase.
An appoggiatura from above, however, is not allowed. The first of the following examples is incorrect, therefore, while the second is correct.

If an appoggiatura (or in its place) a written-out main note should occur in
front of a trill, this does not prohibit another appoggiatura from above or
below from occurring before the next [main] note.

Ser - bami o ca - ra intan - to.

A reason for this is that a certain type of evenness or symmetry of motion, which is never unpleasing to the ear, can be achieved with this kind of trill since it has both an appoggiatura that precedes it and one that follows it. To justify placing the lower appoggiatura at the end of a long trill where no appoggiatura already exists, one could claim that it [thereby] creates a sharper dissonance (namely, the major seventh), or that, by the pitch, it at least implies [to the ear] a chord whose three pitches resolve themselves. On the other hand, if the appoggiatura from above is derived from the ninth chord and if no seventh has preceded it, it provides perhaps too mild a dissonance to continue the fire of the trill. But I do not wish to deceive in order to advance my theories, just as I would not find fault with someone who ended a piece in the following manner:

Exceptions to the rules that are caused by such circumstances affirm the above statement: namely, that there is more than one reason to use appoggiaturas, and that often something that cannot be extrapolated from one rule can quite naturally be justified by another. That which does not seem necessary to intensify the variety of the harmony can, nevertheless, serve to prevent something dull or lacking in the movement of the melody.

Sometimes, but not too often, a small ornament, generally a **compound appoggiatura** or a **turn**, is permitted during the time of a long appoggiatura. The note which follows must then be performed very simply and gently. This occurs most often with appoggiaturas that are incorporated into the rhythm as main notes, and seldom to those which keep their own [small note] configuration.

The **terminations** are located on the opposite [side of the main note] from the appoggiaturas; these are **certain short notes which are attached to the end of a note but are negotiated within its duration**. Their function as an ornament is to connect and fill out the melody. There are two types of **terminations**: **those of one note and those of two notes**. The termination consisting of two notes I shall call **double**; a one-note termination, **simple**. Double terminations are seldom written out by composers; the **simple** ones, never, in so far as they are used (as they are here) as [arbitrary] ornaments of performance.

The first note of the **double termination** is either the note above or below the preceding main note. The second note is the main note itself, which is reiterated. Terminations from below occur much more often than those from above.

In general, all terminations are performed quite quickly and at the very end so that the time of the main note to which they are attached is robbed as little as possible. Similarly, the invariable appoggiaturas should take as little time as possible at the beginning of the main note. These terminations are all slurred to the preceding note.

Terminations from below occur after many [sorts of] trills and contribute greatly to the intensification of the lustre thereof. More pertinent information about trills will follow in the next chapter. Terminations may also be added to appoggiaturas from below, just as terminations from above may in a similar fashion be added to appoggiaturas from above, regardless of whether the latter may be written-out as appoggiaturas [i.e. in small notes] or represented as main notes. One must be sparing with terminations attached to appoggiaturas, especially if the note that follows is in turn followed by a rest. This is because the premature resolution, which occurs because of the dissonance of the appoggiatura, is unpleasant to the ear. Conversely, if a mordent or short trill is gently slurred to the appoggiatura, from above or from below, a better effect results because the entrance of the following note dissipates the dissonance.

If the **terminations of one note**, or the so-called **simple termination**, occur in a leap and belong to the harmony of the preceding note, they are always effective [lit. good] whether they leap up or down. For example:

These notes with terminations.

One also finds terminations that do not belong in the previous harmony occurring a note above or below [the main note].

Some like to call the termination that goes above the note an **Overthrow**[27] (*superjectio*); and the one which goes below the note, a **Backfall**.[28]

A singer has to be careful [not to introduce] terminations a note above or below not belonging to the harmony of the previous chord when the composer for some reason has not notated them, as, for example, when the main notes of a melody descend stepwise:

It would sound very tasteless to affix a termination to each descending note, especially if they are to be performed somewhat slowly and in a pleasing manner. For example:

Although these notes are terminations, their time should, however, be drawn from the time of the following note and performed in the following manner:

It works much better in this manner. Thus, they are no longer mere terminations but become notes taken from the harmony which follows them. The following two terminations:

sound just as lame as the one on the fourth eighth note. It works better to transform it into a leaping one within the harmony of the main note:

It is not easy to perform the termination short, gentle, and legato simultaneously. The termination in the second example makes an ascending leap of a sixth, and the voice must again descend by leap immediately. In this and similar cases, one can reverse the value of the main note and that of the termination, so that the main note becomes short, and the termination long, with a crescendo on the latter. For example:

è quell' af - fet - to.

Terminations of smaller intervals may be treated similarly, and this can be charming.

The **compound apoggiatura** and the **slide** are two essential ornaments of singing, which are introduced, like the appoggiatura, before the main note, and simultaneously with the bass note. They take a little time from the value of the main note. Their goal is filling in and connecting the melody. It would be best to explain them at this point.

The compound apoggiatura that consists of the interval of a second above the melodic main note which it precedes is nothing other than an appoggiatura from below with a termination. The first note of the compound apoggiatura either repeats the previous main note of the melody or introduces a new one. In the first instance, the compound appoggiatura is introduced according to the dictates of the preceding main note and encompasses leaps of various intervals, such as thirds, fourths, fifths, sixths, and sevenths:

In the second instance, however, the compound appoggiatura involves only a leap of a third.

per - dona   se du - bi - tai

117

The latter kind of compound appoggiatura is most common in singing, and those that consist of larger intervals are more commonly used with instruments.

All compound appoggiaturas occur on strong pulses or beats. In every instance, the [antepenultimate] note that precedes must be the same pitch or lower than the [penultimate] note that precedes the note bearing the compound appoggiatura. The note after the one that actually bears the compound appoggiatura must be the same pitch or lower than the previous note. An exception, however, is a somewhat large leap that stays within the harmony and returns again to the previous note. For example:

The compound appogiaturas work best when used in moderate or slow tempos.

Compound appoggiaturas fall into two classifications according to duration. The first classification consists of those with two short notes that are equal in duration. The other classification consists of those in which the first of the two notes is longer than the second, as if a dot stood between them:

I will call the latter **dotted** and the former **undotted**. Many that consist of leaps of a third and all that consist of larger leaps are undotted.

Both notes of the undotted variety are produced more softly than the main note. In the dotted variety, the longer first note is articulated more loudly; and the second note, which should be softer, is performed with the greatest possible brevity. The more gentle the Affect [passion] to be expressed, the longer the first note of the compound appoggiatura is sustained, and the greater the value taken from the main note. **Both kinds are slurred to the main note**. Generally the value of the compound appoggiatura is regulated by the length of the note that it precedes and by the tempo. However, this does not prevent a dotted compound appoggiatura from preceding many a shorter note or an undotted one from preceding many a longer note, as the foregoing third example (showing a compound appoggiatura before the leap of a third) indicates. Since this is impossible to explain with exact rules, it is best if the composer indicates them [the appoggiaturas] by means of little notes in exact values where they are preferred and necessary.

The **slide** moves only in a stepwise manner; whereas, on the other hand, the **compound appoggiatura** always consists of leaps. Nevertheless, the slide is like the compound appoggiatura in that it is always connected in a legato fashion to the main note, from whose value it takes as much time as it needs; in that it moves upwards; and in that it requires after its main note a descending note, or at least not an ascending one. Some **slides** consist of **two**, and some of **three notes**.

The **slides of two notes** are either **fast and equal**:

or **slow and dotted**:

They occur most often right before the higher of two notes of an ascending leap, filling in the empty spaces that lie between these two notes by touching the notes that are the closest to the high note. At the leap of a fourth, the entire interval is filled in. Once in a while, one even encounters [the slide] on stepwise ascending notes:

119

The **fast** slides precede strong [lit. good] as well as weak [lit. bad] beats. The composer often incorporates those that precede strong beats into the rhythm with regularly notated notes. It is perhaps their three-note configuration, in which two preceding short notes and a longer one are followed by a dot, that has given rise to the so-called **Lombardian Taste**, which is preferred.

The two short notes in this figure differ from the slide only in that they are performed very loudly; whereas, a slide that fills in a leap and falls truly within a weak beat will be performed in a softer manner. The singer must use the latter type of slide very sparingly, not as do some instrumentalists who, lacking in the noble simplicity of performance, make all leaps lame and dull by overusing it.[29] Such a slide is rarely allowed when there is no preceding leap. Many keyboard players of the lowest class all too often have the bad habit of using the short slide almost as a cure-all for their dearth of other essential ornaments. Beware of imitating them.

The first of the two notes of **the long and dotted slide** is always articulated loudly; the short one next to the main note, very softly. The length of the first note of this grace is more variable than that of any other. One must also examine the bass and the harmony, and the Affect [expression] to make sure that it [the long and dotted slide] is in accord with them. The main note of the melody thus either receives half the value (λ) or is performed together with the second note of the slide only at the very end (μ). Once in a while, but seldom, it takes some of the time of the main note which follows it (γ).[30]

120

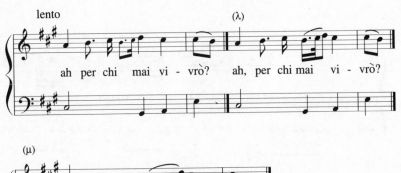

If the note that is preceded by the slide is dotted, [the note] will be heard either at the time of the dot (ξ), or at the end of the second note of the slide (o), or even later if another note is tied to the dot (π). For example:

io son op - pres - sa   io son op - io   son op-

In every instance in triple time (ρ), if the main note occurs at the time of the dot and if the tempo permits, the main note is articulated in a detached fashion, so that between it and the note that follows, a brief space may be noticed. In duple time this is allowed only if the note after the dot is the same note (σ). For example:[31]

In addition, if the tempo is very slow, a **turn** (which will be described in the following chapter) may be introduced in the middle of the dotted slide.

The **slide of three notes** is nothing other than a **filled-out compound appoggiatura**, which, by means [filling in] of the middle note, accomplishes a leap of a third. For example:

Compound Appoggiatura   Slide

Just as the compound appoggiatura may be slower or faster, there are also **slower** and **faster three-note slides**. The very fast ones are more suited to playing rather than singing. In singing, those that are moderately slow or very slow are preferred. The actual duration of each of these three small notes, or of all three together, is not easy to describe, and should rather be left to the tempo indication and the sensibility of the performer. The main note may lose less than half of its value, but never more than that. The three notes of the slide must be of equal value, with the exception that, if the slide is very slow, the middle note may receive a bit more time than the other two. It thus receives a kind of small emphasis. This is, of course, very difficult to indicate with written notes. One must think of the first note as still belonging to the time of the previous main note, and the middle note as dotted and rearticulated; and all three must be performed in a somewhat dragging manner. It is, of course, easier to explain this concept by example.

The performance of this **slow three-note slide** is always gentle and languid. It is always found on a strong pulse or beat before a long note, usually before one at the same pitch as the preceding note, or before a note that is the beginning of a new section of the melody, especially if there is no bass under its first half. This [ornament] is effective in [lit. likes] a downwards moving sequence and may be used with dissonant as well as consonant harmonies, though it is found more often with the former than the latter.

lento

per - do - na,   se du - bi - tai   di   te.

What variation may be achieved by using, at the right time and with good taste, those interchangeable two or three little notes of which the terminations, compound appoggiaturas, and slides consist! What annoyance can be caused the listener by their incorrect, too frequent usage, or their improper placement!

CHAPTER THREE

CONCERNING TRILLS

1. There are two very great obstacles to the perfect production and performance of a trill. The first, that no infallible rules to teach it have yet been found, embarrasses the teacher; the second, that ungenerous Nature endows him with little [ability], plagues the student. The impatience of the teacher unites with the desperation of the student, so that the former abandons the effort and the latter the application. The master is then guilty of a double mistake: first, by not doing his duty and second, by leaving the student in ignorance. One must struggle against these difficulties until they are finally surmounted.

2. Whether it is necessary for one who wants to sing to be able to produce a good trill, one should ask the masters [best practitioners] of the art—for they know better than all others what great obligation they owe to the trill, either when they have been surprised by an unforeseen distraction; or else when, on account of the sterility of the dulled imagination, they are not in a position to hide from the audience the poverty of their knowledge, manifesting itself at just the wrong time—to what extent the trill has come to their rescue.[1]

3. He who can produce a beautiful trill, though he has no store of other ornaments, always has the advantage of acquitting himself with honor at pauses or cadences of the melody where the trill is most indispensable. He who can produce no trill or only a faulty one will never become a great singer, no matter how much else he might understand.

4. Since the trill is so indispensable to singers, the teacher must take pains through oral instruction, through reflection, and through the aid of one or another instrument to bring the student to the point that he can produce a trill, even [lit., equally beaten], clear, flexible, and moderately quick,[2] for these are the principal qualities of the trill.

5. In case the teacher does not know how many kinds of trills there are, I shall tell him that the ingenuity of singers has found such a variety of ways of using them, which have given rise to their nomenclature, that one can confidently name **eight**.

6. The **first** is the **major trill**, which consists of a fast alternation of two neighboring pitches a whole step apart (a). One of these pitches should be called the main note because it has the right to occupy the site over which the trill is to be produced and thus is the ruler.[3] Even though the other pitch occupies the space above it, it is nonetheless only the auxiliary. This trill serves as the origin for all of the others.

7. The **second** is the **minor trill**, whose two pitches constitute a major half step (b). The key of the piece and the directions of the composer determine whether this trill or the preceding one must be used (c). The former, however, is always excluded from inferior cadences[4] (d). If, in some singers, it is not easy to perceive the half-step difference between these two trills, the reason is that the upper, or auxiliary, note is not loud enough; moreover, since the minor trill is more difficult to beat than the other, not everyone knows how to produce it as it should be [sung], and the carelessness eventually becomes habitual (e). He who is unable to distinguish the difference in an instrumentalist can blame only his ear.

(c) Not only must one pay attention to the scale, or the principal key [signature] of the piece, but consulting the ear, one also must always heed the tonalities of the incidental keys into which the piece modulates and, at times, [heed] the preceding and subsequent notes. In **C** major, for example, according to the scale, a trill on **E** is beaten with **E** and **F**. Should a modulation to

127

G major occur – made apparent by an accidental **F♯** occurring before the **E** or immediately afterwards, either in the melody of the voice part itself, in the bass, or in a middle voice – not **F**, but **F♯** must be the auxiliary note for the trill on the **E**. Should the **F♯** again become a natural, the modulation returns to the tonality of C major, and the trill on E is again beaten with **F♮** until a new sharp or flat sign appears. The same [principle] is to be observed when an accidental flat sign appears and then is removed in the melody, bass or middle voices.

(d) [The word] **cadences** [*Cadenzen*] is used here to indicate the last three notes at the end of a main section of a piece. Each of the four main voices of harmony in homophony has its own kind of cadential pattern from which it derives its name. The following musical example illustrates them:

The term "inferior cadence" here designates the discant cadence proper.[5] Since in all major or minor keys, a half step occurs (generally called *Semitonium modi*) in the inferior cadence, it is natural that no trill of a whole step may be introduced before the final note. Only in the discant and tenor cadence is a trill permitted on the penultimate note; for this reason, these [two types of cadences] are the most suitable for ending a piece. Thus they are often confused with one another and lumped together under the name "tenor cadence," even though the piece consists of several voices. If a solo voice is present, even a [solo] alto part, its cadences take the tenor cadence format and, much more rarely, the bass cadence [format]. In a solo bass voice part, while the bass cadences are most common, it [the solo part] especially when it is a baritone [part], may assume the tenor cadence [format].

(e) For some singers, the half-step trill is easier than that of a whole step, without doubt because of an overly soft glottis. In order to learn to beat the

128

trill according to all of the above characteristics and to avoid all bad habits, the beginner should initially try both notes of the trill separately, first in whole steps and subsequently in half steps, alternating and beating them slowly as if they were slurred dotted notes whose second note is equal to [lit., not softer than] the first. Only the beginning note may get a push or aspiration from the chest; the following notes, however, must be connected in one breath without being newly stressed. For example:

The longer he practices this exercise, the faster he should let the notes alternate. At the same time, he should always be careful to pay attention to the proper intonation of both pitches so that neither goes sharp or flat without being noticed. To monitor this, he should from time to time compare pitches with an accurately tuned keyboard instrument or harpsichord. The speed of attack of the two sounds will eventually make the dot between the two notes and the slur imperceptible. Sustaining the main note a bit longer in the exercise assures that the pitch is heard with clarity and does not get lost; and the shorter but equally loud articulation of the auxiliary note insures also that this note retains its clarity but never sounds louder than the main note. It is advisable that the beginner, when he wants to practice the trill, start with the main note in order to become more confident with it. After good progress, he may, however, begin with the auxiliary note, which is the true beginning of the trill and which must be marked by an impulse of the breath. In this way he will become adept at executing the trill both with and without the appoggiatura. The appoggiatura of the trill is nothing other than the auxiliary that is introduced before and held somewhat longer than the main note. After continuing this exercise for some time and noticing marked improvement, the student should endeavor to attach the **double termination** from below at the end of the trill, called by many simply the **termination** (the **essence** of which we have already become acquainted with in the previous chapter), which is executed at the same speed as the pitches of the trill, but without being newly articulated or detached.

The symbol used for the above trills by keyboardists is commonly ᴧᴧᴧ , or **tr**.

129

8. The **third** is the **half trill**, whose name describes it well (f). He who has mastered the first and second may easily learn this one, simply by making it slightly faster than the others and stopping it the moment it is heard, adding to it a bit of brillance (*brillante*) (g). This makes this trill more appropriate to the brisk and lively arias than to the pathetic.

(f) Instrumentalists customarily call this trill the **short trill**. The keyboardists have their own sign which looks like this: ∿. In music its realization is as follows:

If an appoggiatura appears before a short trill, it thereby constitutes the first note of it and must not be repeated. It is another matter if this note, which would otherwise indicate an appoggiatura (but is written out as a main note), is of short duration. For example:

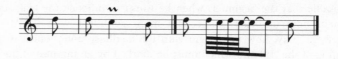

(g) The author here is without doubt referring to the necessary snap[6] of the last auxiliary note of the trill, which must be tossed off, so to speak, with the greatest precision and speed, whereby at the same time occurs a certain special tensing and a flick of the opening of the windpipe, which is more easily felt than described. Understanding the correct manner of executing the short trill on the keyboard will clarify the conception of it. Proper execution greatly depends on the good condition of the opening of the windpipe.

9. The **fourth** is the **rising trill**, which is executed by having the voice, while continuously trilling, imperceptibly ascend from one comma to a higher one without allowing the ascent to be perceived as such.[7]

10. The **fifth** is the **descending trill**, whereby the voice descends likewise imperceptibly from comma to comma in such a manner that its descent cannot be distinguished. Since the institution of true good taste, these two trills are no longer in fashion and they now need to be forgotten. The discriminating ear abhors equally the tiresome old practices and the modern abuses.[8]

Another kind of trill is the so-called *catena di trilli* or **chain of trills**, whereby the trill ascends or descends from one whole or half step of the the scale to the other.

This trill is still in use and is quite effective, especially when each rising trill receives its own clear termination. For the most part, this trill is written out by the composer himself.

11. **The sixth** is the **slow trill**,[9] whose characteristics are also revealed by its name. One can be a good singer, in my opinion, without ever practicing this trill. When this trill stands alone, it is nothing other than an affected wobbling; but when it is gradually united with the first [major] or second [minor] kind of trills, it seems to me that it could please only the first time, at the most[10] (h).

(h) In slow and sad pieces a somewhat slower trill is effective but only in an especially sad expression,[11] but it must not be so slow that it puts one to sleep, nor must it be used too frequently. Therefore the antiquated extremely slow trill of some Frenchmen is not justified.[12] If a singer is in complete command of the trill (as he should be), he will easily see that the place where he sings can prescribe the speed of movement. In a very reverberant location, naturally the tempo of the trill must be somewhat modified. **Quantz** quite correctly maintains that the lower voices should always let the trill beat somewhat slower than the higher voices ; and that therefore an alto must trill more slowly than a soprano, and a bass more slowly than a tenor (**Versuch einer Anweisung die Flöte traversière zu spielen**, p. 85). His distinctions are generally in accordance with the nature of sound.

12. The **seventh** is the **double** trill, which inserts a few notes in the middle of the regular major or minor trill, so that from one trill, three are generated (i). When these few notes, of different pitches,

which by degrees [lit., little by little] separate the notes of the ordinary trill, are sung distinctly and in tune – when this trill is produced pleasantly on the high notes by a beautiful voice, which through rare talent has it under control and does not flaunt it too often, it [the double trill] cannot displease Envy herself, unless she is extremely malevolent (k).

(i) There are two types of double trills. In the first, two notes occur before the regular trill and are introduced from **below**.[13]

The other precedes the trill with four notes which are above and below it:

Like the regular trill, both of the above sometimes have a termination. Keyboard players notate the first kind from below in the following fashion: ᴄᴡᴡ, and the latter from above, thus: ᴄᴡᴡ. Sometimes, particularly in vocal music, when this trill is approached from above, it is indicated in the following manner:

(k) The method [of performance] suggested by the author can be employed only on a long trill occurring either on a very long note or on several shorter

132

notes tied together on the same pitch, and the trill would appear approximately as follows:

But everything must flow without a break. More of importance concerning the double trill appears below.

13. The **eighth** is the **mordent**,[14] which can also serve as a pleasant ornament of song, but is taught more by nature than by art. It arises with greater speed than the others but is over as soon as it is begun (l). Knowing how to introduce it occasionally into the divisions (which I shall treat in the following chapter devoted to the divisions) is a great advantage to the singer (m). And he who understands the art will seldom omit it [the mordent] immediately after an appoggiatura. Ignorance has no right to disdain it.

(l) The Italians always confuse the mordent with the short trill. The mordent proper, called *pincé* by the French, is executed in the following manner:

The following sign is used by the the keyboardists: ✦. Except for the first note, it is simply a **short trill** executed from below. When preceded by an appoggiatura, however, it becomes fully the inversion of a brief trill with its own preceding appoggiatura. The only difference between them is that the mordent in this instance requires an appoggiatura from below, whereas the short trill requires an appoggiatura from above.

133

For example:

(m) In most cases when a main note (preceded by an appoggiatura) is followed by a rest, a mordent or brief trill is permitted on the main note, [and it] must be executed more softly than the appoggiatura and slurred to it.

The mordent can be continued [lit., lengthened] on a long note when space permits. In this instance it is [no different than] a trill that simply takes the lower note instead of the upper as an auxiliary note. For example:

Mordent   Trill

The keyboardists usually indicate it thus: **ᘏ**.

Invariable appoggiaturas can take the place of short trills on descending notes that are not too short to bear them [the trills]. For example:

The Italians tend erroneously to call these mordents – which is probably why our author is not very definite about the matter.

14. The teacher must largely direct his attention to a few very necessary trills, [isolating] them from the many kinds of trills examined above (n). I know and hear all too often that one can sing without trills; but nevertheless one must not follow the example of those too lazy to try.

(n) If this is understood in its truest sense, the author is not altogether incorrect. Nevertheless, since there are various graces that bear some similarity to the trill, including some with which we are already familiar, a good teacher ought not neglect them. He must ask the student to devote more practice to those that seem the most difficult to him. In some singers the short trill may be well executed, while the longer trill may be performed either lamely, overly fast, or bleatingly. In other singers, the reverse is true.

15. To be beautiful, the trill must be prepared. However, it does not always require an appoggiatura, for at times, neither time nor good taste permits it. It [the trill] requires an appoggiatura in almost all final cadences and at various other places, with the tonality prescribing whether a whole or half step is required above the main note.

16. There are many defects of the trill to be avoided. The very long sustained trill not infrequently [used] at the wrong time,[15] was very popular in the past, just as the divisions are today. Since the art of singing has become refined, it [the long trill], however, has been left to trumpeters, or to those singers who dare to risk exploding in order to wrest shouts of approval from the plebes. Employed too often, the trill does not please, regardless of its beauty. The trill beaten with an uneven speed pleases even less. The **goat trill**[16] is ridiculous because, like laughter, it is produced in the mouth and, if it is high-pitched, [it is produced] in the roof of the mouth [palate] (o). The trill consisting of two notes a third apart engenders annoyance. The trill that is too slow becomes boring, and the trill that is not purely in tune makes one want to cover his ears.

(o) When the interval of the trill is smaller than a half step, or when the two notes of which it consists are beaten with unequal speed and strength, or quiveringly, the trill sounds like a goat bleating. The precise place for production of a good trill is at the opening of the head of the windpipe.[17] The movement can be felt from the outside when the fingers are placed there. If no movement or beating is felt, this serves as a sure indication that one is bleating out the trill only by means of the vibration of air on the palate. Such a trill is never more obvious, nor more unbearable, than in a large place or from a distance, because the outer air is not made to vibrate evenly or with enough force.

17. The importance of having a good trill obligates the teacher to encourage the student to practice it diligently on all vowels and on all pitches that are comfortable to his range, not only on long notes but also on the short notes, whereby one learns in time to produce the short trill and the mordent and attains the skill to execute these, even in the middle of the fastest divisions.

18. When the trill is mastered, the teacher should make sure that the student can also let go of it easily and at will. The error of not being able to finish the trill as quickly as it should be is not an uncommon one.

19. The understanding of where or where not to introduce the trill outside of the main cadences of a piece comes with experience, good taste, and insight.

Here I would like to add a few remarks to better elucidate **Tosi's** thoughts.

The specific trills designated by the author as the **first** and the **second** nowadays are more freely heard than formerly. They can occur not only before cadenzas and with appoggiaturas but also completely freely and without appoggiaturas (α). They may even occur at the beginning of the piece (β). Many trills may also occur consecutively (γ). They can occur also over sustained notes, over a long note, and (in general) every place where a note seems not to have enough movement or brilliance, especially in a lively expression (δ). They may be found on all beats and in all meters.

on - da   per   for -

mar   e   let -   to e   sponda   etc.

(γ)

(δ)

Since, according to the current custom, composers themselves tend to indicate the trills where they are desired, the singer should concern himself more with good execution than with the rules which specify placement.

Just like the long sustained notes, a long trill may be performed crescendo–decrescendo [lit., alternately loud or soft]. To acquire this facility, it is necessary to practice the trill in all degrees of softness and loudness.

Where no appoggiatura occurs before a note, as has been shown in the preceding chapter, neither can one be employed before the trill that is indicated over that note. Right from the beginning, the trill must be beaten rigorously and evenly, especially when it occurs after a pause or a leap. Also, not all notes that have an appoggiatura before them permit the trill.

Terminations of two notes, described in the previous chapter, occur after fairly long trills, no matter whether the following notes ascend, descend, or leap.

The tonality – in which the held-out [trilled] note occurs, or that of the preceding, or the subsequent notes – determines whether or not the termination consists of a whole or half step. The termination is always very closely connected [rhythmically] to the note which follows; it is connected without pause to that note. The only exception occurs when the trill and its termination are indicated over a dotted note whose subsequent shorter note ascends.[18] Between the termination of the trill and the following short note occurs a small almost imperceptible lingering, which cannot be exactly expressed in the notation. On two dotted notes that descend a second, the termination is not allowed.

A trill on a note that makes a so-called half cadence and is followed by a fermata does not permit the termination because, in that instance, it is impossible for the termination to make the lively connection, between the following and the preceding – which is its function.

Some Italian singers employ it [the termination] as in the above piece and, even worse, add as many as two or three terminations to such a trill. They perhaps have not learned to adhere to the above-mentioned rule of **Tosi**: **that one must know when it is proper to terminate the trill**.

The proper, or long, trill should last the full length of the note on which it occurs, especially when right before a cadence.[19] In this case, the termination should occur preferably later rather than earlier, joining [directly] to the final note. If one were to end the trill midway through the penultimate note of the cadence, as some singers do, the brilliance, which is the purpose here of the trill, would be totally lost.

After a long trill of a so-called cadenza, especially in a slow piece and where the instruments resume playing only after the last note, the last note of the termination may be held slightly, and the final note very briefly anticipated if there is no syllable before the last note to be pronounced.

In a very lively piece, however, where the accompaniment enters on or before the last note, it is more appropriate to the necessary fire of the execution that the singer sustain his trill [in the cadenza] until the attentive accompanists interrupt it by the entrance of their instruments; but neither the termination nor the final note should be clearly obvious to the listener. If the trill occurs on the third syllable from the end of the cadenza of a very lively and fiery piece, it is better to omit the termination since its place is already taken by the short syllable that precedes the final note.

While the termination of a long trill may not as a rule be softer than the trill itself, at least it must not be louder. It is therefore a mistake when some singers strike the first note of the termination too loudly, slow it down, or even add the upper note of this termination to the invariable appoggiatura from above (ε).

139

It is even worse to add a third note to the termination (ζ).

Often the time allotted to the trill is not sufficient to permit the termination. Short written notes that follow the main note and take the place of the termination, as it were, prohibit it, as in this example:

In tender and sad pieces and above slurred notes, one must be especially cautious in adding a trill because a careless accumulation of trills can easily express the opposite of that which was intended.

The **half** or **short trill**, which **Tosi** designates as the third type, is distinguished from the normal trill not merely by its shortness and clarity but in particular, by the fact that when it occurs on a rather long note, it does not occupy the entire duration of the long note.

It occurs only before a descending second and may be generated from a written-out note or an appoggiatura.

When descending appoggiaturas occur before long notes, especially when followed by either a pause, a fermata, or a cadence, it is customary to gently connect the sustained and louder appoggiatura to the short trill.

No **termination** is permitted after the short trill. Those which have terminations, however, should be properly included among the category of **turns**, discussed below.

If there is too little time on short descending notes for the short trill, such as [those] illustrated by the second example above, the invariable appoggiatura may be substituted.

Double trills from above and below occur very seldom in singing, except in the example cited by **Tosi**. The most frequent use of the **double trill from below** is at the end of an improvised cadenza, where the beginning two notes, once in a while but not very often, may be repeated several times ever faster (η). It may also be employed in this special fashion (δ) when it precedes a fermata. It may be noted that when preceding a fermata the second note of the termination (consisting of two short written-out notes), which is normally connected without pause to the **double trill**, may be lengthened somewhat if the tempo is slow; in other instances both [notes of the termination] may be lengthened in different degrees of slowness, as is illustrated in this musical example:

The practice of occasionally beating the final trill of a cadenza **in the minor keys** on the sixth above the bass (instead of the customary fifth above the same) serves to make it end in the manner demonstrated above.

The small embellishment preceding a fermata over a progression of six-four and five-three chords also originated in this.

The first note is thus held an arbitrary amount of time, and the following notes are gently and quietly slurred to it.

141

The **double trill from above** is usually on the penultimate note of a cadence when it has made a leap of a third from the seventh to the fifth above the bass (ι).

Whereas the **mordent** proper, that is, one whose auxiliary is a half step or whole step below the main note, appears quite often in instrumental music (and as serviceable as it is for those instruments whose sound cannot be gradually increased), its use in singing is much more limited. On certain strong beats following a rest or a leap, the singer can, instead of a mordent, more comfortably employ the **compound appoggiatura**. As already mentioned, the mordent usually occurs after the appoggiatura from below.

On some appoggiaturas – if they precede an ascending leap, and if enough time can be spared for them from the main note, particularly in a recitative – an extended mordent can be used. However, it must not be employed too often.

Even where the tonality requires a whole step, as in the preceding example, it is customary to beat the mordent with the half step to make it more biting.

Like the short trill, the mordent must always be beaten as quickly as possible. The only instance in which it can be performed very slowly and gently is in certain slow arias on the starting note of (any main section) that is followed by a downward leap, which in turn, is followed by a fermata or a pause.

Ca - ro,   ca - ro.   Ca - ro,   ca - ro.

The **turn**, despite the author's omission (perhaps he categorized it with the mordent), is another ornament related to the trill. It nevertheless deserves special attention and study because of its great usefulness.

In the strict sense [lit., actually] it consists of an invariable appoggiatura, a main note, and a termination, all of which are connected. In the execution of the turn, one follows the rules for the performance of appoggiaturas and terminations in that one more sharply strikes the appoggiatura, but slurs the main note onto it and the main note to the termination. The first and second notes must always be in quick succession. The last two notes of the turn which constitute the termination, can, however, be performed at various speeds. This engenders three main types of execution.

For keyboard players, who generally observe the ornaments most exactly and correctly, the sign is as follows: ∾. Except in keyboard music, the sign of the trill is generally used, or it is written out thus:

Once in a while, the first two notes of the turn are repeated quite quickly and with a sharp snap, or in other words, by placing the short trill over the main note instead of the invariable appoggiatura. For example:

At this speed, this kind of turn takes the place of a short trill with a termination. Because the last two notes are not always beaten at the same speed and not slurred quickly to the following note – both of which are important qualifications for the termination of a tril – **Bach** classifies this ornament more precisely as a **turn** in his **Versuch über die wahre Art das Clavier zu spielen**.[20]

Thus, two main types of turns exist: the **simple turn** and the **short turn**.

Whether the pitches of the turn should be half steps or whole steps must be judged mainly from the tonality, and the modulation of the piece [judged] as one does with trills or other ornaments.

One of the main properties of the turn – that its last two notes are not bound to the following main note but are always provided with a little space between them – has already been mentioned and can be observed in the preceding musical example. In most cases, however, the first three notes of the turn are performed quickly, and the remaining time value of their main note is taken up by lingering on the last note of the turn. Consequently, the note on which one wants to make a turn should be neither too long, so that too much time remains; nor too short, so that there is sufficient time to make the turn roundly and clearly.

In general, the turn may be introduced in both slow and fast pieces and on either slurred or articulated notes. It not only serves the purpose of filling out; but it can also be used also for fiery or brilliant expressions, as well as for calm or flattering expressions.

The simple turn, in particular, occurs above or following its main note.

One finds it indicated **over** the main note in stepwise movement as well as in the leaping progression, and on strong pulses as well as weak ones.

fù già fin - or   per   no - i   etc.

fù già fin - or per   no - i   etc.

For the most part, however, it occurs in [lit., prefers] an ascending rather than a descending sequence of notes.

When three consecutive ascending notes occur, the simple turn works very well on the middle one [of these] thus:

144

A turn can be applied to the repeated note, either at the beginning of the measure, or on the beat when it is followed by a rising pitch. Thus:

If the repeated note is followed by a descending second, it is better to introduce a **compound appoggiatura** on it instead of a turn. If the [rhythmic] movement of the measure is very lively, one can substitute, for the compound appoggiatura, an invariable appoggiatura or a short trill–although the turn itself is not absolutely prohibited here as this example shows:

Just as a note can be repeated several times throughout a short measure, the simple turn which belongs to it can be repeated as well (χ). It is also possible to place a turn on each note that arpeggiates a chord (λ).

A turn may be employed above each one of consecutively rising notes of equal value.

Sen - za l' a - ma - bi - le   etc.

In singing, the fast turn can generally take the place of a shorter trill.

145

This can apply to trills in an ascending **chain of trills** when the note values are somewhat short. It is, however, not as successful on descending notes, nor in the following instance:

nor in many other similar instances. It is immaterial whether one uses a turn or a trill, unless the throat of the singer is more comfortable with the turn than with the trill. Here are few more examples in which it makes no difference which ornament is used:

Trills that appear above notes which are so long that a turn would leave too much empty space, or those that do not tolerate a termination (as was seen in previous musical examples) must be excluded from those that are interchangeable with the turn. Most final trills, as well, belong to this category [i.e. must be excluded], especially in lively and fiery pieces.

After the main note, a turn may be employed if the duration of the main note is somewhat long, either because of its [notated] value or its tempo (μ); or if, in the flattering mode of performance, in moderate tempo, it is lengthened by means of a dot (γ). One can also include in this category notes that are tied instead of dotted.

(μ) grazioso

(γ) lento

A simple turn may even be introduced above a rising or leaping appoggiatura, or between an appoggiatura and its main note in a similar [moderate] tempo and [flattering] expression.

Between the dotted first note and the short second note of a dotted slide, the turn is readily allowed in a calm and tender expression.

In a moderate tempo the **trilled turn** may be placed over a falling second when either a written-out note or an appoggiatura is notated (ξ). Whereas a short trill might occur in a faster tempo it [the trilled turn] might similarly be employed in a somewhat slower tempo [lit., on somewhat longer notes] (ο).

A **trilled turn** with an appoggiatura may be introduced over the middle note [of a group] of three descending notes in a very slow tempo, especially if there are no words to be pronounced, and if the singer's throat has sufficient agility. Another appoggiatura consisting of a third from above may be introduced before the last note.

The last appoggiatura in this case belongs to the time of the following note [as accurately indicated here] and, after the turn, functions to support more movement than that found in the main notes and to provide the higher note that is generally needed after the turn.

In pieces that are slow and rich in Affect [expression], with short segments after which a short pause follows, one can quite gently and slowly introduce the simple (π) turn after an appoggiatura from below. In a similar manner [i.e. gently and slowly], the trilled turn may be introduced on an ascending appoggiatura whose last two notes of course concur [with the written notes] (ζ).

In tender and sad pieces – or if one finds it desirable to conceal a trill that is difficult to articulate at the final cadence of a piece, with or without an improvised cadenza – both [of the above figurations] can substitute for this otherwise essential trill.

If simple turns are introduced above unslurred notes that are articulated separately – and especially if they are not descending seconds and are intended to enliven a cheerful expression – they receive a special clarity if the main note is sounded beforehand [as the grace note], and the turn over the written main note connected directly to it with the greatest possible speed:

The execution is as follows:

For the sake of clarity, **Bach**, who was the first to classify this type of ornament among the essential ornaments, designates it as the **snapped turn**.[21] I
do not see why a singer whose glottis is otherwise flexible enough should be
prevented from availing himself of this figure in suitable places. One must be
careful, however, not to confuse the manner of execution of this ornament
with that of a turn that appears on the second half of the note, since that turn
is executed in a fashion more appropriate to the flattering style and could be
expressed in notes approximately as follows:

The **vibrato** on one note – which is achieved on stringed instruments by
rocking the fingertip back and forth on the same note, making the pitch neither higher nor lower, but gently beating it – is also an ornament that in
singing is especially effective on long sustained notes, particularly when
applied towards the end of such notes. It is quite impossible to express the
vibrato in musical notation. It is more easily grasped with the help of oral
instruction, but not all throats are capable of this type of execution.

The ornaments of song, whose nature and use have been described
in this and the previous chapters, are the so-called **essential ornaments**
that no good performer, be he singer or instrumentalist, can do without. The
more exactly and cleanly the singer, in particular, performs them, the more
praise he deserves, since many of these are much more difficult to execute
with the voice than with any instrument. Should this not inspire everyone
who is dedicated to the art of singing to practice these with all greater diligence? Having read the instructions contained in these chapters, he will find
that many things that are impossible to clarify by mere words and notes will
subsequently become much clearer by the careful observation of good singers.
The singer must also not be ashamed to pay attention to good instrumentalists. Nevertheless, it is also certain that the singer, even more than the instru-

mentalist, should avoid amassing ornaments unnecessarily. He possesses that instrument of sound–the voice–to which even the most appealing [flattering] instruments made by human hands, give precedence, since it [the voice] is an instrument that can doubly enliven sound through words. A singer should therefore, above all, endeavor to master for himself his sound and the loudness and softness of his voice; thus he will be in command of many notes for which instrumentalists must seek to compensate, not only because of their lack of words but also partly because of their limited control over the duration or over the loudness and softness of their sound.

CHAPTER FOUR

CONCERNING DIVISIONS

1. Although divisions[1], in themselves, lack the power to evoke the charm that touches the heart, since they serve mainly to engender admiration of the singer for his good fortune in having a flexible voice, it is, nevertheless, very necessary that the teacher instruct his student well in them, so that the latter learns to execute them with ease, speed, and the correct intonation. For when they are performed at the appropriate place, they certainly deserve applause and make the singer generally capable of singing, and in all styles.

2. He who has allowed the voice of a student to be so lazy that he always drags teaches him only the smallest part of his craft and incapacitates him for learning the greater part. With pieces that must be performed in a fast tempo and probably even with those in moderately fast tempos, whoever does not have an agile voice bores [lit., annoys] the audience into such sleepy indifference that they almost fall out of their seats [lit., down]; and the constant lagging causes everything he sings almost always to sound out of tune.

3. It is commonly agreed that there are two types of divisions: the **detached** and the **slurred**. Because of its slowness, the **drag**[2] deserves to be classified more as an extempore ornament than as a division.

4. For the detached [division], the teacher must seek to teach the students that very light movement of the voice in which the notes that constitute the division are all articulated with the same speed and clarity and are equally distinguishable, so that the [notes of the] division are neither overly slurred [lit., stuck together] nor overly detached (a).

(a) To achieve this, one must, when practicing, imagine that the vowel sound of the division is gently repeated with each note; for example, one must pronounce as many **a**'s in rapid succession as there are notes in the

151

division–just as with a stringed instrument, [where] a short bow stroke belongs to each note of the division; and in the transverse flute and some other wind instruments, [where] each note receives its own gentle impetus by the correct tongue stroke, whether single or double (see **Quantz, Versuch**, chapter VI). During this gentle articulation of the vowel in singing, however, the tongue must not make any special movement; and the air necessary for the divisions that is emitted from the lungs is subdivided into as many small parts as there are notes – which are, as a result, articulate and clear.

One must take care, however, that the air in the mouth is not reflected improperly. One must feel, as it were, the articulation of each note in the glottis. Some singers, to be sure, allow the air to push against the palate, much as one does in a rather quiet laugh. In this fashion, they can produce the divisions somewhat more easily and faster. There is almost no other way to execute many reiterations of the same note[3] very rapidly, particularly if there occurs at the head of the windpipe a certain and special tensing of the muscles–which, on a small scale, bears some resemblance to the tensing of the muscles and nerves of the arm when a chord has to be struck many times consecutively in a very fast manner. This can be much more easily felt and experienced, of course, than accurately described. The listener in a large room (or at a distance) is made very uncomfortable by this manner of performing the divisions because, in the first place, the air does not receive its natural direction for singing; and, rather than real singing, is heard a bleating sound which resembles the cackling of a chicken (which the Italians call *sgagateata*[4]). In the second place, the notes have no duration and immediately dissipate. For this reason, singers who employ this manner of execution can make the divisions only at very great speed, or not at all; whereas, a singer who has become accustomed to singing the divisions in the correct manner, as above, and has otherwise practiced sufficiently can succeed in all gradations of speed. In the third place, because the opening of the windpipe and neighboring parts of the mouth have become accustomed to moving incorrectly, this type of singer loses the ability to sing a slow, sustained adagio, which does not permit many decorative fast notes, and whose nature dictates that it be performed in a touching manner. Singers who are confident in the naturally beautiful sound of their voices have never resorted to artifices of this kind. Generally, they are used only by those who seek to cover the none-too-pleasing natural sound of their voices by means of the many notes and wish to arouse admiration rather than to touch [the heart]. There are others who do not have enough patience by diligent practice to make their voices flexible in accordance with the correct method. Others whose glottis is somewhat soft (of whom there are many) do not articulate the divisions with enough definition. A certain great female singer[5] – who for a long time had delighted audiences in Italy, England, and Germany (but retired from the theater six years ago), and who was admired for the extraordinary crispness, clarity, and speed with which she executed all sorts of fast notes – was believed to have availed herself of none other than the techniques described above. I do not know

152

whether this is correct, but this much I do know: the sound of her voice when executing these passages was almost as full and strong, if possible, as the sound of the natural chest voice in others. Those persons who wish to emulate this famous singer only in this respect, perhaps without attention to her many other merits, will find that the result confirms the following statement: two persons often undertake the same matter with very unequal results. If unsure whether his palate is arched enough for this kind of division, as it presumably must be, he should, according to my modest counsel, perform this kind of division in the usual manner. He then stands less chance of committing errors that were never heard in this great singer.

5. The second type of division [i.e., the slurred] is performed in such a fashion that all the notes of a stepwise passage are closely and evenly connected from the first note on. One seeks hereby to express, in singing, an imitation of a certain slippery smoothness. Experts in music call this type of division **slurring**. The effect of this is very pleasant indeed, if the singer does not avail himself of it too often (b).

(b) In this type [of division], if one articulates the vowel only on the first note and sustains it (without repetition and on one breath) through as many of the notes which follow as are to be slurred – instead of having to repeat it [the vowel] gently on every note, as in the case with the detached division – he will perform slurred notes correctly. The flutist does not repeat his tonguing with such notes, no matter what his type, nor the violinist his bowing. However, the singer must guard against allowing the notes to become unclear; he must, despite the slur, bring each to the listener's ear in its correct intonation. For those who endeavor to perform detached divisions in the inadvisable manner described toward the end of the preceding remark, [i.e. the **sgagateata**, or quiet laugh] the proper performance of the slurred [divisions] becomes almost impossible. We have heard demonstrations of this. They always sound detached. This seems to work best for those who do not unduly force their natural chest voices. However, those whose glottis naturally has very soft and flexible parts would be the most successful in the execution of slurred divisions, if they did not otherwise have to make their weakness evident with the detached divisions.

6. Since the detached divisions occur more often than all the others, they require the most practice.

7. The domain of the slur is very limited in singing. It is confined to a few stepwise ascending and descending notes that, in order not to displease, may not encompass more than four notes. It seems to me that the slur is more pleasant to the ear in descending than in ascending (c).

(c) In the following staves [lit., lines] appear examples of short descending slurred divisions, such as are probably meant by the author.

va - da pur ne' fos - chi or - ro - ri

frà   le fie - re ad a - bi - tar

Exceptions to **Tosi's** thoughts concerning the ascending slurred divisions appear, especially in the adagio, where once in a while occur slurred notes that comprise an entire octave or more. For example:

m'ingan   ni.

He who wishes to learn the correct execution of these must always begin by learning how to slur the notes together two by two. In this way he will become skillful with more notes.

8. Finally, the **drag** consists of the execution of certain notes, which, with the greatest of skill, are slowly and pleasantly dragged, as it were, one after the other, alternately becoming loud and soft (d). I will speak about its inherent beauty elsewhere.[6]

(d) The drag is distinguishable from the slur primarily by its slowness and by the fact that at times one allows the voice gradually and almost imperceptibly to become ever higher or lower until one has reached the higher or lower pitch one wants.

9. If the teacher almost imperceptibly increases the tempo while the student is singing the divisions, he will discover that there is no more effective means of making the student's voice light and capable of fast movement. Care must be taken, however, that this imperceptible alteration of the tempo does not in time become a bad habit (e).

(e) So that the student does not get in the habit of rushing. In general, one must practice the divisions with varying degrees of speed, in order to be capable of executing them equally well in all tempos. Many singers have only one speed, into which all divisions must fit in order to succeed. It is an advantage, not only for the sake of clarity but also for the steady maintenance of an even tempo, to always give the first of four or three [groups of] fast notes a slight emphasis, which I indicate here with small marks.

10. The teacher should require the student to beat the divisions with equal ability in both ascending and descending. Even though this instruction properly belongs to the beginner, not all singers master it.

11. After the stepwise divisions, he should have those [divisions] that are interrupted with all manner of difficult leaps practiced with the greatest accuracy. If such divisions are to be intoned purely, precisely, and confidently, they rightfully deserve special attention. The industry that should be expended herein demands more time and trouble than any other lesson, not only because of the excessive difficulty but also because of the necessary consequences that those efforts imply. A singer who has become familiar with the most dangerous leaps has no occasion whatsoever to be baffled by any difficulty (f).

(f) One should note here that in the execution of the division with leaps, it is especially necessary to be careful that the notes are equally loud. The lower the pitch the wider open the windpipe and the more air thus emitted.[7] Consequently, a singer who produces the lowest notes possible in his range must make every effort with these low notes to set as much air in motion as he can without overly forcing. On the other hand, the higher the notes the more he must save his breath.

12. So that no adornment of the art remain hidden from him, one should not neglect to teach the student how, at times in divisions, the loud may be employed as well as the soft and slurred notes as well as those that are detached; and how especially on dotted notes (if they are not too fast), a short trill can occasionally be introduced.

13. It is also a very good exercise with divisions to have the student learn to add the mordent from time to time – that is, if the student has it [the mordent] in his grasp, by nature or by art, and if the master has sufficient insight to point out the right places where it achieves an especially beautiful effect. Since this is information that perhaps is not suitable for one who teaches beginners, and even less suitable for the beginners themselves, it would perhaps have been better to save it for another place, as I would have done, had I not known that there are students with such fine powers of discrimination that in a few years they will become the best of singers, and that there is no dearth of teachers whose knowledge and insights are well suited to the most capable minds among their students. Moreover, I would have thought myself remiss in a chapter on divisions had I neglected to mention the mordent, since it is one of the most beautiful ornaments thereof (g).

(g) According to the author, the mordent, as noted above, consists of invariable appoggiaturas, which, in divisions that are not too fast, can be executed on strong-beat notes (α). Where a longer note precedes two shorter notes in very fast divisions, mordents occur, for the most part, only before the longer note. In this location they are usually indicated by the composer himself (β).

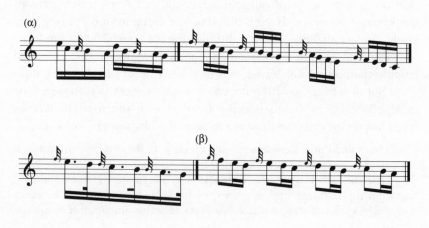

14.   The student should not be allowed to sing the divisions in an uneven or irregular tempo; neither should he be allowed to mark time with the tongue or the chin or the head, or with movements of the whole body.

15. Every teacher knows that the divisions sound unpleasant on the third and the fifth vowel (the **i** or the **u**).[8] But not everyone knows that, in good schools, they are not permitted even on the **e** and **o**[9] if these two vowels are pronounced closed (h).

(h) He who has command of the Italian language knows that the **e** and **o** are at times pronounced more brightly or open, and at times more closed [lit., more darkly]. In the German language divisions are permitted (besides on the vowels where they are not forbidden in Italian) also on those diphthongs that begin with an open [lit., bright] vowel, especially **a** and **e** – whereby the first [vowel of the diphthong] is held to the end of the division, at which point the second is pronounced. The same rule should be observed in all languages for the pronunciation of consonants at the end of the syllable bearing the division. For these [consonants] likewise must not be pronounced until the end of the division; otherwise, the mouth would be prematurely closed, and the sound of the voice would become dull and unpleasant.

For the sake of the divisions, it is always a mistake in pronunciation to change a closed vowel to an open one, since vowels must be pronounced in singing just as in speaking, if one is to be understood.

16.   There are many errors to be aware of and to avoid in performing the divisions. Besides those involving the nose and throat and some other ones with which we are familiar, one finds also the very ugly faults of those who neither detach nor slur the divisions; for then a singer does not sing, but howls (i). Even more ridiculous is when a singer articulates so loudly and with such forceful aspiration that, for example, when we should hear a division on the **a**, he seems to be saying **ga ga ga** (k). This applies also to the other vowels. The worst error of all, finally, is to sing the divisions not purely in tune (l).

(i) Slurring the division when it should be detached is an error that, especially in Italy, has currently begun to spread with many singers from the most modern schools. They tend to slur almost all, even the liveliest divisions, although they lack the patience and effort required for properly learning the slurred division. Thus one may easily judge how close they often are to howling.

(k) This is a typical error of those poorly instructed basses, many of whom seek fame by bellowing instead of singing, especially on their highest notes. When they wish to sing divisions, they put an **h** in front of every note, which they then aspirate with such force that, besides producing an unpleasant sound, it causes them unnecessarily to expend so much air that they are forced to breathe almost every half measure.

(l). Another error consists of exchanging one vowel in the course of a division for another one, such as making an **a** into an **o**, etc. The same vowel with which a division is begun must be maintained unchanged to the end [of the division].

17. The teacher should bear in mind that, after a good voice has been well exercised in the sustaining of notes, it becomes better through training in the gradual development of speed. On the other hand, a good voice forced to sing the fastest runs, without the necessary time for the instrument [lit., tools] to be trained properly, becomes worse; and sometimes, due to the neglect of the teacher and to the great loss of the student, becomes one of the worst (m).

(m) Some of our German teachers of insufficient experience should be apprised of this.

18. In the **siciliano**, the divisions and trills are faults [lit., errors], but the slurs and the drags are things of beauty (n).

(n) This rule is not generally valid in the current style of composition. There are pieces in siciliano style in which the brilliant is combined with the flattering in the most beautiful way. The composer does not neglect, however, to indicate trills where he wants them.[10]

19. The whole beauty of divisions consists in their being purely in tune, distinct [lit., detached], round[11] and clear, even, articulated, and fast (o).

(o) The best touchstone by which to test the execution of a division is an **echo** (if one can have it) that does not answer too quickly but permits the delay of at least eight fast sixteenth notes. This [echo] reveals most reliably where one note is produced the slightest bit unevenly or weaker than the other, even if it is not noticeable in the singer himself.

20. Divisions share the same fate as trills. Both give pleasure if they are in the right place. However, if they are not reserved for suitable occasions, their too frequent use engenders disgust; disgust engenders contempt; and, finally, even hatred.

I should like here to draw attention to [lit., take note of] some special figures, in the execution of which mistakes are often made, and to describe their correct execution.

Short notes in slow or fast tempos – especially sixteenths or thirty-second notes or eighths in the alla breve – that occur after a dot are always executed very short, whether there may be one or several of them; the note occurring before the dot, therefore, is held so much the longer. For example, these [notes]

slow

are executed as if they were written thus:

The note before the dot is stronger [in emphasis]; the one after the dot, weaker.

If a short note precedes and the second note is dotted, the first note is executed as short as possible, and the remainder of the time [of the first note] is assigned to the dotted note. For example:

Slow:

Execution:

In these figures, however, the first note is sung loudly; and the one before the dot, which is always slurred to the previous note, is sung more quietly; and, if time permits, a crescendo is made.

159

The three notes of a triplet must always be exactly equal in length, so that they may be distinguished from three other notes of other figures whose first notes are longer or shorter than the others. For example:

Triplet: Incorrect execution.

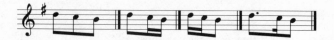

Each note of the triplet must receive an equal impulse from the chest; the first note must not be detached and the others slurred. This equality of impulse must continue for the entirety of the triplet division, so that no break or other figure may be perceived between them [the notes of the triplet]. For many singers the correct execution of triplets in general is difficult; but for many others, only certain types are troublesome.

In a very fast tempo, triplets whose middle note is a step higher and whose last note is the same as the first (γ), while [they are] not actually slurred, must not be strongly detached either. One must be careful, however, not to shorten the middle note, as often happens. The first note, in particular, must be very clearly defined. In those triplets, on the other hand, whose middle note is a step lower (δ), every note must receive its own impulse; otherwise, the latter [the middle note] would sound too soft, and the former [the first note] too loud. One may easily try this himself.

When several consecutive notes on the same pitch occur in moderate tempo, above which there is a slur sign and under the slur sign there are dots (ε), one must neither separate nor detach the notes, but execute each note instead with a slight pressure from the chest.[12]

160

In figure (ζ) the last two sixteenths should not be slurred but should be very evenly and clearly detached. The first note, however, is slurred to its invariable appoggiatura.

Notes that are tied to other notes by a slur sign should be neither rearticulated nor marked.

Special attention should be paid that the second part of a syncopated note (η) not be emphasized in such a manner as to indicate the beat but sustained without rearticulation.

Some of those requiring slurring have been identified above in connection with various categories of ornamentation. The question of slurring or detaching on other notes is a matter of personal choice, dependent on the context [in which the notes are found] or the passion expressed by them. The composer is obligated to indicate these notes with their own slur sign. Those notes which are not included in the specific rules for slurring, and not specifically indicated by the composer, must actually be detached. Some cases, however, are left to the sensibility of the performer himself. It is as great a mistake in fiery or lively pieces to introduce many slurred divisions as it is to fill a slow and sad piece with many detached fast runs.

21. Once the student is totally versed in the trills and the divisions, his teacher must teach him how to read and enunciate words correctly, which is to say, devoid of the ridiculous errors that rob a word of its doubled consonants, only to bestow them upon another word that should have only a single consonant.

22. Once the pronunciation is improved, the master should take care that the student pronounce the words without affectation, so that they may be clearly understood without the loss of a single syllable (p). When one cannot understand the words, the singer robs the listener of a great part of the charm that the song derives from the words. If the words are not heard, the singer excludes truth from art. Finally, unless the words are understood, the human voice is indistinguishable from a cornetto[13] or an oboe. This error, though very offensive, is little short nowadays of being universal, to the great disadvantage of singers and the art of singing. It should be clearly understood that the words are the only thing that give singers the advantage over instrumentalists–if both are otherwise equally knowledgeable. The modern teacher

should put this fact to good use. Improvement on this point has never been more necessary than it is today. The student must be helped to greater and greater security in this matter, so necessary to the pronunciation of the syllables under the notes, so that he neither stumbles nor is uncertain.

(p) **Mr. Bérard**, the author of a book dedicated to Madame Pompadour, *L'art du Chant* (Paris, 1755), has made a great effort to clarify the correct pronunciation of French words in singing, by the change or addition of some letters that are not a part of the written word.[14] I leave it to experts on the French language and to experts on the art of singing to judge whether he has been successful in all respects. In the German and Italian languages, which are by far less difficult to pronounce than the French, there is no need, it seems to me, for so much ado for one who has learned to read properly (as a singer is supposed to have done). Nevertheless, it is an undeniable truth that the correct pronunciation of the **consonants** contributes greatly to the clarity of speech generally, and is even the origin and cause thereof. To produce the vowels, the parts of the mouth remain motionless in the position that the pronunciation of each vowel necessitates, and as long as air flows through the windpipe, the same vowel is continuously heard. The consonants, on the other hand, are not produced like the vowels, with a continuous uniform position of the parts of the mouth and the expulsion of air from the windpipe. They are instead produced by a momentary new impetus, pressure, or vibration of one or the other of the parts of the mouth necessary for speech, such as the tongue, palate, teeth, etc. – through which the air, continuously forced out of the windpipe, takes on in an instant a modification or a different direction. The vowel sounds, therefore, may be compared with the continuous sound of a flute or an organ pipe; and the consonants, with the sound of a hammer on an anvil, which is heard for only a moment. By means of the different momentary directions that the air takes in the pronunciation of various consonants preceding or following a vowel, are formed the various syllables and the words with which we give every idea its own symbol. The syllables are articulated by the consonants and thus made clear and distinct from each other; otherwise one would have no syllables other than the [sum total of the] vowels that could be invented, together with the diphthongs composed of these vowels. It is obvious therefore how concerned and careful the singer must be with correct pronunciation not only of the vowels but also of the consonants. If a singer is remiss in clear enunciation of one or the other, a lack of clarity results, made more obvious by singing than by speech because of the constantly changing pitches, because the syllables are held longer and because of the variety of different pitches that can appear above the same syllable, etc.–all of which are responsible for the unintelligibility.

In large buildings or in the open air (as [Wolfgang Caspar] **Printz** has already indicated in his **Musica modulatoria vocalis oder manierliche**

162

oder zierliche Sing-kunst[15]), the consonants must be pronounced more crisply [lit. sharply] – in fact, almost excessively so – than in common speech, but with close attention to their individual hardness or softness [in the context of sounds preceding or following them]. Close at hand, such crisp enunciation would not be especially pleasant to hear and would sound somewhat affected; but it is greatly effective at a distance, delivering all words clearly to the ear and simultaneously losing all unpleasantness. A singer accustomed to the precise pronunciation of the consonants will always be better understood at a distance, if he does not sing too loudly, than one who yells with all his might but does not enunciate the consonants crisply and clearly enough. If I am not mistaken, I have been more aware of this kind of vigorous pronunciation of consonants by **Faustina** than by many other singers.

Some singers make the mistake of introducing certain vowels with a consonant or certain consonants with a vowel that does not belong to the word. For example, **Lamen** or **Namen** is sung instead of **Amen**; or **äsollen** and **äschwert**, instead of **sollen** and **schwert**, and the like. A careful teacher should strive to prevent or seek to correct such bad habits from the very beginning.

Since Nature herself teaches the attentive student that the various Affects [passions] demand different sounds of the voice; but since the numerous instances of raising and lowering of pitches in the music have already been prescribed by the composer (and thus nothing remains of improvisation for the singer but to express the Affect through the various sounds of his voice) – [since this is true] if opportunity and place do not allow him to combine the art of gesture[16] with it [vocal expression], I consider it indeed unnecessary to describe in detail and individually how one should sing **vigorous**, **abrupt**, **majestic**, and **hollow**, etc. tones. It is very necessary, however, for a singer to learn from the art of speaking or from oral instruction by good speakers (if they are available) or through careful attention to their lectures what kinds of vocal sounds are necessary for the expression of each Affect or each rhetorical figure.[17] In addition to the abovementioned rules concerning good diction for a speaker and [those] provided in thorough detail by [Johann Christoph] **Gottsched** in his **Ausführliche Redekunst**[18] (in the chapter concerning good diction for a speaker) (λ), the singer should diligently practice the reading or declamation of Affect-rich passages from good speakers and writers – in short, he should **learn to read well**. If, when he sings, he will carefully and attentively combine this [ability to read well] with those comprehensive rules as applied to the singing voice, he will not fail in good pronunciation in the arias as well as in the recitatives.

(λ) He who is fluent in the French language may also read [Jean Léonor le Gallois de] **Grimarest**, **Traité du récitatif** [19] and apply the essentials in that book to the language in which he wants to sing.

One pitfall against which the singer must guard and into which he may easily fall, especially if he has a lively temperament, is overly exaggerating the strong passions, as, for example, converting a vigorous note into a scream or a howl, or a sad or muted note into a whine or a moan. If this is unseemly in a speaker, it is certainly ten times more offensive in a singer.

It is absolutely necessary that Germans, who are not fluent in Italian but (as the current fashion dictates) want to sing in that language, must learn (if not the entire language from the ground up) at least the correct pronunciation and the proper accents of that language. It does not sound exactly elegant when a German singer who cannot read Italian butchers an aria or even a recitative in this language, garbling it so that even an Italian would not be able to understand a single word of it. And yet nothing is more common than this.

One necessary rule of Italian pronunciation in singing is the following: when one word ends with a vowel, and the following word begins with another one, and no punctuation [lit. distinctive] mark occurs between the two words (namely no period or comma or the like), both syllables, according to the rules of the mechanics of Italian poetry, are usually set to only one note of music; thus one must not swallow the last vowel of the first word and let only the first vowel of the second word be heard; but one must, instead, pronounce both, quickly but distinctly and in succession on the same note. If the note under which the two vowels come together is long, one must hold longer the vowel that would be the longer in reading. If the longer vowel is in the first syllable, one must not pronounce the second syllable until the end of the note. In a preceding chapter, one can find various examples of this, for example, p. 94, in the bottom lines of **gli affetti a moderar**, one holds the **a** longest in both instances; on p. 95, in **Se il mio duol se i mali miei**, etc., one holds longer the syllable **se** and in **farei**, the **e**. The remainder of that which is appropriate to good Italian pronunciation I leave to expert language teachers.

24. The student must be prevented from breathing in the middle of a word, since making two words out of one is an error that Nature does not tolerate. Nature must be imitated to avoid being ridiculed. This rule is not so strict in an interrupted progression of notes or a long division if either one or the other cannot be performed in one breath. In olden times, it was necessary to give this instruction only to the very beginners. Nowadays, however, this abuse, which has been fostered by the modern schools, has become entrenched in those who wish to be regarded as something special. The teacher can prevent this in the student by teaching him to make good use of the breath, always providing himself with more breath than seems necessary, and by advising him to avoid overly long divisions if the chest is not strong enough (q).

(q) Right from the beginning, one must strive to take in as much breath as possible without harming himself. Further, one must strive to continue singing in one breath as long as possible without ever forcing and to vary [the volume of] the voice from soft to moderate to loud. However, in doing so, one must not exhale forcefully and frequently, especially in the detached divisions but only in the amount required by the loudness or softness for a clear tone, holding back the rest [of the air] as much as possible without impairing the sound. The lungs hereby become capable of taking in and holding more air than previously, and it becomes possible to sing more on one breath. No sound should be made during inhalation, nor should the breath be inhaled too fast nor too energetically but rather in a relaxed fashion and slowly, making it possible for twice as much air to be inhaled. To that end one must not carelessly pass over those places in the melody where there is time to breathe; an experienced and careful composer has presumably provided an opportunity for breathing, so that one might not feel compelled, at an inconvenient place, to take too fast a breath, which, of course, cannot last very long.

25. In all musical pieces, the teacher must teach his student to recognize those places where he can take a breath without effort (r). Some singers seem as fearful as asthmatics and take such labored breaths every moment that the listener himself becomes anxious; or they arrive at their final notes completely out of breath (s).

(r) Needless to say, it is most comfortable to take a breath at a rest or after a long note. Where there are no rests or long notes, however, one must do this always **after the strong beat**, and **not after notes on weak beats**. Consequently, one cannot breathe after the last note of the measure nor after a principal part of the beat, unless its [note value] is longer than that of the preceding and following notes; but one must always include the strong beat of the following measure and not take a breath until then. However, very fast stepwise ascending or descending triplets are an exception to this. After the last note of the triplet, one may breathe if necessary. If the triplets consist of leaps, a breath may be taken between the leaps, as is most suitable between great leaps in general, when it is impossible to take a breath elsewhere.

If a shorter note is tied to a long note, a breath is possible after or even during the shorter note without rearticulating the short tied note.

If there are frequent short rests, as for example, in the following phrase:

it is obvious that one should not breathe at every rest.

It is a great error to breathe between an appoggiatura and its main note, between a long trill and its termination, or between the termination and the note that follows it, since this negates the binding together of the melody that it is the purpose of these ornaments to achieve.

If in the middle of a melody, a long note is to be held for one or more measures and no rest precedes it, a breath may be taken before such a note. If, however, the long note occurs on the last syllable of a word and does not follow a division, it is always better to breathe before the first syllable of that word – thereby shortening its duration very little.

Before an improvised final cadenza, the composer generally provides time for the necessary breath. If, however, the sense of the words does not allow this, either the singer must breathe before the last word, but not in the middle of it; or, if the cadenza occurs upon the first syllable of the word, he must breathe on the first note of the measure where the instruments generally accent the note strongly, after which they rest. Some of the most modern of the Italian singers, in some of these cases, omit some of the syllables in the penultimate measure, leaving it to the imagination of the listener to fill them in. They clear their throats at this point a few times, with all of their physical strength inhale their breath like a bellows, and thereby give the signal that a wonder is about to commence. Some do even worse. For example, in an aria that ends with the words *il lido guarda e il mar* preceded by a rest of an entire measure wherein they would have enough time to strike a pose, nevertheless they wait until the instruments have come to rest; then they bray out the syllables *il lido guar-* (which were to be sung in quarter notes while the instruments were still playing) after the rest with as much speed and vehemence as if they had started up out of their sleep. Not until then, during a general silence, follows the big breath and then...a long cadenza. This fashion is said not to have been introduced as yet in **Tosi's** time.

One must pay careful attention to saving the breath immediately after inhalation. On the first note after the breath, particularly if it is not one of the fastest, generally too much breath is expended all at once – which results in a rough and harsh attack.

In general, if a singer pays careful attention to what he performs, he can readily sense which notes can be slightly separated if necessary and which cannot be separated at all. Having missed taking his breath in the right place, his own sensitivity will tell him which note he may unobtrusively omit within a long division of very fast notes. The first note of the measure is often the most suitable, especially when it is preceded by a leap.

s) Some even lose time by taking a breath and start to drag.

26. For the student who has difficulty understanding or trouble remembering, the master should seek opportunities of noble emulation so that he might motivate him to study out of jealousy (which is sometimes more powerful than genius). If, instead of one lesson, the student hears two and does not allow himself to become depressed by

166

the progress of the other [student], he will perhaps first learn the lesson of his fellow student and thereafter his own.

27. He should never allow the student to hold the paper in front of his face, so as to keep him from blocking the sound of his voice and from making it sound timid.

28. He should accustom the student to sing often in the presence of persons who, because of their prestige or their insight into music, are well regarded; so that the student may gradually lose his timidity and thus become self-assured but not arrogant and bold. A noble bravery is the first-born daughter of happiness and in a singer it becomes a real advantage. On the other hand, the timid one is very unhappy. Because he is burdened by the difficulty of correct breathing, his voice shakes constantly. He has to swallow on almost every note thereby losing time. He is hurt by the fact that his skill does not serve him outside of his house. He irks the listener and ruins the compositions in such a way that one no longer recognizes them for what they are. A timid singer is as unhappy as a poor miserable prodigal.

29. The teacher should not forget to make clear to the student what a great error is made by those who beat trills; or make divisions; or take a breath on syncopated, tied, or long spun-out notes. What a wonderful effect, on the other hand, is made by allowing the voice on such notes gradually to strengthen or swell, so to speak. Instead of losing something, the composition thereby gains greatly in beauty.

30. He should instruct him well in what must be performed loud and what soft (t) and how this should be accomplished, with one proviso that he practice more the loud than the soft. It is easier to teach one who sings loudly to sing quietly than it is to teach one who sings quietly to sing louder. Experience teaches that one must not trust the piano [soft] because it entices only to deceive; and whoever wants to lose his voice, let him sing piano. At this point I am reminded of the prevailing opinion among singers that there is an artificial piano which is heard and perceived as easily as the forte. But this is only an opinion, which is to say, the mother of all error. The piano of the good singer is heard, not because of some kind of applied artifice but because of the deep silence of those who are attentively listening. As proof of this, one should notice that when even the average singer is quiet in the theater for only a quarter of a minute when he should be singing, the listeners, out of eagerness to know the reason for this unexpected pause, become so quiet that if the singer at this moment produces a word very quietly, even the most distant listener will certainly understand it.

(t) In general, a pleasant balance must be struck between the loud and the soft. The matter of which notes are to be loud or soft in connection with the use of ornaments has already been discussed in its proper place. Any note of considerable length must be begun softly, then gradually strengthened, or made to swell, and then ended piano. The only notes that are excepted from this are those requiring a vigorous expression, or an exclamation, or those on which a staccato is indicated – all of which one must immediately articulate loudly, of course. Certain [places for the] raising or lowering of [the volume of] the voice will, as it were, be obvious to those who can read correctly and with Affect [passion]. The rising forte and the diminishing piano are intermediate shades of the performance, and neither should be employed in its most extreme degree without a special reason. Fast notes preceded by a note of longer value or a dotted note are performed more softly than the longer note. The first of four fast notes, as has already been mentioned, should always be somewhat marked. If the notes are otherwise flattering, and their movement is not overly fast, they may be diminished, especially if they descend after a leap. However, with fiery and lively runs and leaps, no diminuendo is to be introduced. In general, the strong beats on which the harmony changes must be louder and accentuated more than the short passing notes. In the case of a fast ascending run, whether in an adagio or an allegro, the beginning lower notes must be performed especially loud and vigorously. The subsequent higher notes can diminish somewhat. Long spun-out notes that ascend stepwise may gradually undergo a crescendo. Those that have an accidental sharp must especially be brought out. In the case of stepwise descending spun-out notes, some may be performed crescendo, others descrescendo.

He who would sing all fast divisions very softly, allowing the power of his voice to be heard only here and there on longer notes, would have the advantage, of course, of concealing many faults of the voice, as well as that of being able to perform the divisions much faster than usual. I doubt whether the listener is satisfied, however, to hear little or nothing of the divisions, especially if he is in a large place [e.g. auditorium].

However, it is not possible to express in mechanical rules how to increase and decrease the loudness of a note. Much depends upon the discretion or the sensitivity of the performer, and especially upon the main Affects [passions] that dominate the entire piece. What little that I have mentioned may give rise to further thought for one who is attentive. Without industrious listening to good singers and instrumentalists who perform with taste, no one will be able to attain proficiency in this matter.

For the sake of those who are unable to form an adequate idea of abstract rules without having examples before their eyes, **Quantz** has performed the laudable task, in his **Versuch einer Anweisung die Flöte traversière zu spielen**, of prescribing most explicitly the loudness and softness of almost every note of many individual phrases and even for an entire adagio. This is to be found on pages 145ff.[20] Though all of this is actually meant for the flute, an aspiring singer may find these examples very useful as he goes through them and tries to put into practice that which is possible for his voice, according to the rules. It will be easier if he takes the trouble to copy in detail examples from the charts and to place above the notes those symbols [lit., abbreviated words] which indicate the degree of loudness and softness, since in the charts these are indicated only with letters of the alphabet that refer to the chapter of the book proper. I recommend even more highly [lit., refer even more widely to] this work of **Quantz** because a singer will find therein a tremendous amount of material that he can make use of, especially if he does not shrink from reading through the whole book carefully instead of [merely] **leafing through it**.

The loudness or softness, especially on long and serious notes, must be observed even by those who sing the supporting voices [not the soloists] in choirs. The sound of a long note that is made louder or softer by all voices at the same time is a truly beautiful effect. Of course the Ripieno[21] voice is not capable of all the refinement of solo singing. One must nevertheless try to apply as much refinement as possible, but with this difference: that above all, one keep in mind the power and the [proper] emphasis of the notes. Just as the lines and brush strokes of a painting to be viewed from a distance differ from the fine lines of a piece for a very small room, so must the performance of a chorus differ from that of an aria. Emphatic and powerful are not by any means to be confused with clumsy and boorish. To sing strongly and emphatically is a long way from bellowing and screaming. I would like to repeat here the admonition that one of our old German voice teachers, who had visited Italy, gave to the choir singers of his time in his own somewhat quaint words. I am referring to Printz in the **Musica modulatoria vocalis**, who wrote (p. 8): "The *Prefectus* (conductor of the choir) should pay special attention that none of the singers should scream too much. Not only is it dreadful when the singers open their traps[22] so wide that one could drive in a hay cart, and shout so loudly that they turn blue and their eyes roll up like a stuck goat's; but it also sounds exceedingly ugly and could be taken for the yelling of drunken peasants or for the howling of dogs rather than for elegant music."

I hope that such reminders are not necessary for the German choirs of our time.

31. The teacher should keep in mind that he who does not sing in strict time can hardly gain the respect of cultivated people. Therefore he should take care during his instruction that not only does each note receive its [proper] value, but that there be no alteration or aberration in the overall tempo of the movement, if he wants to teach properly and educate the student well.

32. If, in certain schools, the moldy old books with the large notes in chapel style, and the fugues, and bound pieces (u) are buried in the dust, the good teacher should seek them out again, since these contain the most powerful means to make the students confident in matters of

pitch and rhythm and likewise in the ability to find the notes, If current fashion did not require the singer nowadays almost always to sing from memory, I wonder how some singers would be able to command the name of great virtuoso.

(u) The word *Madrigali* appears in the original text. The Italians generally tend to call by the name of madrigal those many-voiced, bound [23] contrapuntal movements consisting of short poetry of free and uneven verses for voices without instruments. Some, especially those by [Antonio] **Lotti**, are very much praised. Well into advanced age, the famous **Francesco Gasparini** also crafted some quite beautiful madrigals in which enjoyment reigns side by side with art. To my knowledge, these are not very well known to the public, at least in Germany.

33. The teacher should encourage his student when he progresses; he should humble him, however, without beating him, when he persistently resists learning. He should be more strict with negligence. He should never end a lesson without good results.

Young males, at the time when their voices change, must not be taxed by too much singing, much less by too loud singing, until such time as the [newly] acquired deeper voice becomes steady. The same rule should be applied to young women at about the age when the male voice changes and indeed under certain circumstances that their mothers will best be able to notice.[24] Failing to pay attention to this could cause good voices of both sexes to be, if not lost, at least impaired.

34. One hour of practice a day, even at the beginning, is not enough, even for the most capable. The teacher should consider how much time he would have to spend with one who is not so talented and how great his obligation is to accommodate himself to the student's ability. In a teacher who teaches only for his bread, one cannot be assured of this necessary dedication [lit., accommodation].[25] His other students are waiting for him. He is in a bad humor over the daily grind. Necessity drives him. He thinks the month stretches long before him. He looks at the clock and leaves. If he teaches for a fairly good fee, we wish him luck.

CHAPTER FIVE

CONCERNING RECITATIVE

1. There are three different kinds of recitatives; and in three different kinds of recitatives must the teacher instruct his students.

2. The first kind is the **church recitative**, and [is first] for a good reason. It is performed in a manner suitable to the sanctity of the place. It does not permit the lightheartedness of a free composition style but rather requires here and there a long sustaining of a note[1] [*messa di voce*], many appoggiaturas, and a noble seriousness that is constantly maintained. The art of expressing it cannot be learned in any other way than out of a conviction of this truth: that one is speaking to **God**.

3. The second kind is the **theatrical recitative**. Because it is inseparably connected with the action of the singer, this recitative requires the teacher to instruct the student in a certain imitation that is true to nature and that cannot be beautiful unless it is performed with the stately decorum with which princes and those who consort with them speak.

4. The third kind, called the **chamber recitative**, is, according to the judgment of knowledgeable men, more capable than the others of touching the natural emotions of the human heart. This almost always requires a special artistry with regard to the words, which, since they are largely devoted to the expression of the strongest feelings of the heart, oblige the teacher to teach his students that lively art of participation [assuming the role] that can convince [the listener] that the singer truly feels that which he is performing. If the student has missed this lesson, he may very well need it later on. The extraordinary pleasure that musicians find in the chamber recitative arises from the acquired insight into those artifices which, without the aid of the customary ornaments, are in themselves capable of giving pleasure. And

certainly where [true] passion speaks, trills and divisions must remain silent and yield completely [lit., alone] to the power of beautiful expression united with melody in the persuasion of the heart.

5. The **church recitative** allows the singers more freedom than the other two and releases them from an exact observation of the time[2] (a), especially in the final cadences. They [the singers] should, however, make use of it [this freedom] as singers, not as violinists (b).

(a) If it is correctly performed otherwise, it could free many directors of German church choirs from the trouble of beating time.

(b) A certain amount of sustaining (which is filled in) in places rich in Affect [passion] is permitted at times for the purpose of improvised ornamentation. This ornamentation, however, is not allowed to be as extensive or extravagant as that which is permitted in arias. In place of the usually notated recitative ending (α), the shortest and easiest kinds of ornamentation are those given on p. 141, illustrating the double trill before the fermata (β); or a gently executed trilled turn provided with a long sustained, crescendoed appoggiatura, p. 147, on the second from above before the last note of the recitative, which is introduced at the location of the written-out fourth over it or of the twice-repeated [lit., written] ending note (γ).

One can also perform the ending very simply, arbitrarily sustaining one of the other preceding short notes. An example occurs on the syllable *men* in the word *pentimento* of the previous musical illustration, which also in this place seems actually to have been the intention of the composer.

At such cadences or on such arbitrary sustained notes, a few notes (but for the most part some slow spun-out notes) could still be introduced at the discretion of the performer. Occasionally they will already be notated by the composer, perhaps to limit the opportunity for digression – as is elucidated by the following example (δ) on the penultimate note of which could also be introduced in any case the two ornaments mentioned above (β) and (γ).

(δ)

per me si fà dol - cez - za o -   - gni tor - men - to.

6. Since this might impede the natural art of the narrative, no improvised ornamentation is permitted in the **theatrical recitative**, with the exception of certain sentences in many a soliloquy (*soliloquio*) (c) that are set in the manner of the chamber style.

(c) These [soliloquies] are provided, either completely or in part, with an accompaniment of several instruments, whereas the other theatrical recitatives, for the most part, have only the continuo for accompaniment. Such a movement, in a special sense, is called an **Accompagnament**[3] [instrumental accompaniment]. It does not necessarily follow, however, that all recitatives sung by one person alone on the stage are performed with instrumental accompaniment; it is of course permissible to provide other passages in the recitative that express certain emotions with an accompaniment of various instruments.

7. The third type [the chamber recitative] is less serious than the first and has more in common with the second (d).

(d) All three types of recitative share in common that which the author has specified above for the church recitative: that it is not sung in strict time. One must be guided more by the length and shortness of syllables in common speech than by the written value of the notes in the recitative. To be sure, these notes must be adapted by the composer to the duration of the syllables, but there are instances in which one holds the notes for a longer or shorter time than their prescribed value requires. It sounds especially tasteless when some German choral singers burst out with three sixteenth notes – very often in a recitative after a short rest – rapping them out so anxiously and so fast that no one will recognize the recitative as the imitation of common speech that it (even more than the aria) is supposed to be. To be sure, the short phrases that the instruments play between [the sung phrases of] the accompanied recitatives must be performed in strict time. However, the singer is not bound to this, but he must wait out the short phrases if he is not supposed to enter as they are playing, just as the instrumentalists, on the other hand, must always wait for him. When, however, as often happens, ariosos or other phrases that can and should be performed in strict time and that the composer generally indicates with the words *a tempo* or **in measured rhythm**, occur in the recitative, the singer is obliged to follow this direction, whether he be singing from memory or with the music.[4]

It is customary to change some notes in all three kinds of recitatives and to add a small supplement [ornament] to others. This practice, however, is more common in the church and chamber recitatives than in the theatrical ones.

(1) The recitative cadences are usually written out in the following manner (ε): the penultimate note is sung a fourth higher and thus repeats the preceding note (ζ). Some composers prefer to write them as they are to be sung. If the cadence ends with a single long syllable, one simply changes the fourth before the last note to an appoggiatura (η).

(2) Before a note making a strong-beat descending leap of a third, especially if it is followed by a short break expressed by a comma or another punctuation mark, there is a tendency to introduce occasionally either an appoggiatura of the second from above [and] to accompany this appoggiatura in tender places with a gentle short trill (δ), or to use only the appoggiatura instead of the first note in places that are not with feeling, especially if another note follows on the same pitch (ι).

The same procedure may be followed in similar cases when the two notes descend a second instead of a third (χ).

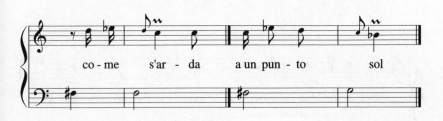

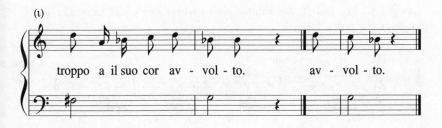

175

(3) When several notes are repeated on one pitch, a mordent proper may be sometimes introduced between the strong notes and the passing notes of the same. Here are some examples of this:

At (λ), (μ), (γ), and (ξ) are similar places where one could introduce these mordents notated as follows:

But since too many ornaments of the same type become offensive, these should not be used all the time.

(4) One can also introduce lengthened mordents over leaping appoggiaturas from below. In the middle two staves on p. 142 one may place the words **mio ben** or other similar words under the written-out mordents; this is an example of what can be introduced in church and chamber recitatives.

Whoever has read the above and then listens attentively to good singers will get a better idea of the small ornaments that occur in the recitative and will be able to imitate them more easily. In this matter [as in all aspects of the study of singing] one cannot gain full understanding without live examples of this matter.

8. The errors and insufferable abuses that are heard in the recitatives and not recognized by those who commit them are almost innumerable. I shall point out some that occur especially in the theater, so that the teacher might correct them (e).

(e) It is easy to see that these corrections can be made good use of in chamber and church recitatives as well.

9. Some sing the recitative on the stage in the same manner as in the church or in the chamber: with a constantly droning sound that could make a person sick. Some howl it out[5] because they are too greatly preoccupied with Affect [passion]. Some utter it almost confidentially; others, as if confused. Some stretch out or force out the last syllables, while others make them inaudible. Some sing it as if they had no heart for it; others, as if they were deep in thought. Some do not understand it; others do not let it be understood. Some act as if they were begging; others, as if they were only glancing at the listener over their shoulders. Some drag it out; others rattle it off. Some sing through their teeth; others, with open-mouthed exaggeration [lit., affectation]. Some do not pronounce correctly; others miss the appropriate expression. Some laugh it; others weep it. Some speak; others hiss it. Some shriek; others howl; and some sing out of tune. And among the errors of those who have become so removed from nature, the greatest is that they do not reflect upon their obligation to do better.

10. Careless modern teachers neglect to instruct their students in all kinds of the recitatives, for nowadays the effort expended on expression is either regarded as unnecessary or is disdained as old-fashioned. And yet they should be aware every day that it is not only absolutely necessary to be able to sing the recitatives, but also that one should know how to recite[6] them. If they do not believe this, they may look honestly [lit., without deluding themselves] among those whom they have trained, for an actor worthy of the encomiums of a Cortona for tenderness or of a Baron Ballerini for fire; or [let them look] on the musical stage at the present time and try to find an equal of various others famous for their acting. In my remarks here, though I do not name any of these, however consummate their artistry might be, I do not want to fail to attest to the esteem that they deserve and that I owe to them (f).

(f) The author undoubtedly means, if I can guess correctly, **Nicola Grimaldi**, generally known by the name of **Nicolini**, who was elevated to the rank of a Venetian cavalier; also the famous **Francesco Bernardi**, called **Senesino**, and **Madame Faustina Hasse**, who was indisputably as great an actress as she was a singer. Concerning **Nicolini**, even **Addison**, who was not particularly well disposed toward Italian opera, writes the following in the thirteenth issue of the *Spectator*: "It gives me just indignation to see a person [viz. Nicolini] whose action gives new majesty to kings, resolution to heroes, and softness to lovers, thus sinking from the greatness of his behaviour and degraded into the character of the **London Prentice** (o). I have often wished that our tragedians copy from after the great master in action. Could they but make the same use of their arms and legs, and inform their faces with as significant looks and passions, how glorious would an English tragedy appear with that action, which is capable of giving a dignity to the forced thought, cold conceits, and unnatural expressions of an Italian opera."[7] (π)

(o) In his role in a certain London opera at that time, **Nicolini** had to fight a lion – first portrayed by a choleric candle-snuffer, then by a gentle tailor, and finally by a gay country squire [playing merely] for [his own] amusement – during which fight, the lion found more admirers among the public than **Nicolini** himself.[8]

(π) It is obvious that **Addison** is not referring here to the music, but to the libretti of the London opera of that time; and in this, he is absolutely right. **Metastasio** and his lucky successors were not writing Singspiels[9] at that time.

11. Whoever is unable to teach delivery of the recitative does not understand the words, it would seem. How can a teacher who does not understand the words constantly teach the student that expression which is the soul of singing, and without which it is impossible to sing well?

O,[10] weak gentlemen teachers, without considering the great damage that you cause to Music by shaking the very pillars on which she rests, how can you take students under your wing when you do not know that the recitatives, particularly in the mother tongue, must be so taught as to suit the expression of the words? I would advise you to give over the name and office of teacher to others who are equal to [the task of] benefiting both the singers and the music (g). Otherwise, it is no wonder that students who have been sacrificed to your ignorance cannot distinguish the humorous from the sad or the fiery from the tender, and thus appear stupid on stage and without sense or sensibility in the chamber. I say it as I see it: your fault and theirs is inexcusable. For the torment that one has when one hears the recitatives sung in the taste of Capuchin choral singing is intolerable.

(g) In his teaching, **Porpora** in particular has constantly and seriously kept in mind and inculcated the correct delivery and expression of the words in the recitative as well as in the aria. He also possesses the rare (and in many teachers who are not actually composers almost unknown) gift of understanding exactly the ability of his students and directing his teaching thereto. He allows none to sing anything beyond the quality and capability of his voice. I believe that no impartial music scholar, also considering his composition, will deny the fairness [of this statement]. Among many other singing teachers and composers, those have always been the most successful whose voices were most like the voices of their teachers.

12. But the reason the recitative is no longer given expression in the fashion of the famous Ancients is not only [lit., not always] to be sought either in the ineptitude of the masters or in the negligence of the singers. It stems rather from the limited understanding of certain modern composers – fine composers are exempted – who compose such unnatural and tasteless recitatives that they can neither be taught nor be accompanied by the right action nor be sung. Good sense herself reaches out a hand to rescue [lit., vindicate] the teachers and the singers. This same good sense prevents me from blaming the composers and entering a subject that is above my limited understanding and orders me very wisely to return to my limited and superficial singer's understanding, which is barely enough for elementary counterpoint. On the other hand, when I consider the necessity of placing various benefits at the disposal of singers, as I have undertaken to do with the publication of these remarks, [I realize that] I would commit a double error if I had nothing to say about the composition of the recitative to those who need it so badly. My doubts in this matter would indeed leave me confused and undecided had I not been aided by the timely insight that the recitative has nothing to do with artificial counterpoint. If it is indeed true that the art of composing fugues does not belong in the recitative, then I would like to know the singer who would not be benefited by the knowledge that many theatrical recitatives would be improved if they were not [so easily] confused with one another; if it were possible to learn them by heart; if they were not deficient in the adaptation of the music to the expression of the words; if they did not shock the singer and the listener with the most dangerous leaps from white to black keys; if they did not insult the ear and the rules with the worst modulations; if they did not torture good taste by being constantly the same; if they did not cause heartburn because of the disgusting changes in tonality; and, finally, if the phrases were not dislocated by people with insufficient knowledge of periods and commas. I am astonished that certain gentlemen do

not try to imitate and turn to their advantage the recitatives of those composers who represent the truth most vividly through the expression of certain notes that sound [lit., sing themselves] as if they were speaking. But what good is served by my being troubled over this? Can I demand that all these reasons, however obvious they may be, are to be recognized as good, when reason itself in music (h) is beginning to go out of style? Custom has such great strength! It liberates its followers from the rules through a power outside of the rules [lit., illegal] in order to direct their industry toward nothing but artificial refrains [ritornellos] and accompaniments (i). It does not wish them to waste their precious time on recitatives, which according to its principles, are supposed to fall from the pen and not from the head. Whether it is ignorance or negligence I do not know, but this I do know: that the singer never profits from it [custom] in the least.

(h) The author wrote this in the year 1723. I cannot really say how matters now stand in Italy concerning this point because of insufficient [updated] information.

(i) This complaint would certainly not be made if **Tosi** were to see the ritornellos of many of the contemporary composers of Italy. I rather suspect that he would find reason to complain about the opposite [lack of attention to the ritornello]. I will let others judge how far his most modern compatriots have come since **Tosi's** time with the improvement of the recitative style.

13. About the composition of the recitative, in general, much would remain to be said, especially on account of the irksome monotony that assaults the ear in every opera with a thousand truncated cadences[11] (κ). To be sure, custom introduced cadences of this type, but they are, for the most part, without taste or art. Abolishing them all would be a worse remedy than the ailment. To introduce nothing but final cadences (λ) would be disgusting. If in any case between these two extremes, a middle ground would have to be found, I believe that among a hundred broken cadences, ten fully completed endings with punctuation to end musical sections would not be unreasonable [lit., bad usage]. But the experts do not discuss this and their silence counsels me to speak no further.[12]

14. I return now to the teacher to remind him again that it is his duty to teach music; and that if a student, before he has been released from the teacher's care, is not certain of his science, the injury falls upon the innocent; and he who is the cause of it cannot make reparation.

15. If the master finds, upon completion of the above lesson, that he has enough ability beyond this to teach the student more important things that contribute to his further growth, he must introduce him immediately to church arias, in which all theatrical and feminine decoration must be set aside; and he must sing as a man. For this reason, he must provide the student with various motets suitable to his capabilities (m), motets that are set naturally and with noble grace and in which the happy and the pathetic alternate. The teacher must go through these with the student as often as necessary for the student to perform them with assurance and with liveliness. He should take care at the same time that the words are well pronounced and even better understood; that the recitatives are executed with expression and without affectation; that in the arias precision in tempo is not lacking; that, on the other hand, a talent for finer and more tasteful singing may shine forth; and, above all, that the divisions that end the motet are well detached, sung in tune, and performed rapidly.

(m) In Italy the **Motet** is a certain spiritual cantata in Latin for solo voice and instruments, sung in church during mass between the Credo and the Sanctus. Motets consist generally of two arias and two recitatives and end with an Alleluja usually containing many divisions. Nevertheless, all of the above instructions of **Tosi** are excellently suited to German Protestant church cantatas.

Thereupon, one should instruct the student also in the manner of singing that the style [lit. taste] of the chamber cantata requires, so that he might learn through practice the difference between the style of the church cantata and that of the chamber cantata.

Even if the master is satisfied with the progress of his student, he should not presume to allow him to be heard in public without the student's having heard beforehand the sage advice of men who know more about singing than they do about flattering. Not only will they suggest compositions by which the student can gain the most honor, but they will also reveal to him the shortcomings that, out of negligence or lack of knowledge on the part of the teacher, have not been corrected or even recognized.

16. If all teachers [lit., those occupied with teaching] would bear in mind that whether we are to win or lose a good name and confidence depends on our first step into the great world, they would not so blindly and haphazardly expose their students to the danger of falling with the first step.

17. Finally, if the master has no more insights than this, to put into practice the rules presented up to this point – which, if necessary, might be barely sufficient – he is bound by his conscience not to venture further; he himself should rather advise the student, for his own good, to submit himself to more learned instruction. But before it comes to that, perhaps it would be useful to address a few words to the student himself. If he is too young to understand, then let that person who takes care of him, or in some way is responsible for him, hear me in the following chapters.

CHAPTER SIX

REMARKS INTENDED ESPECIALLY FOR THE MUSIC STUDENT

1. Before making the extensive and difficult effort such as must be expended on the finer and more artificial type of singing, it is necessary that the student examine his own calling, without which all diligence would be in vain. It is impossible to resist the obstinacy of our natural inclination when, with subversive power, it pulls us toward something else. When it beckons, it immediately persuades and thereby spares the beginner half the trouble.

2. I assume therefore that the student is anxiously desirous to attain for himself such a beautiful science and that he may have already received adequate instruction in the previously taught tedious fundamentals, of which some may perhaps have escaped my weak memory. At first, he must principally strive toward the possession of ethical virtues; afterward, he must apply himself to the perfection of his art, [lit., the art of singing well]; so that he might, through good progress in both [i.e., virtue and art], arrive at the happy state of having united in himself the noblest spiritual qualities with the rarest gifts of genius.

3. When a student makes singing his principal work in life, he should consider that upon his voice depends inescapably his success or failure. In order not to lose it, therefore, he must not permit himself excesses or reckless pleasures.

4. He must learn to read perfectly, so that he will not suffer the embarrassment of having to be prompted [lit., begging for the words] and not lapse into absurdities that have their origin in shameful ignorance. Oh, how many still need to go back to [lit. take in hand] their primers!

5. If his teacher has not succeeded in correcting his faulty pronunciation, he [the student] should try on his own initiative to learn the

best [pronunciation], since the excuse that one was not born in Tuscany is not sufficient to excuse one's ignorance.

6. He should seek with equal diligence to rid [lit., cleanse] himself of all other errors that the teacher in his negligence might have overlooked.

7. Besides music, he should learn at least something of the Latin language, so that he might understand the words that he has to sing in church, and so that he might give them the same power that is needed in any other language. I might almost believe that many singers do not even understand their mother tongue, to say nothing of Latin (a).

(a) At this point our German singers should reread the note, pp. 162ff.

8. He should untiringly exercise his voice in agility [lit. rapidity] of movement, so that it becomes obedient in every instance. In this manner, he becomes the master rather than the slave of his voice, and without this he will not deserve the reputation of an excellent pathetic[1] [-style] singer.

9. He should not fail from time to time to make some *messa di voce* [2] (b), so that the voice always remains adaptable to the one [agility] and to the other [sustaining].[3]

(b) See above, p. 84.

10. He should repeat his lesson at home until he is quite sure of it and it has become imprinted upon his memory. He will thereby spare his teacher the trouble of repeating it, and himself the trouble of learning it again.

11. Singing demands such great diligence that one must study it with his mind when he cannot study it with the voice.

12. Young people have the distinct advantage, with their tireless energy, of being able to overcome all of the obstacles that confront them, even if they were errors sucked in, so to speak, with their mother's milk. Although this opinion of mine has met with strong objections, experience defends me, subject to the following condition: that one correct oneself in time. If the rooting out of defects is constantly put off, they grow with the years, and the more deeply they take root the uglier they become.

13. The young beginner in the art of singing should try as often as possible to listen to the most famous singers and the best instrumentalists. From listening to their performance he derives more benefit than from any other instruction.

14. Thereafter, he should try to imitate first one and then the other, in order, through the diligence of others, imperceptibly to arrive at good taste. Although this precept is very necessary for the student, it may, on the other hand, cause infinite damage to the mature singer. The reason for this I will give elsewhere in this book.

15. He should often sing the most agreeable works of the best composers, since these are the sweet incentives for him to become ever better acquainted with good taste and to accustom the ear to what is truly pleasing. He who studies music knows that, with the imitation that is recommended and with the stimulation that good composition provides, the sense of taste develops with time into knowledge, and knowledge into second nature.

16. He should learn to accompany himself at the keyboard if he wants to learn to sing well. The harpsichord invites the student, with such great attraction, to diligence that with it negligence may be overcome, and insight into music becomes ever deeper. The obvious advantage that singers enjoy in this agreeable instrument relieves me of the effort of using further persuasion. Besides this, it often befalls singers who cannot play the keyboard that they cannot be heard without the help of another; and, to their great disadvantage and greater embarrassment, they cannot even obey the commands of persons of high rank.[4]

17. So long as a singer does not please himself, he will certainly never be able to please others. If one considers that singers with more than ordinary understanding feel deprived of this pleasure [in singing] by not having learned enough, what then is a beginner to do? Study, and keep on studying, and not consider himself finished [i.e., sufficiently taught] when he has just barely mastered a few pleasing trifles.

18. I might almost assert that all effort that is expended on singing is useless if not accompanied by insight into composition. He who can compose can give account of that which he does, but whoever understands nothing of composition, works in the dark and cannot sing for long without falling into error. The most famous Ancients recognized the intrinsic value of this principle from its effects, and a good student must imitate them, without being concerned whether or not the lesson given here is fashionable. Nowadays one occasionally hears here and there beautiful ideas that a fortunate natural talent expresses, but they all come by chance and await the chance applause of the listeners. On the other hand, when one examines closely the inventions of many singers, they are [found to be], if not unbearable, at least rather bad. They often clash with the rhythm or with the fundamental bass, since

Fortune cannot always cover up defects. Even though insight into the art of composing is essential, I stop short of counseling [the singer] to go into it very deeply, because this would be to show him the easiest way to lose his voice. I admonish him urgently, however, to learn at least the most important rules of musical composition, so that he does not sing blindly.

19. To study very hard and still preserve the full beauty of the voice are two things which are almost incompatible. Compatibility may develop between them, but it can hardly endure without prejudice to the one or the other [lit., without selfishness and jealousy].[5] Considering that in nature, perfection of the voice is given freely; but that in art, it is dearly bought, one will recognize the truth of [lit., so follows] the saying that Art takes precedence over Nature both in merit and in praise.

20. The student should always look for the best wherever he may find it, without caring whether it was in fashion fifteen or twenty years ago, or whether it may be found in the latest compositional style. The good as well as the bad may be found in all ages, if one only knows how to look for it, recognize it, and make use of it.

21. To my irreparable misfortune, I am already old. If I were still young, I would try as much as possible to imitate the cantabile [tunefulness] and the pleasing quality of those now called by the nasty name of Ancient. But in matters which concern fast singing, I would follow those who bear the beautiful title of Modern (c). Though my ideal may be impossible to realize at my age, a clever beginner will nevertheless do himself no harm by trying to acquire skills in both the Ancient and the Modern styles. That is the only way to perfection. If, however, he wanted to choose only one of the two styles, I would boldy advise him [lit., without fear of being accused of bias] to hold more to the taste of the former [the Ancients] (d).

(c) How much the times have begun to change on this matter in Italy!

(d) Instead of all the other instructions, at this point one should remember what the author has said further back: that the old dullness should be avoided as much as the newer excesses. Nonetheless, it is certain that a singer who was hardly considered to be of even average competence in music in former times has already starred on several theatrical stages today. The Ancients took more time to learn the principles.

22. Every kind of singing has its own level. For example, the manly should be distinguished from the childish, just as the sublime [noble] should be distinguished from the common [vulgar].

23. The student should never hope to win acclaim if he does not abhor ignorance.

24. Whoever does not strive with all of his might to climb to the highest level within his discipline, has already begun to relinquish second place; and gradually he will [come to] be contented with the last.

25. Even if one possibly does not hold it against many weak female singers (because of the liberties once allowed them) for having the improvised changes written out by others, a student who would be a good singer should not follow their example in this. Whoever becomes accustomed to allowing all the variations to be stuffed into his mouth like pabulum [lit., gruel] becomes dry and barren and makes himself a slave to his memory.

26. If a student has defects, especially of the nose, the throat, or the ears, he should not sing unless his teacher or someone else who understands singing is present to help correct him; otherwise the faults will become more pronounced, and effective remedies against them will become useless.

27. If he practices his lesson at home, he should stand in front of a mirror from time to time. Not to admire his own beauty with fascinated vanity, but rather to guard against or to free himself from convulsive movements of the torso or the face. (I tend to refer to all grimacing of an affected [lit., ridiculously forced] singer in this manner.) Once they have gained a foothold, it becomes impossible to be rid of them.

28. The most comfortable hours to practice singing are the early hours. The other hours, with the exception of those that are spent on the care of the body, are suitable for other things that a singer has to learn in his profession.

29. If a beginner has mastered intonation, *messa di voce*,[6] trills, and divisions, and has practiced a long time in expressive recitative singing and has it completely under his control; if he considers that the master cannot teach him that perfect execution demanded by the most refined art in the arias, and is also unable to be constantly at his side, then I say he will begin to realize how very much he needs that discipline with which even the best singer in the world must always continue to be his own pupil and his own teacher. If his judgment is mature enough, I advise him, as the first means of expanding his knowledge, to read the following chapter, so that he will be able thereafter to gain the greater benefit from those who can sing and teach arias. If his judgment is not mature, the fruit of it would only be sour and bitter.

CHAPTER SEVEN

CONCERNING ARIAS

1. If the person who introduced the practice of repeating an aria from the beginning intended to give the singers an opportunity to show their skill in varying the phrases already performed, the music lover cannot find fault with this invention; nevertheless, a great part of the expression of the words is lost thereby[1](a).

(a) This is chiefly a matter of an able and musically inclined poet's so arranging the arias that they can be repeated from the beginning without prejudicing the sense and the power of the words. Through the repetition from the beginning a new emphasis is perhaps achieved. In crafting the poems to be set to music, if the poet bears in mind that he wants to express thoughts and feelings, not for themselves alone, but in close unity and liaison with the music, he will not find it difficult to sacrifice, if necessary, a few poetic embellishments in the arias and choruses, which, after all, consist of only a few lines. Besides, the music allows him a free hand in the more expansive **recitatives**, forbidding him little or nothing except a few quite inappropriate verse forms. If Italian librettists of **Tosi's** time have been culpable, the blame for this must not be placed on the music. But have not some contemporary Germans proven through rules and practice that poetic and musical beauties do not necessarily neutralize each other?[2]

2. Arias were sung in three different styles by our famous Ancients. On the stage, the art of singing was lively and varied; in the chamber, more artificial and refined; in church, however, serious and full of Affect [passion]. A great number of the Moderns are unaware of this difference.

3. A singer is obliged to expend the greater part of his effort on the arias because they can either establish his good name or destroy it. A few oral instructions would suffice, however, to show the way to such a valuable asset. It would not be particularly useful to the beginner to

possess a number of arias in which the most excellent optional ornaments were written out in thousands of ways. In spite of [the seeming value of] all that, these would not suffice for all arias; and, moreover, they would always lack the benefit of that fresh interpretation [lit., pleasant performance] by the author's own voice, in which Nature and Art are best expressed without conflict. All I can do, in my opinion, is to persuade a beginner to pay careful attention to the beautiful design that the best singers exhibit in their performance, in accordance with the rules of the bass and of harmony. Just as the ability of the beginner increases, so will he gradually be able to develop this inherent art and insight. However, if he did not know how to learn by observing the design of these worthy people, he should follow the example of one of my most trusted friends who never went to the opera without taking along the score of all the arias that the best singer was to sing. Here he contemplated with close attention [lit., wonder] the choicest, most refined concepts of the art that were applied above the harmony, tailored, however, in the most exact fashion to the strictest laws of time; and thus he learned something.

4. Among other things that are worthy of consideration within this intended design, the first to be considered is the manner in which all arias consisting of three parts must be executed. In the first part, nothing but quite simple ornaments are required, which, however, must be tasteful and sparse (b), so that the work of the composer may be heard in its natural beauty. In the second part, one wants to hear, along with that noble simplicity, still more ornamentation, so that the knowledgeable listener may perceive that the singer is possessed of a greater breadth of knowledge. And finally, with the repetition from the beginning, he who does not by means of variation make what he has already sung, better and more beautiful than it is written is certainly no great hero.

(b) For this purpose [i.e. the ornamentation of the first part], the ornaments described and explained in the second and third chapters [of this book] are almost sufficient, if one chooses carefully among them.

5. The student should strive to sing through the arias very often and always with variations. The average singer who has at his disposal a wealth of small ornaments deserves (if I am not mistaken) far more respect than a better singer with a limited imagination [lit. dry head], since the latter can delight the connoisseurs only once. However, even if the former does not astound by the rarity of his inventions, he at

189

least engages attention by the diversity of his improvisations [lit., sudden ideas].

6. The best singers among the Ancients indulged every evening in the caprice of changing not only all of the slow arias in the opera but also some of the faster ones. A student who is not making the effort to gain a firm footing on the most basic foundations of the art of singing will not be able to bear the heavy burden of [emulating] such important models.

7. If no variations were allowed in the arias, it would be impossible to discover the intelligence of the singer. On the other hand, one can easily recognize by the quality of their variations which of two singers of the first rank is the better.

8. I now return from this little digression to the design of the variations in the arias. A beginner must observe therein not only the rules of the art but the skillful distribution and application of his own inventions as well. They [the rules] teach that taste, insight, and the observation of time, no matter how good [lit., for all that], can be practically useless to a person whose head does not overflow with impromptu [lit., unexpected] embellishments. On the other hand, the art of making proper use of invention does not permit the abundance of good ideas to be detrimental to the composition and to assail the ears to the point of distraction.

9. A student should first strive to acquire an extensive knowledge of musical embellishments, but once in possession of them, should seek to use them wisely. To further convince himself of this, let him note that the most famous singers never parade all of their talents in just a few arias. If the vocalist displays on a single day everything that he possesses in his booth for the crowd [lit., populace] to look at, he stands in the greatest danger of going bankrupt.

10. In the performance of the arias (as I have already stated), one can never be too diligent. If one neglects certain things that either seem to be or really are of minor importance, how then may the art be perfected if there is always something missing?

11. With those arias that are set for voice and bass alone, the student of ornamentation should concentrate mainly on the rhythm and the fundamental bass. For those arias that are provided with instrumental accompaniment, however, it is necessary to observe precisely their movement in order to avoid those errors that are frequently committed by those who have not learned to recognize them.

12. So as not to make errors in a public performance of the arias,

190

two important rules are illuminating to the man who reflects [as he works]. The first of these wise counsels is a reminder that, (if it cannot be [accomplished] otherwise) it is better to make mistakes a thousand times by oneself at home if one thereby gains the assurance that he will not make them in public. The second rule demands, with reasons against which there is no argument, that one perform the arias for the first time in public with none but the most essential ornaments; nevertheless, one should firmly resolve to reflect at the same time where one might add improvised ornaments the next [lit., second] time [one sings the arias]. Thus from rehearsal to rehearsal, by constant polishing, one gradually becomes a great singer.

13. One of the most necessary and most difficult challenges in the attainment of the completely perfect execution of the arias is this: that one seek facility, especially in the ornamentation [lit., beauty of the improvisation]. Whoever succeeds in combining such rare gifts with a pleasing delivery of the voice[3] is the most fortunate of singers.

14. He who, possessing little talent for invention, studies the art of singing in defiance, as it were [of this limitation], should remember that pure intonation; expression appropriate to the words; effectively spun-out held notes[4] [*messa di voce*]; well slurred appoggiaturas; crisp trills; clear divisions; and, finally, the ability to accompany oneself at the keyboard are indeed very necessary qualities of a singer, but are not insurmountable difficulties. I know well that all of this [the above] does not suffice to make one an accomplished singer, and that he must be very foolish if he is merely satisfied not to sing badly. Despite that, the matters noted above tend to invite art to come to the rescue most accommodatingly: it is seldom completely absent, but often appears of its own accord and uncalled. But one must not tire of studying these matters.

15. Let the student avoid all of the abuses that have, of late, crept in and become entrenched in the singing of arias, if he wishes to preserve the established and proper essence of music.

16. Every singer (not to mention the beginner) must be careful not to mimic the singing style of others in a ridiculous and exaggerated way. Otherwise, he had better be ready for [lit., will have to expect] very bad consequences. One who makes people laugh will hardly merit high esteem. This sort of aping insults everyone who does not want to be considered foolish or ignorant. This [sort of error] arises mostly from that same false pride [lit., ambition] that compels us to point out the mistakes of others in order to seem greater in our own

knowledge. May heaven prevent them from being further puffed up by [lit., deriving more nourishment from] poisonous envy and jealousy! That they [the imitators] are not always ineffective is confirmed only too well by examples. They are, however, rightly punished by the law of retaliation; and in their punishment they deserve no pity. Such aping of the arias of other singers has discredited more than one singer.[5]

17. I do not possess enough of the art of persuasion nor enough words to instill, as I would like to and should, in the student, the importance of the strict observation of correct rhythm. And if I speak about it more than once, I consider it necessary in more than one instance, because even among the best of singers, there are a considerable number who imperceptibly change the rhythm, tending either to drag or to rush. Although one is hardly aware of this at the beginning of an aria, the longer the piece progresses the greater [the discrepancy becomes]; and by the end one really notices the difference unmistakably; and with the difference, the error.

18. If I do not counsel a student to imitate certain moderns in their way of executing an aria, it is only the exact observance of the rhythm that is responsible. This [the exact observance of the rhythm], since it has been made by knowledge and experience a principle of the art of singing, forbids me seriously to give such advice. Truly, the contempt in which many modern singers hold the rhythm, sacrificing it to their absurd fancy for their beloved divisions, is too unjust to be passed over in silence.

19. Insufferable is the weakness of certain singers, in demanding that an entire orchestra stop playing during the most beautiful course of the regularly defined movement of the aria, in order to give them time to unpack their poorly grounded inventions, which they may have memorized anyway so that they can drag them from one theater to another; or which they may have stolen from some female singer, more lucky than learned, who has received the applause of the populace for them, and with whom one does not expect the exact observance of the rhythm. **Easy, easy with the criticism**! I hear a singer who hates restraint say. **This, if you do not know, is called singing with style**. Singing according to style? . . . I retort: You are wrong. In the arias, pausing over each second or fourth and over all sevenths and sixths[6] of the harmony was the worthless practice of the very oldest of singers; and it was rejected more than fifty years ago by **Rivani,** called **Ciecolino** (c), who with inarguable and incontrover-

tible reasons (which should always be adhered to), maintained that he who can sing will find enough appropriate places, even in the correct rhythm, to attach artistic ornaments, without having recourse to begging for or inventing the pauses. Whether or not this was a teaching that deserves to be put into practice can be observed in those who have availed themselves of its use, among whom **Signor Pistocchi**[7] (d), the most famous singer of our time and of all times, was the first. His name has become immortal because he was the only inventor of a well-rounded and perfect taste and because he taught how to use all of the embellishments of the art without going against the observance of time. This example [of Pistocchi] alone, which is worth a thousand of those of the newest fashion, should be enough, Honored Sir, to disabuse you of your error. If you still do not believe me, I say further that **Siface**[8] (e), in his touchingly flowing melody, takes advantage of this advice; that **Buzzoleni**[9] (f), with an incomparable insight, almost worshiped his teaching; that **Luigino**[10] (g), with his pleasant and charming way of singing, walked in his footsteps; and that Signora **Boschi**[11] (h), to the honor of her sex, let it be heard that a female who enjoys studying may also teach men of note the rarest refinement of the art; that Signora **Lotti**[12] (i), under the guidance of these same rules and [possessed of] a penetrating loveliness, stole our hearts through her singing – and one cannot deny the same honor to her. If such highly regarded persons, among whom I must also count very famous singers whose names are currently known all over Europe without my having to name them (and whom I have tried not to exclude unwittingly, at least in thought if not with pen) – if all those, I say, and others besides, who practice the art of singing only for their pleasure but are nonetheless capable of making the most skillful professional singers envious, are not enough to make you understand that without rhythm one cannot nor may not sing, you should at least recognize that, along with the error that you cherish as regards the observance of the rhythm, you may fall into another perhaps even greater one. That is, you simply do not understand [lit., know] that if the voice is not accompanied,[13] it is robbed of all harmony; and consequently, very little of your so-called artistry may be perceived. Instead, the connoisseurs will start to yawn. More as an excuse than as a justification, you perhaps will object that few listeners are so discriminating, but that there are a great many who blindly heap praises upon everything that has the semblance of novelty. But who here is in the wrong? The listeners who would perhaps praise even this disgrace do not cover up your errors when they expose their ignorance to the light of day. It is your duty to undeceive them [lit., pull them out of their ignorance]. You should abandon your ill-grounded stubbornness and freely admit that the liberties you take are at odds with reason and go against its precepts. Your obstinacy makes you, as well as all those instrumentalists, punishable as partners in crime; and they yield to you and wait for you at the expense of their own dignity. Since obedience is only the action of a vassal, it is not appropriate in this matter for you to make one who is your colleague and your equal, recognize any other master than the tempo. Finally, remember that the principles we have discussed will always be useful to you. For if you, though you are in the wrong, are now so happy to receive the applause of the crowds, you will then [as soon as you learn the above rules] be in agreement with the *cognoscenti;* and [your] approval will rightfully become universal.

(c) I have been unable to find out who he was.

(d) His given name was **Francesco Antonio**. He was a castrato, but besides his great ability in singing, he was also a good composer of his time. Among his works, I am familiar not only with many of his cantatas but also with many operas, among them *Il Narciso*, 1697. Among his compositions he left four cantatas: two Italian and two French, as well as two (nota bene) **German** arias engraved in copper, which **Roger** published in Amsterdam.[14] From about the year 1697 and later, he was the Margrave's Capellmeister in Ansbach. The art of singing is incontestably indebted to him for many improvements. Most of the famous singers and teachers who succeeded him in Italy had been his students. He also possessed the secret of allowing each one to sing according to the capability and special qualities of his voice. Therefore, many of his students differed from one another in their manner of singing; yet they were always good because he knew well how to distinguish the essential from the improvised embellishments. One of his most famous students is the contemporary great singer, good actor, and talented voice teacher, **Antonio Bernacchi**.[15]

(e) About him, other than the fact that he was a good singer, the only thing that is known is that he was murdered on a journey near **Ferrara** by disguised persons, probably because of his rude impertinence.

(f) He was a tenor.

(g) I have been unable to find out anything about him.

(h) She also went under the name of **Francesca Vanini**. She performed in **London** in the year 1710 in **Handel's** opera **Rinaldo**.

(i) She was the wife of the famous *maestro di cappella* **Lotti**[16] and was still performing in operas in the years 1718 and 1719 in Dresden.

20. The errors against the rhythm are not, however, reasons enough in themselves for counseling a student not to imitate the singing style in the arias of our gentlemen Moderns. It is obvious that all of their efforts are directed solely to mutilating and mangling the arias in such a way that it is no longer possible to hear the words, thoughts, or modulations – much less to distinguish one aria from another – since the variations that they insert everywhere are so much the same that when one has heard one, he has heard a thousand. **And yet Fashion keeps the upper hand**? A few years ago it was thought that in every opera, one aria that was provided with runs was sufficient for the singer who had a very agile throat, to satisfy his desire for divisions. Today's singers are not of this opinion. Just as if they could not be satisfied with turning an aria utterly and in a frightful manner into nothing but passages, they hurtle headlong toward their final cadenzas with redoubled energy, as though to recapture the time they imagine they have lost during the course of the aria. In the chapter on cadenzas we will shortly see whether or not this fashion is in good taste. In the meantime, I shall return to the abuses and errors in the arias.

21. I do not really know who among the Moderns was the ungrateful composer or singer who could have had the heart to ban the pathetic quality, rich in Affect [passion] from arias, just as though, after a long and faithful service, it no longer merited the honor of its services. No matter who he was, this much is certain: he has robbed the art of singing of the best that it possessed. My weak insight does not suffice to discover the reasons for this; and even less so when I ask all singers what they think about the pathetic (k), and they answer in general agreement (as they very seldom are) that it provides the greatest pleasure to the ear, the sweetest touching of the heart, and the strongest pillar of harmony. **Must we be deprived of even one note of all these charms without knowing why**?...Now I understand. I must not ask singers about this but rather the people who, in their foolish stubbornness, are the fickle protectors of fashion. The pathetic will perhaps not be able to survive this...Or does my imagination deceive me? Fashion and the populace are like the water of an overflowing stream, which, no sooner having overflowed its banks, very often changes the direction of its bed; but, finally, on the

first warm day resumes its previous course [lit., returns to nothingness]. The evil, of course, stems from the source; the greatest blame, nevertheless, lies with the singers. They praise the pathetic, but sing the joyous [allegro]. He who could not guess their thoughts must have very little understanding. They acknowledge the pathetic as the best; but since they know that it is more difficult than the joyous, they put it aside.

(k) The term "pathetic," as it is generally understood, means everything that is filled with strong passion. Thus, some of the fast, even furioso, arias, in a certain sense, can be called pathetic. The practice has been established, especially in Italy, of identifying in a special way the slow arias – which are generally expressions of a high degree of tender, sad, or otherwise nobly serious emotions – as pathetic arias. Their character is usually recognized by the performer at first glance by means of the terms *adagio, largo, lento, mesto, grave*, etc., which allow the performer to identify immediately their character as pathetic. This is what is meant here by the author.

22. In former times, one would occasionally hear arias in the theater, set in this most pleasant style – arias that were composed with ritornellos[17] well modulated, and rich in harmony, and accompanied by various instruments – arias that delighted the sensibilities of all those who understood the art [of music] and singing. When these arias were sung completely by the five or six famous persons whom I have named, it was humanly impossible under the spell of such powerful emotions, to refrain from [being moved to] passion, tenderness, or even to tears. O strong evidence of the ignominy of idolized Fashion! Is anyone nowadays, even with the best of singing, moved to tears? No, the listeners all respond. No: because the constant allegro that the Moderns sing, even if deserving of admiration because of its strength and perfection, goes no further than the exterior of a sensitive ear, if even that far. The taste of the Ancients I have named was a mixture of the joyous and the tender, an alternation that was sure to delight. The current taste has such a high opinion of itself that it is content just to deviate from the older taste, even if [in doing so] it should lose the greater part of its charm. The study of pathetic arias was the favorite pursuit of the earlier singers; but practicing the most difficult passages is the only goal of today's singer. The former labored with more thoroughness; the latter perform with more agility and fire. However, having found the courage to compare the most famous singers in the former and the latter styles, may my audacity now be excused if I finish this comparison by saying that the Moderns are inimitable when they

sing for the ear, and that the art of the Ancients was unattainable (l) when they sang for the heart (m).

(l) He who has heard the pathetic arias of a **Hasse** or a **Graun** sung by a **Salinbeni**[18] or a **Carestini**[19] (not to mention other skillful male and female singers), or who was so very fortunate as to hear **Graun**[20] himself execute his touching pathetic arias, if he [the hearer] possesses a sensitive soul, will not deny that everything that **Tosi** missed in good taste in the art of singing, during the years in which he wrote this book, reappeared several years later in a greatly improved form.

(m) The heart and the ear are, even today, very vague concepts in music. It is laughable to the person who is wise to the world, to be confronted in certain musical books with a representation of the ear and the heart as half enemies. Is there a way other than through the ear to arouse the soul to tenderness with musical notes? Do courage, daring, and other such passions reside only in our ears? Or do they [the ears] perhaps approve of a musical noise with no soul, introduced inopportunely and devoid of all expression?

23. It is undeniable, therefore, that the best among today's singers, in a certain sense, have improved and bettered the taste of former times through inventions, and that they are worthy of being imitated not only by a student but also by an already mature singer. As evidence of my esteem for the Moderns, I must publicly acknowledge that, if they cared for expression and the pathetic a little more and the divisions a little less, they could boast of having brought the art of singing to the highest degree of perfection.

24. It could also be that the extravagant ideas now heard in many compositions are responsible for depriving the frequently mentioned singers of the opportunity to show their ability in the cantabile. The types of arias now in fashion put them into such a violent temper and apply, so to speak, such sharp spurs to them that they are quite out of breath. How are they then to have the composure to bring out their fine and penetrating power of discernment? But, Good Heavens! Now that there are so many new composers, among whom there are more than one who has a head that is just as good as, if not better than those of the most famous Ancients, what is the reason for always excluding from their extraordinary inventions the greatly longed-for adagio? Why does this never occur to them in their inventions that are so beautiful? What sin would they commit by holding back their hot blood somewhat? Since it is not seemly in the arias to always ride courier [lit., ride as a very fast messenger], as it were, why can they not invent one that would allow us to relax a little or, perhaps at the very least, one that

197

might enable us to assist the unlucky hero with compassion when he is supposed to cry and perhaps even die on the stage?...**No, dear sir, the current fashion demands that this hero cry and die and at the same time sing fast and merrily** (n).[21]

(n) I hope that none of my readers interpret these ideas of **Tosi's** as derisive toward all singing by a dying theatrical hero. In any case, this is not the place to cite the librettists who have demonstrated through argument that in certain performances one may, while singing, give orders, carry on a conversation, fight, and die without becoming absurd. Our author is here chiding only some young singers of his time, who were impelled by their extraordinarily facile throats to constantly sing fast; he is chiding those listeners who, because of their fondness for innovation, forget all of the other embellishments of singing upon hearing the divisions of these singers; finally, he chides those composers who inopportunely accommodated themselves to the caprice of the singers and the listeners, in defiance of good taste and sound reason. They should indeed have had them sing, but only in a way befitting the circumstances in which they found themselves in the theater. **Who were these singers?**...I cannot answer that question. This much I do know however: that they all acquired with time a more sober and serious taste. The excessive fire of youth is eventually brought within bounds.

24. (cont.) But how? The fury of the new taste is not appeased by sacrificing the pathetic and its inseparable friend, the adagio. It goes so far as to demand that arias without the major third should be banned forever, as though that were the resolution of a general conspiracy. Can anyone imagine anything more absurd in the whole world? Gentlemen composers (to the famous among you I speak only with due respect), musical composition has changed style three times within the span of my memory. The first style, which pleased on the dramatic stage and in the chamber, was that of **Pietro Simone**[22] and of **Stradella**[23] (o). The second style is that of the best composers who are still alive – whether or not they are young and in fashion, I leave to the judgment of others. But your style, dear sirs, which has not found sure footing in Italy and is not appreciated at all on the other side of the mountains, in a short time will only be alluded to by the next generation; since fashion, in any case, does not last very long. However, if the art of singing is to last until the end of the world, either you yourselves will become more clever, or your descendants will invent a different style of composing. Would you like to know how?...They will do away with the abuses and will revive the first, second, and third church modes in order to get rid of the already worn-out fifth, sixth, and eighth. They will seek to restore to life the

fourth and seventh, which, thanks to you, along with their **finales**, have died out and are buried in the church(o).

(o) It is not our intention to explain the author's thoughts on church modes nor to discuss the degree to which they are sound or unsound. The key in which he sings is irrelevant to the singer. If the aria lies comfortably in his voice, he may leave the rest to the composer. His veneration of the Ancients seems to have taken possession of **Tosi** here.

24 (cont.) For the pleasure of the singer and the connoisseur, a mixture of the allegro and the pathetic is sometimes heard. The arias are not suffocated, as it were, by the overly loud sound of the instruments, which often cover the more artistic fine shadings of the piano [soft], the gentle tones, and indeed also [the voices of] those who can sing loud enough, but do not wish to scream (p).

(p) When this happens, it is often not the composition that is to blame but the performance of the instrumentalists, who cannot get used to playing softly.

24 (cont.) In the future it will no longer be tolerated that the instruments play constantly in unison with the singing voice – an invention of ignorance designed to hide from the people the weakness of so many singers, both male and female. The arias will recover the almost lost harmony provided by the accompaniment; they will be composed more for the singers than for the instrumentalists. The voice part will no longer have the disadvantage of yielding its place to the violins; the soprano and the alto voices will no longer be expected to sing all arias in the style of the basses, in spite of a thousand consecutive octaves (q).

(q) To what extent the accompaniment may be effective or ineffective, as the instruments play the notes in unison with the voice or an octave higher, has already been thoroughly examined by [Johann David] **Heinchen** in his **General-bass in der Composition**,[24] pp. 60ff., but also has been amply reinforced through the practice of great composers. In **Tosi's** time, indeed, the instrumental accompaniment was poorly worked out and too monotonous when it was in unison with the voice. Nowadays, however, the instruments tend, in certain parts of the aria, to unite with the voice; whereas in other parts they distance themselves, thus achieving great diversity. It is unnecessary for the singer to delve more deeply into this matter.

24 (cont.) Finally, one will hear arias that are more tasteful and less similar to each other, that are more natural and singable, and that are better crafted and yet less laborious. The more they distance themselves from the [taste of] the common people, the more stately and

noble they become. But methinks I hear it said that, "theatrical license is great and fashion pleases, but my audacity is constantly increasing." And should I not answer: that abuse causes more mischief than the already harmful invention itself, and that there are a great many who concur with my opinion. Am I the only one among the singers who should not know that a beautiful composition contributes to good singing, and that a poor one is very disadvantageous to the singer? Have we not more than once heard that the quality of the composition is capable of making a good name for an average singer in some arias, but that it can cost another singer the good name he has already really earned? Music composed by men of insight and good taste instructs the student, improves one who already has some understanding, and delights him who hears it. Since I have taken up this matter, I must speak my mind fully.[25]

25. He who introduced music to the theatrical stage probably had the intention of performing it triumphantly and placing it upon the throne. Who could have imagined that, in the course of a few short years, music itself should take part in the sad tragedy of its own downfall? You magnificent theater buildings! Whoever looks upon you without becoming angry does not realize that you are erected upon the precious ruins of harmony. You are the cause of the abuses and the errors. From you stems the current fashion of writing and the multitude of ballad makers. You are the only reason that the number of well-grounded music scholars, deserving of the prestigious title of *maestro di cappella,* is nowadays so small. Since poor counterpoint has been condemned by this corrupt age to beg a piece of bread in the church, since at the same time ignorance triumphs in many theaters, the greater part of the composers have, either through avarice or through the very hard law of necessity, felt themselves forced to abandon thorough study; thus, is it to be feared (unless heaven comes to the rescue in the form of certain great spirits or of those few who, to their credit, are still holding to the true principles) that music, having lost the name of science and companion of world wisdom, is in real danger of being declared unworthy of being heard in church – in order to ward off the scandal caused by [the performance of] gigues, minuets, and furlanes in the temple? Indeed, in some places where good taste has been corrupted, who would be able to distinguish between compositions for the church and those for the theater, if one paid to enter the church?

26. I know that the world applauds a certain few great masters who

are perfectly in command of both styles of composition. Those I recommend to him who wishes to learn to sing well. Should their number be not so small as it is thought to be, and as I suspect it is, I beg forgiveness of those whom I have perhaps unjustly excluded. I hope to receive their forgiveness readily, since an involuntary error is not an insult, and because a great spirit possesses no other jealousy than that which is a virtue. The ignorant, on the other hand, tend not to forgive willingly. Indeed, since they, rather [than forgive], disdain and bear ill-will toward all that they do not understand, they will be just the ones from whom I cannot expect a pardon.

27. Unfortunately, I once asked one of these gentlemen from whom he had learned composition. "**From the keyboard**," he answered immediately. "Good. In which tonality," I continued, "did you craft the beginning movement of your opera?" **What tonality? what tonality?** he interrupted me disdainfully. **Why do you wish to make me angry by such moldy old questions? It is clear what kind of school you come from. The modern school, in case you do not know it, does not concern itself with tonality. One laughs with good reason at the foolish fancy of those who believe that there are two tonalities; since those, on the other hand, who maintain that they should be divided into the authentic and the plagal (the main and the subordinate), and that there eight of them (even more if necessary), quite wisely allow one the liberty of composing as seems to him right and good. In your time the world slept, and you should not be offended if our exceptionally singular style has reawakened it through mirth that pleases the heart and makes the foot want to dance. Wake up before you die and lift up your hard neck bowed by the burden of so many perverse whims. Show me one thing that has been invented by youth that is not disapproved of by old age. Otherwise, you will find that your own words condemn you in the statement that ignorance makes enemies of all that is good. The fine arts are becoming ever more refined; and if I am challenged, I will undertake to prove, sword in hand, that music can rise no higher than it already is. Wake up, I say, and if you have not lost all sense of judgment, listen to me. You must admit that I am right. To prove it, I state the following:**

28. **One cannot deny the fact that our so exceptionally**

pleasing style of composition has been invented, in the excellent name of the *new fashion*, to suppress the overly difficult rules of counterpoint.

29. It is quite true that we have an irrefutable law among us to ban the pathetic forever, since we hate sadness.

30. But if old moss-covered graybeards should say that we compete with each other as to who can bring forth the most offensive and the most unheard-of deviations, so that we could claim to be creative geniuses, that is a malicious black lie [told] by those who recognize with bad grace how exalted we are. Let jealousy die! You can see very well that the regard that we have won according to the general consensus is decisive; and if a singer does not hold with our guild, he will surely find no protector to even look at him or pay the slightest bit of attention to him. But tell me (since we are speaking in confidence with sincerity on our lips), who can sing or compose well without having had our approval beforehand? No matter how much merit he has (as you know), we do not lack the means to bring him down. Yes, only a few syllables are necessary to bring down all of his merits: *he is old fashioned*.

31. Tell me, I pray you, who, without us, could ever have brought the art of singing to the highest peak of felicity by the simple means of removing from the arias the annoying competition between the first and second violin and the viola? Can anyone dare to deny us this honor? We, we are the ones who, by virtue of our cleverness, have freed the singer to ascend to the highest degree of perfection, by ridding the arias of the thundering din of the fundamental basses: so that...(hear and learn it well), even if there were a hundred violins in an orchestra, we are still capable of composing in such a way that they are able to play at the same time the same part that the singer is performing. What do you say to that? Do you still have the nerve to find fault with us?

32. Oh, how beautiful is our style of composing! It forces none of us to the tedious learning of the rules; it does not trouble the soul with thinking; and it does not give us the illusion that makes us want to put into practice everything that we might have discovered through much racking of the

brain; it does no harm to our health; it charms the modern ear; and it finds enough admirers who treasure it and are willing to pay richly for it. And you would presume to find fault with it?

33. On the other hand, what can we not say about the obscure and most tiresome compositions of those whom you trumpet forth as the most exalted among men, though you do not deserve the honor of speaking? Have you not noticed that the stale stuff of these old grouches makes us sick? We would be utter fools to study until we are sick and paralyzed to learn the harmony, the fugues, their reverse, and double counterpoint, and the many connecting main themes: to place them in stretto in order to cull from them the canons and other such dry stuff no longer in fashion; and, what is even worse, ourselves become poorly praised and even more poorly paid. What do you say now, Sir Arbiter of Art? Have you understood me well? *"Yes, dear Sir?"* What do you answer me now? *"Nothing."*

34. I am surprised, you singers, my worthy friends, at the deep lethargy in which you seem to lie buried, to your great shame. You should finally wake up – it is high time – and tell this brand of composer, whom we have just heard, to their faces, that you wish to sing and not to dance.

CHAPTER EIGHT

CONCERNING CADENZAS

1. There are two types of final cadences in the aria. Composers call these the **one from above** and the **one from below**. To make this [distinction] more comprehensible to the student, I will say that in C major, the notes of the first type of cadence would be **La Sol Fa** (**E D C**); and those of the second, **Fa Mi Fa** (**C B C**) (a). In solo arias or in recitatives, the singer may choose the type he prefers. If, however, other singing voices or instruments are combined at the cadence, he may not interchange them, but must strictly adhere to the one that has been prescribed (b).

(a) The various types are already given in music examples on page 128. The most common cadence nowadays in arias is the following: **C D C**.

(b) Because the two voices, or the voice and the instrument, that were to perform the cadence and the trill together, either in thirds or in sixths, would then be in unison. What is said here about instruments is to be understood as [referring to] one instrument accompanying the voice. For if there are only violins accompanying [during] the final cadence, as seldom occurs, the singer is also free, especially in the final trill, to sing the trill from above or from below, since one of the instruments will always be playing one of the two [kinds of cadences] in unison with him.

2. It would be superfluous for me to discuss the truncated cadences[1] (c). These have become very common, to be sure, but they are useful only in the recitative.

(c) See pages 180–81.

3. In earlier times, cadences that fall a fifth were not used for a soprano in an unaccompanied or an accompanied aria, unless the imitation of a word made it necessary for the composer to use them.

Nowadays, these are the most in vogue, although their only virtue is that they are the easiest for both the composer and for the singer (d).

(d) In our time, no longer so much for the soprano and the tenor. It would be ridiculous in a unison passage with the instruments and the basso continuo to give them their own cadence in opposition to the splendor of the unison. In general, defiance and other [passions] can be well expressed by this **bass** cadence in all voices.

4. In the chapter concerning the arias where I have warned the student to beware of the torrent of modern divisions, I promised to disclose my humble opinion concerning the now common ornamentation on cadences (e). I submit them, as [I do] all my other ideas, to the critical judgment of reason and [good] taste, so that these, as the highest arbiters of music, may condemn either the abuses of modern cadences or the error of my thinking.

(e) Formerly, the main endings – **literally called cadences** – were performed in rhythm just as they were written. A trill was made on the middle note. Later, a small improvised embellishment began to be attached to the note before the trill, if there was time for it without disturbing the rhythm. From this point on, the last measure of the voice part began to be sung more slowly and to be held back somewhat. Finally, there was an attempt to adorn this delay with all kinds of improvised divisions, runs, drags, leaps – in short, all the possible figures that the voice is capable of executing. These are still in use today and are now **preferably** called **cadenzas**. They are said to have originated between the years 1710 and 1716. In the course of this chapter, I will, for the sake of clarity, translate the true cadences with the word **cadences**, [*Schlüsse*], but the embellishments that it is fashionable to attach to them I will simply call **cadenzas** [*Cadenzen*].

5. Every aria has at least three cadences, all of which are final. The singers of our day usually try to discharge a barrage [lit., running fire] of improvised divisions at the end of the first part while the orchestra waits. With the cadence of the second part, the throat is doubly loaded and for the orchestra, time stands still. When finally the fermata arrives with the third cadence, the whole fusillade, painstakingly loaded to bursting, explodes with so many divisions that the orchestra is almost driven to swearing from impatience.[2] Why deafen the world with so many divisions? I beg the modern gentlemen to forgive me if I take the liberty of saying, in the best interest of music, that good taste does not lie in the continuous speed of a voice wandering about without guidance or purpose, but rather in the fact that it expresses itself in a manner appropriate to singing: by the sweetness of the *portamento*,

by the appoggiaturas in artistic and evenly improvised ornamentation, and by seeking to move from one note to another with unusual and unexpected rubato (*rubamento di tempo*)³ – **which, however, must be tailored to the exact movement of the bass**. These are the highest and most essential qualities of good singing, which, however, no human intelligence will find in the extravagant cadenzas of the modern singers. I have yet more to say. An unbearable practice in the most ancient times (as my solfege teacher taught me) was that of adding to the cadences a multitude of divisions, which, as is now the case, went on forever and were repeated again and again, as are those in our time. Finally, these runs were so greatly despised that they were banished as disturbers of the aural peace, before the work of correcting them could begin. A similar fate will befall those of our times as soon as a well-regarded singer, who is not led astray by the empty praises of the rabble, shows the way. As a result of the improvement mentioned above, the famous descendants [of these ancients] made a law, which perhaps would not have been abolished if they were still capable of being heard. But excess and its consequences, the passing of time, old age, and death have robbed our present times of that which was most admirable in singing. Now, singers laugh aloud about the abolition and at those who abolished the divisions in cadenzas. Instead, they have recalled them from their exile and have allowed them to reappear on the stage with even more overblown additions, so that they may be perceived by the naive as rare inventions. They earn great sums for this and, moreover, they do not care whether these divisions have been discredited [lit. abhorred] for fifty, sixty, or a thousand years. Who can blame them for that? Neither Jealousy nor Folly have the heart to do it. Would that Reason, which is neither envious nor foolish, would take the singers into her confidence and whisper into their ears: **Under what pretext do you use the name of Modern since you sing in the ancient style? Do you seriously believe that your wealth and praise come from your facile throat? Stop this deception and thank the overwhelming number of theaters, the dearth of excellent singers, and the ignorance of the listeners.** What answer would they give? That I do not know. But we will come closer [to reconciliation].

6. My Gentlemen of the Modern style: in order to beg applause from the blind ignorant, are you not deceiving yourselves by taking refuge in your overly extended divisions? You really do beg, in that

you ask for the Vivat almost out of charity – the Vivat that you realize you do not deserve. In return, you ridicule your patrons if they do not have enough hands, feet, or voices to praise you (f). Where is good order? Where is gratitude? What if they were to find out [that all you care about is applause]? My dear friends, if these abuses of the cadenzas are useful to you, they are all the more harmful to your profession and are the greatest [abuses] that you can commit because you commit them consciously and in cold blood. For your own sake, convince the world that there is a better way and use the splendid gifts that God has given you for something that is worthy of you. In the meantime I return with more determination to my opinions.

(f) This concerns the Bravo and the Eviva yelling, the clapping of hands and the noises that occur in Italian theaters when a singer has performed anything that seems worthy of applause.

7. I should really like to know the reasons that some Moderns of great names and reputations have for placing the trill in cadences from above on the third above the final note, since the trill, which must be resolved in this case, cannot be [resolved] on account of this self-same third (which, since it is the sixth above the bass, prevents [resolution]) and the cadences consequently remain unresolved (g). Even if they believe that the best lessons come from fashion, it seems to me that, once in a while, the ear should be consulted as to whether it is satisfied by a trill beaten with the seventh and sixth above the bass that is hurrying toward the cadence. I am convinced that the answer would be **No**. The rules of the old masters require that the trill in a cadence must be prepared by means of the sixth above the bass, so that afterwards it [the trill] might be heard on the fifth above the bass, that being its proper place.

(g) See above, pages 141 and 142.

8. Other singers of the first rank make these cadences in the manner of the basses, that is, by means of a descending leap of a fifth with a stepwise division of rapidly descending fast notes; and they pride themselves on their beautiful singing and their adroitness in avoiding the octaves, which, although masked, can still be heard; and thus, the singers deceive themselves (h).

(h) If a bass cadence is prescribed, the octaves that are here regarded as unisons, are expressly to be heard; and then it would be a mistake to interfere with the impact of this leap by means of a run in between its notes, which would fill it in. But if a bass cadence is used instead of a prescribed tenor cadence, it is doubly wrong to disguise the octaves by means of the run, in that, to the obvious, here forbidden [octaves] is added one more filled-in disguised [octave].

9. It is an infallible rule [lit., undeniable truth] that a good singer may not introduce a trill or a division on every cadence on the penultimate syllable of such words as *confonderò, amerò*, etc., since on short syllables such as these, this type of ornament is not suitable; those ornaments, however, are suitable on the antepenultimate syllable (i).

(i) A syllable that provides a comfortable vowel[4] is a prerequisite for the improvised cadenza, which, however, is never permitted on a short syllable. The location of the comfortable syllable can be at times still further back than the antepenultimate – for example, *la sciami dubitar* and die **P s a l m e n eurer Pracht**. The singer in such cases must not neglect to pronounce clearly the remaining syllables upon finishing the cadenza and to connect them with the cadenza. How ridiculous it would be if the singer were to forget these syllables and, in our example, sing: *la a a a a a...ar* or **Psa a a a a a...acht!** Many Italian singers often make this mistake. Sometimes they snatch an *a* out of thin air, although one is nowhere to be seen. Reread at this point pp. 165–66 and p. 139.

10. Many singers of the second rank finish the soprano cadences in the manner of the French, without trills, because they are incapable of executing them, or because this ornament is easily imitated, or because they are looking for something that seems to be modern. They are mistaken in this, however, because the French do not leave out the trill in these [soprano] cadences except in slow and tender arias; and our Italians, who are used to exaggerating all styles, exclude it from everything, even though it belongs in the allegro. I know that a good singer may be justified in abstaining from the trill in pleasing and flattering arias,[5] but this must not happen too often. Even if the cadences are bearable without this beautiful ornament [the trill], it would be impossible not to be annoyed eventually by the abrupt ending of a large number of cadences (k).

(k) The ornament needed when the opportunity permits is the **trilled turn**. See pp. 147–48.

11. I notice that most Moderns (whether friends or foes of the trill), on the frequently mentioned inferior cadences from below, add before the final note an appoggiatura on the penultimate syllable of the word leading to the final note. This seems to me an error because I believe that the appoggiatura in this instance is tasteless on any syllable other

than the last and that it does not conform to the style of the Ancients and of those who understand the art of singing (l).

(l) [The point] – that the syllable indicated for the main note (which follows) must already be pronounced on the appoggiatura before it – has already been made in the chapter on appoggiaturas. See pp. 92–93.

12. If the best modern singers do not believe that they are in error by singing the final note before the bass in cadences from below, they are all the more mistaken. This is an error which offends both the ear and the rules. It is doubly an error when, as is often the case, they attach an appoggiatura to a final note that is anticipated too early. A bad effect is always the result if the appoggiatura, whether ascending or descending, does not enter simultaneously with the bass, and the main note [is not] accordingly sounded afterwards (m).

(m) This may be found in the chapter on the appoggiatura, where it actually belongs.

13. Is it not, however, worse than all the errors to plague the listener with a thousand cadenzas that are all the same? Where does this barrenness come from? Every singer knows that there is no better way to earn high regard for his singing than fruitfulness of ideas and [new] turns of expression.

14. If among all cadences in the arias, the last allows the singer some freedom to introduce a kind of improvised ornament, so that one can hear that the end is approaching, this small exception to the rule is tolerable. However, it becomes unbearable when a singer clings stubbornly to his boring gargling with the intention of becoming obnoxious to the connoisseurs, who the better they know that composers regularly leave a note free with every main cadence the more they suffer. This note provides an opportunity for a modest embellishment without the need of straying from the correct tempo without taste, without artistry, and without understanding (n).

(n) It is obvious that our author has declared himself in favor of the style of cadenza that exhibits the continuation of the bass without retardation, as I have already mentioned in my note (e) above [in this chapter].

15. I am even more astonished when I think that the modern style of composing, after it has exposed all the cadences of theatrical arias to the torture of long runs, is also so cruel as to condemn the arias of the cantatas to the same punishment and furthermore, not to spare even the recitative cadences in the cantatas. Do the singers who make no

distinction between the singing style of the chamber and the exaggerations [lit., excessive agitation] of the theater style seek to obtain the crowd's roar of applause by begging in the chambers of distinguished persons of rank? O poor notes! You are no longer the signs of music. For if you still were, your dictates would be followed more precisely.

16. A well-bred beginner in the art of singing should shun such bad examples, together with the abuses, the errors, and everything that is low and common in the cadenzas, as well as elsewhere.

17. Since one of the worthy pursuits of the Ancients was the inventing of special cadenzas without retarding the rhythmic movement,[6] the student should seek to reintroduce these (o) and to learn from the Ancients their skill of stealing a little time for ornamentation on the final cadence. He should consider the fact that the connoisseurs of the art of singing do not perceive as beautiful all of the basses falling totally silent.

(o) This style of providing the final cadences of arias with improvised ornaments, without holding back the movement of the bass and the other accompanying instruments, is nowadays at times applied, and not without good effect, at the end of the first part of an aria (especially if it is an adagio, but also on a cadence within the aria) that provides preparation for the final cadenza by singers who possess the [necessary] competence. This effect is more easily learned through attentive listening than through prescribed notation.

18. In cadenzas may still be heard many errors that were ancient, and are now modern. They were ridiculous then, and they are ridiculous now. If one considers that the changing of a thing does not necessarily improve it, he will probably come to the conclusion that that which is incorrect might be improved through diligence, but not through fashion (p).

(p) **Tosi** is thus an enemy of our current improvised cadenzas. Am I to contradict him to please the fanciers and admirers of cadenzas and become their champion? It is true that many abuses occur, some of which have been rightfully censured by the author. It is true that one would rather hear no cadenza at all than poor one that is often rushed through. Now and then many a singer spoils all the good that he has achieved in the aria with an absurd ending. It is really burdensome for those who are poor in invention, not wishing to repeat the same one again and again, to have to create new cadenzas so often. It is also true, on the other hand, that a fiery person of talent can take his listeners by surprise and add, so to speak, a new degree of strength to the passion the aria is intended to arouse. He can bring to the ear of the listeners certain notes that were not always permissible in the aria by including [lit., clothing them in] a skillful cadenza, and thus he can acquaint the listeners with the entire range of his voice. The surprising, as well as the expected, has a place in music. As long as reasons for the cadenza are to be found that are not absolutely outweighed by reasons against them, a singer is not to be reproached for not letting slip through his fingers an opportunity to give free rein to a felicitious idea. He must, however, pay attention to the following rules: (1) Cadenzas must not be too long nor too frequent. (2) They must always be related to the main Affect [passion] of the aria. It is so much the better if possible, to include some of the most beautiful individual phrases [lit., places] or periods [from the aria]. Furthermore, this similarity is a means by which one may always have good ideas in reserve. (3) Similar figures should not be repeated nor transposed too often; rather, one should seek to connect different figures and skillfully alternate them. Yet the cadenza must not be an actual arioso melody, but only a skillful weaving together of broken phrases that are not enlarged upon. Therefore, (4) no rhythmic movement is to be observed therein. It must seem as though the singer has been overcome by passion in such a way that he could not possibly be thinking of being limited by the rhythm. (5) Though one is very likely to touch some notes that are outside of the [indicated] scale, one must still not stray too far into distant keys; and the foreign pitches, which would be dissonances in an ordinary melody if the bass were provided, must be given their proper resolution. (6) The cadenza of a lively and fiery aria may consist of large leaps, trills, triplets, runs, etc.; but that of a sad and pathetic aria prefers the slurred and dragged manner intermixed with some dissonant intervals. (7) The more unexpected elements that can be brought into a cadenza the more beautiful it is. (8) One may not breathe in a cadenza that is sung by the singer alone; therefore, it may not be held longer than is possible in one breath, and some breath must be left over for a precise trill.

Double cadenzas, especially those that are executed either by two voices or by a voice and an accompanying instrument, must, of course, comply with everything that has been said above about cadenzas, but they are (1) more closely bound to the laws of harmony and correct imitation. They must (2) not always consist of figures entirely in thirds and parallel sixths, since one soon tires of these; but instead, they must contain properly connected and resolved figures and especially adroit imitations, since one imitates that which another has sung, though this may occur in various intervals. Whoever is desirous of inventing such double cadenzas must well understand the rules of preparing and resolving dissonances, and of imitations. Though they are also (3) not bound to any specific beat, it is nevertheless self-evident that a beat must be maintained during the imitation of those figures that the other singer has performed. (4) Those figures that have been presented for imitation must be crafted in such a way that the second [lit., other] performer is able to imitate them equally well with his voice and with his instrument, with regard to both skill and range. Consequently, it is necessary that one singer yield to the other and adapt his voice to the other's capabilities. It is especially important that the instrumentalist not perform something that is impossible for a singing

211

voice; nor a singer, something that is impossible for many an instrument. (5) It is permissible to take a breath in the double cadenzas, since it is difficult to craft them in such a way that one breath will suffice; and this is true also, since while one is singing, the breathing of the other is not so easily noticed. However, both singers must not take a breath at the same time. (6) To invent double cadenzas on the spur of the moment without prior agreement is rarely successful because it is seldom that two people possess the same insight into the harmony, the same mental adroitness, and the same patience and courtesy. In Italy, many absurd disputes have arisen over this matter. It is better, therefore, that the musicians understand each other very well beforehand; if this is not possible, they must leave the invention of the cadenza to the composer and adhere exactly to what he has written. He will arrange it in such a way that it will not be apparent to the listener that it has been memorized.

Whoever gives close consideration to the above will see, in general, that it is probably impossible to write out good cadenzas in advance, just as it is hardly possible to teach someone to memorize clever ideas beforehand, because both the writing and the teaching are partly elicited and partly determined by the circumstances and the opportunity. Through diligent reading and observation of the clever ideas of others, however, one can awaken, sharpen, and improve his own wit, and he can keep it under control by [following] the dictates of reason. In the same way, one can develop his own musical wit by paying careful attention to the clever ideas of other good singers. All that remains is to show him the pitfalls to be avoided and to put before him, as guides, the precepts of good and reasonable taste. Whoever is already possessed of a fruitful inventive faculty, and familiarizes himself with my observations concerning the improvised cadenzas, and listens attentively and diligently to good singers and instrumentalists will, in a short time, have an overabundance rather than a dearth of cadenzas, even if he does not possess a single one that has been written down. With regard to the double cadenza, however, whoever wishes a detailed description of the runs and phrases suitable for imitation, and of their various types and turns of phrase, will find it, along with an extensive explanation of that which can hold the invention of the simple cadenza in check, and various plans for good and reasonable cadenzas, in Chapter XV of Quantz's **Versuch über die Flöte traversière zu spielen**. I refer him now to this treatise because I believe it not permissible to have it reprinted here.[7]

Nevertheless, the listening music lovers, if they have considered it worth their while to read what I have written, will be able to determine rather well the value of most of the cadenzas that many of our Italian singers so avidly collect.

Once in a while, within a piece, occur the so-called fermatas, where one must linger somewhat, as the name indicates. They are indicated by the usual sign for sustaining: ⌒. In these, the last note of the bass, after which the small pause occurs, is always the fifth of the main key. Sometimes one lingers on the penultimate note of the bass, which then has a seventh followed by the sixth above the bass (α); and at other times, one lingers on the last note of the

212

bass, which is either the six-four above the bass and its following root-position chord (β), or the root-position chord alone (γ) (δ) (ε). Sometimes such a fermata occurs immediately at the beginning of an aria above a tonic root-position chord [lit., final] of the key (ζ).[8] Following all of these fermatas is always a rest on which one tends to linger anew.

Here at one's discretion, an improvised ornament that is in character with the main passion of the piece and that is not bound by rhythm may be introduced on the note of the strong beat. It must always be based, however, in the incipient harmony of the bass note above which it is placed and must not wander into any other chord. Example (α) illustrates the chord of the seventh; (β), the six-four chord; and (γ), (δ), and (ε), how the root-position chord has been arbitrarily filled in and changed by the added notes. If the note that follows descends only one step as in (α) and (β), one should try to return adroitly at the end of the ornament to its beginning note and to close as in (α) with a long trill on the **c♯**; and in (β) with a long trill on the **e** itself; or, instead of the trill, perform a trilled turn on the same pitch, followed by a slow termination. See p. 148. The ornament mentioned on p. 141 is also suitable above the fermata in (β). In the case of the fermata on the root-position chord, however, if the last note makes a leap of a fifth, or an octave, as in (γ) and (ε) or a filled-in leap of a third as in (δ) below it, the improvised ornament above it is ended with a long or double trill **beaten on the third above the bass**. To this trill is attached, not the usual termination but a type of languid termination, that is used only in this particular instance. For example:

o   ca -   - ro

Par -   -   -   -   -

-          -   -   - to.

When the fermata occurs above an accented last syllable, or above a similar one-syllable word, such as *vedrà, mar*, etc., and this word occurs on the last strong beat before the fermata, one finishes simply with the trill, but without a termination. See pp. 138–39.

Whoever does not wish to ornament examples (γ) and (ε) may make a long crescendo on the first note and slur it to the slow mordent, as described on p. 142.

214

19. But now let us once more put aside for a few moments the opinions of the famous Ancients and the alleged Moderns in order to be able to note what our beginner in the art of singing has learned. Surely he must be eager to be heard. We will hear him but, at the same time, we must not neglect to instruct him in the most important lesson; so that, at least, he may rightfully earn the name of a good singer, should he not have the good fortune to be called a great one.

CHAPTER NINE

REMARKS FOR THE USE OF THE PROFESSIONAL SINGER

1. Behold our singer appearing in public, having happily put behind him the previous lessons by virtue of his diligence. But what good does it do only to be seen? Whoever does not play a worthy role on the great stages of the world is no more significant a figure than a minor character who has no lines.

2. Judging by the cold indifference toward their profession that many singers exhibit, one might conclude that they are only waiting for the moment when Music might prostrate herself before them and with gestures of humility request the boon of being taken magnanimously into their favor as a most humble and obedient servant.

3. If so many singers were not so thoroughly convinced they had already learned enough, the number of truly good ones would not be so small; and on the other hand, the number [lit., heap] of bad ones would not be so frightfully great. Those who have memorized four **Kyries** already believe that they have reached the heights [lit. the *ne plus ultra*]. But give them a very simple cantata, which is copied cleanly and clearly, and instead of being grateful for this favor, they say with shameless audacity: **Great souls are not obliged to sing in their mother tongue on the spur of the moment.** Who could refrain from laughing at this point? A singer who knows that words, whether Latin or Italian, do not change the notes will suspect at once that the ready evasion of this great personage [lit., soul] stems from the fact that he is unable to sing [lit., hit] the notes, or does not know how to read – and he will have guessed the truth.

4. Many others long for the moment when they might be rid of the drudgery of learning the fundamentals, in order to enter the swarm of those at the middle level. Should they find thereafter, however, through the grace of divine providence, someone who will give them

their bread despite their meager knowledge, they immediately bid a fond farewell to Music and do not care if the world knows whether or not they dwell among the living. These do not consider that for a singer to be merely competent [lit., middle-level] means to be ignorant.

5. Others study nothing but errors. They are gifted with an admirable ease of learning all of them and retaining them with an excellent memory. Their natural inclination drives [so relentlessly] toward the bad that even if they had been blessed by nature with a beautiful voice, they are quite inconsolable if they cannot discover the trick by which they may transform it into one of the worst.

6. A person whose thinking is on a higher plane will seek out nobler though less numerous company. He will realize his need for other insights, other lessons, and other teachers. From these he will seek to learn, besides the art of singing well, how to live well, and how to conduct himself properly in society. When this knowledge is combined with his accomplishments in the art of singing, he may then hope for the favor of great men, as well as for general recognition.

7. To have the reputation of a well-behaved and prudent young man, he should be neither vulgar nor insolent.

8. He should shun disreputable or low company, especially distancing himself from those who allow themselves scandalous liberties.

9. He should avoid the company of those singers who have vulgar and objectionable manners, however famous they may be; for as long as they make their fortunes, they do not care whether they do it in the most sordid fashion.

10. Consorting with persons of higher rank is a good school for developing courteous and proper manners. Since no rule is without exception, however, I counsel the singer to withdraw from gatherings in which he does not belong so that he may suffer no embarrassment. Leaving or staying away will make the proper statement.

11. If he is not remunerated by the great, he should never complain about it because in so doing, he may lose a great deal instead of gaining a little. There are more than a few examples of this. The best way to deal with this circumstance is to serve them with even greater attention. Perhaps the day will come when they will recognize him.

12.[1]

13. The golden age of music would already have passed if the swans [i.e., the singers] had not taken up residence on a few stages in Italy and on the banks of the royal Thames. O pleasant **London**! No longer do the swans sing about their own death with touching sweet-

ness on the other rivers, as they used to do; rather, they mourn bitterly the dying out of great princes worthy of high esteem, by whom they have been tenderly loved and regarded (a). This is the usual course of human events, and it is seen daily that by divine providence everything in this world is in a state of flux; and [fortune], having reached its peak, must of necessity decline. But let us leave our tears to our hearts and return again to the singer.

(a) The author wrote this in the year 1723, and I do not actually know the identity of the great prince to whose death he was alluding. How many changes music has experienced since then! In how many places has she nearly died out, only to be revived by the highest and most honorable connoisseurs and patrons, is so well known all over Europe that I will not presume to broadcast this information again by means of my weak praise.

14. The singer who has good judgment will never, without just cause, utter the words that are so often used and are so repugnant to everyone: **Today I cannot sing because I have caught my death of cold**, and, as he is saying **I beg to be excused**, coughs a little. I can attest to the fact that in all the days of my long life, I have never heard a single singer pronounce this happy truth: **Today I feel well**; although honesty would require this admission. They save this unusual candor for the following day, when they have no trouble whatsoever in saying, **In all the days of my life I have never been in such good voice as yesterday.** Of course, under certain circumstances this pretext can not only be excused, but is necessary. Some miserly people who love music believe that the musician is indebted the very instant that they ask him to wait on them without remuneration, and that it costs them nothing more than a thank you to him. A refusal [they think] is such a grievous insult that the musician deserves nothing but hate and revenge. Since it is a human and divine law that everyone live on his honest earnings, what uncharitable order of things has condemned Music to serve everyone gratis? That is too much to ask. This type of frugality is inexcusable [lit., excessive].

15. A singer who knows the world distinguishes between the command and the way it is given. He knows how to refuse graciously and how to enhance his reputation by obeying. He knows that even one with the greatest self-interest must sometimes seek to serve without recompense.

16. One who sings out of desire for honor sings well and with time will sing even better; but the singer who thinks about nothing but gain learns little more than how to remain a poor ignoramus.

17. Who could ever believe, if experience did not teach it, that the finest virtue could hinder a singer? Ambition and pride always triumph; whereas the greater honorable humility is, the more it is beaten down.

18. At first glance, it seems to me that pride, through its audacity, has taken over the place of knowledge and insight. Upon closer inspection, however, it seems that nothing occupies their place but ignorance covered by the mask of pride.

19. Pride is nothing but a certain artificial exercise in certain gestures of the body, cleverly used to hide the weaknesses of the mind. Certain singers, who are so incompetent as to be incapable of singing four notes extempore, would not seem so confident and fearless if, in their increasingly presumptuous perversity, they could not use shrugs, rolling of the eyes, and malicious shaking of the head to make the audience ascribe their own flagrant errors to the keyboardist or the orchestra.

20. To humble pride, one need only blow away the smoke of flattery.

21. Who would be able to sing better than one of these arrogant ones, were he not contemptuous of study?

22. One who becomes arrogant at the first applause, without considering whether this applause is the result of blind chance or flattery, is a fool; and if he believes that he is deserving of this applause, there is no hope for him.

23. If a singer cannot regulate and adjust his voice according to the place in which he sings, he must seek to correct this because it is simple-minded not to be able to distinguish a large theater from a small chamber.

24. It is worse if a singer, when singing with two, three, or four others, drowns out the voices of those who are singing at the same time; if he does this, not out of ignorance [but on purpose], it is all the more reprehensible.

25. All pieces for several voices must be sung just as they stand [are written], demanding only the art of noble simplicity. I recall (or was it a dream?) having heard a famous duet sung by two great singers, who, spurred on by jealousy, repeatedly presented each other something new to do before and after [each was to sing] and [required] each to answer the other alternately. The duet was so hacked to pieces that all this contest amounted to was [to see] who could play the most foolish tricks (b).

219

(b) Carefully chosen and previously agreed-to changes are, however, not forbidden in a duet. One should observe the rules for double cadences. See p. 211.

26. The correction by experienced friends of established reputation can be valuable for learning. The poisonous attacks of the envious, however, are even more valuable. The more pointed the malicious intent to expose the errors of others, the greater the benefit that may be derived from it; and no thanks are owed for it.

27. Every singer should hold this for an evident truth: those errors that have been corrected by enemies are much more easily purged, so that they are wiped out without a trace. They quickly fade out of sight and out of mind. Those errors that one seeks to correct through one's own initiative, however, are almost impossible to correct [lit., become completely without remedy]; [even when healed] the scars remain, threatening to break open at any moment.

28. Whoever is applauded for his singing in only one locale should not think he knows more than he does. Instead, he should often change the place of his residence – for only then will he realize, with a more mature insight, how far his talent goes.

29. In order to be appreciated in all places, as Reason counsels, one should sing well in all places. Should Reason, however, remain silent, our own self-interest should admonish us very strongly to accommodate ourselves to the taste of the nation that is listening to us and paying us, insofar as this particular taste is not corrupted.

30. Although one who sings well provokes envy, he will put it to shame by endeavoring to sing even better.

31. I do not know whether or not a perfect singer can also be a perfect actor, because the person going in two different directions at the same time tends to prefer one to the other. Since, however, it is incomparably more difficult to sing than to recite, singing is a greater accomplishment than acting [lit., reciting]. How fortunate is he who is perfect in both (c)!

(c) To become more closely acquainted with the art of good acting, one should consult the **Art du théâtre**[2] of **François Riccoboni** [lit., Riccoboni the Younger], of which there is an excellent German translation in the fourth part of the **Beyträge zur Historie und Aufnahme des Theaters**. He should also consult the **Pensées sur la déclamation**[3] of **Luigi Riccoboni** [lit., the Elder] and his Italian poem on the art of acting, a translation of both of which has been promised. If he is unable to find the **Comédien**[4] [Schauspieler] of **Rémond von Sainte Albine** in French, the article in the first issue of the **Theatralische Bibliothek** of **M. Lessing** will be useful. Besides reading these excellent writings, one should not hesitate to diligently and carefully observe the acting of the good actors, particularly the tragic actors. The acting of Senesino, during the time of his stay in Dresden in the years 1718 and 1719, was reputed to have become even better after he had repeatedly observed the presentations of the incomparable troupe of French actors who performed frequently at that time in Dresden.

32. Above I have stated that a mature singer should no longer [slavishly] copy others. Here I would like to reiterate the admonition and add my reasons for it. Copying is right for the student, but for a master only invention is appropriate.

33. Laziness seeks to copy, and one cannot do worse than copy that which stems from ignorance.

34. Before insight and experience can produce a single good singer through diligence, ignorance has already produced a thousand bad ones through copying. And yet there is not one among the bad ones who would wish to acknowledge ignorance as his teacher.

35. If only many of the female singers (among whom I duly honor the deserving) would realize that when they copy a single good singer out of self-interest, they all become bad singers, they would not, because of their foolishness in singing the arias of good singers with exactly the same variations, expose themselves in the theater to much cruel [lit., sharp] derisive laughter. They miss their purpose (if it is not their teachers whom they are trying to deceive) by following the instincts of sheep and cranes, rather than that of reason; for reason, which teaches us that there are various paths leading to applause, causes us to understand, not only through examples from former times, but also through what we hear at this very hour, that a given pair of female singers would not be equally great if one copied the other.

36. Since the respect accorded to the fair sex does not excuse in them the abuse of copying, which is to the disadvantage of the art of singing, what can possibly be said about the weaknesses of those male singers who, instead of invention, copy not only whole arias of other men but even those of women? O great blindness that robs good taste of all light! It would be assuming the impossible to imagine that a singer could succeed in copying in such a natural manner that one could no longer distinguish the original version [from the copy]. Can the singer possibly believe that he could, on that account, claim merit that is not his own, and that he could attend the ball in another's costume without the fear of being stripped naked?

37. Whoever understands the correct way of copying makes use of nothing more than the design, because all embellishments that are heard with admiration, if they are natural to the singer, immediately lose their beauty as soon as the listener realizes that they are only imitations.

38. The best art of a singer must certainly be imitated (but not copied); but even then only with the proviso that not the slightest similarity to the original remain; otherwise, instead of beautiful emulation, he produces only ugly distortion [of the original].

39. I do not know who deserves greater scorn: the singer who cannot imitate one who sings well without exaggeration, or the singer who cannot imitate anyone well except one who sings badly.

40. If many singers would only realize that bad imitation is a contagious plague that spares only him who studies diligently, the world would be spared the pain of never seeing anything better than a carnival filled with good fellows, and yet being without hope that the play would soon improve (d).[5] However, it is the world's own fault. It should learn to praise merit but not to sugar-coat that which in reality is worthy of reproof (if I may understate the case).

41. Whoever does not know how to stretch out the notes (*rubare il tempo*) can certainly neither compose nor accompany himself, and remains deprived of the best taste and the finest insight (e).

(e) Distorting the note values[6] (*rubare il tempo*) actually means to take away from a prescribed note some of its value and add it to the next one, or vice versa. For example:

distorted:

or:

And this may be applied to various kinds of notes, figures, and rhythms.

42. The stretching out of notes is an especially praiseworthy robbery, especially in the pathetic, which enables one singer to sing better than another, providing he has the insight and wit to replace that which has been taken away (f).

(f) One must take care that the notes whose values are to be distorted are not so wrenched or pulled out of shape from their original value that the melody thereby becomes unclear or unintelligible. Good and permissible stealing of time[7] may best be learned from accomplished and knowledgeable performers.

43. Even more necessary is the pleasant exercise of the **portamento**[8] (g), without which all other diligence falls short. One who would like to be firmly grounded in this should listen more to the precepts of the heart than to the laws of the art.

(g) **The putting forth of the voice** (*portar la voce*) means to bind one note to another while constantly sustaining a crescendo and decrescendo,[9] without stopping or breaking off. See pp. 85–86 and 153.

44. What a great master is the heart! Admit it, beloved singers, and acknowledge with due thankfulness that you could not have become

the most distinguished in your profession had you not been its student. Acknowledge that in a few lessons, it taught you the best expression, the finest taste, the most noble action, and the most ingenious artifice. Acknowledge (even if it should not seem believable) that it improves the shortcomings of nature by making the raw voice more pleasant, the middling one better, and the good one perfect. Acknowledge that when the heart itself sings, it is impossible to dissemble; and that truth never possesses greater powers of persuasion than at that time. Finally make it known (because I myself cannot say it) that you have learned from the heart alone the special indescribable charm that steals softly through the veins and finally reaches the seat of the soul.

45. Though the way to touch the heart is long, difficult, and little known, the difficulties are nevertheless not insuperable for those who do not tire of studying.

46. Even the most highly [lit., first] ranked singer in the world has to continue to study just as much to maintain his reputation as he did to acquire it.

47. As everyone knows, there is no other means than study by which one may attain this desirable [lit., laudable] goal. But study alone is still not enough. One must also know how and with whom to study.

48. Nowadays there are as many teachers as there are people who make music their profession. Everyone wants to teach, and not merely the fundamentals. Heaven protect us! This would insult ambition in its most vulnerable part. Leaving this aside, I will speak only of those who presume to pose as petty [lit., minor] legislators in the most advanced art of singing. How can we then wonder that good taste is lost and the entire art of singing comes to naught. Such shameful audacity is as prevalent among those who, the first time they open their mouths, already imagine that they sing well, just as the least skilled of the instrumentalists [imagine themselves to play well]. These, even if they have never sung in their lives nor could ever sing, presume not only to teach singing but to bring the student to perfection. They find plenty of simpletons who entrust themselves to their care. Furthermore, there are reputable instrumentalists who believe that the most beautiful variations that they can execute with their fingers might produce the same effect in the voice, even though this is not at all the case. I would perhaps be the first to repudiate as presumptuous the liberty I have taken in criticizing, if my remarks were directed toward insulting those singers and most worthy instrumentalists who can not only sing but can also teach singing. But I take this

liberty because it is my intention to punish with a few words those who do not have the necessary ability: *Age quod agis*. For one who does not understand Latin, these words mean: **You** [the singer] **learn first to sing the notes; and you** [the instrumentalist]**, to play your instrument** (h).

(h) Some of our worthy German singing teachers will kindly search their consciences at this point.

49. If it occasionally happens that a bad teacher produces a good student, there is no question but that the natural gifts of the student have prevailed over the inadequacies of the teacher. One should not be greatly surprised by this; for if, from time to time, even the best of teachers were not surpassed, the finest arts would be lying in ruins.

50. Many believe that every perfect singer must be totally suited to the teaching of the art of singing. This is not actually true, however. For no matter how great his insight, it will be insufficient to the task, if he has not the ability of making himself readily understood; if he does not adapt his teaching to the ability of the aspiring student; if he does not possess some knowledge of composition; if he does not have such an even temper that the student hardly believes that he is in school; and, finally, if he is not sufficiently attentive, imaginative, and experienced to bring out the strengths of the singer and to cover his weaknesses. These are the most noble and necessary qualities of good instruction.

51. The teacher who possesses the qualities mentioned above can teach. By these qualities he inspires the student to be eager to be taught by him. By precept he corrects the errors, and by example he awakens the desire to imitate him.

52. He knows that a dearth of ornamentation is just as undesirable as an excess. He is aware that with too few ornaments the singer causes a yearning; and with too many, disgust. Of these two defects, the first will be more serious [lit., despised], although it is less insulting, because the second is more easily corrected.

53. He will pay little attention to those who can execute nothing better than a stepwise run of an octave; rather, he will say that such ornaments, aptly called rockets, which they resemble, are best suited to beginners (i).

(i) Since there must be variations in all parts of music, they must occur also in the divisions. Whoever is capable of executing only one type is unfortunate indeed. Executing a run that ascends and descends over two octaves and performing it in tune [lit., on key], evenly loud, round, well articulated, and clear, is not as easy as many might conclude from the author's words. Everyone, however, can test his ability in this to see how he succeeds. These rockets are especially conspicuous in singers whose voices do not have a wide range or are not even. With many singers the rockets take on a particularly crooked flight [lit., course] and tend to burst by the time they are halfway up.

54. A good teacher will have little respect for those singers who believe that the listeners will be moved to the point of fainting if they change in a dull manner of their own invention from the major third above the bass into the minor [third].

55. He will judge a particular singer to be unfit who tries every evening in the theater to get the listeners to memorize his arias. This can easily happen if the listener hears the arias always performed in the same manner without any variation whatsoever.

56. He will be astounded by the audacity of the singer who, with little skill and even less knowledge of the musical art of sailing, ventures out upon the sea of notes. When the sky becomes cloudy he loses his way; and, although he is still too far from the harbor to be heard, he shouts for help and is actually in danger of shipwreck if he is not rescued.

57. He [the good teacher] will not praise the singer who insists on singing two thirds of an opera by himself, and who firmly believes that he can never become tiresome, just as though on this earth he should always please by divine right. This singer does not know the first principles of musical politics. Time will teach him, however. Who sings but a little and well, sings best.

58. He will laugh at the singer who imagines that the listener is pleased by the splendor of his clothes, since splendid attire aggrandizes ignorance as much as it does merit. Those singers who have nothing but outward appearance pay the debt to the eyes that they have borrowed from the ears.

59. He will be revolted by the nauseating artificial style of those singers who imitate the waves of the sea and who force the blameless notes out with coarse, ugly bursts. This is a disgusting, ill-bred custom. But since it has come to us from France, it passes for a rare new fashion [lit., modern rarity].

60. He will be amazed at this seemingly bewitched century in which many male and female singers are paid well for singing poorly. If only Fashion had a good memory, she would remember, perhaps not without revulsion, that he who sang at at an average level of com-

petence twenty years ago played the part of a bad character in second-rate theaters. Nowadays people who, like parrots, have to be spoon-fed [lit., have everything put into their mouths], are collecting a fortune in the first-rate theaters.

61. He will censure more harshly the ignorance of men, since they are obliged to study more than women.

62. He will not be able to abide one who to the detriment of rhythm, seeks to imitate certain persons so as to be known as a modern.

63. He will be astounded at the singer who, despite a correct understanding of rhythm, is nonetheless unable to make use of it because he has never applied himself to the study of composition and accompanying. He imagines quite falsely that in order to be called a great singer, it is enough to be capable of a little sight-singing. He does not realize, however, that the secret of its beauty [the beauty of the tempo rubato] in the art of singing consists of precisely that which he still lacks. He has failed to learn the art of gaining time in order to lose it again. This is an art [lit., fruit] that evolves from the knowledge of composition, but it is not as tasteful as that art by means of which one loses time [by holding the note a bit longer] in order to regain it [by slightly speeding the time up in the succeeding notes]. This is the ingenious invention of those who understand the art of composition and possess the best taste (k).

(k) These somewhat puzzling words of the author all seem to point towards the so-called **tempo rubato**, which during his time seemed to have been made too much of.

64. He will be offended by the senselessness of those who allow sacred texts to be placed under the most wanton of theatrical arias in order to sing the same music with approval in church, just as if no difference existed between one style of composition and the other, and as if the picked-over scraps of the stage were good enough for the worship of God.

65. What would he say about those who have invented the astounding trick of singing like crickets! Who could ever have dreamed that it would become fashionable to take ten or twelve consecutive eighth notes and break them up into small pieces by a certain shaking of the voice? And yet in a very short time, this device will pass for the modern mordent.

66. He will have even greater reason, however, to abhor the invention by which one sings in a laughing manner [lit., laughs singing] or

sings in the manner of hens that have just laid an egg. Are there per-haps some other animals that should be [lit., are] imitated to make the art of singing seem even more ridiculous (l)?

(l) Oh yes. In the meantime, however, until this has been arranged, I pro-pose as a diversion a pretty instrument for imitation: the **posthorn**.

67. He will disapprove of the malice of a reputable singer who chats or laughs in the theater with his companions to make the public believe that a certain male or female singer, who is just about ready to sing his first aria and who is only beginning to come into his own, does not deserve his attention and whose anticipated applause he begrudges or fears.

68. He will not be able to tolerate the vanity of that singer who is so full of himself for the little that he has learned that he listens to himself with such delight that it seems as if he were transported in an ecstasy of self-worship. He worships himself to such a degree that he is willing to lord it over the whole human race and now demands noth-ing less than this: **Be still and admire**. The first note he utters seems to say to all who are assembled: **Hear this and die**. Those assembled, preferring, however, to live and not wanting to listen to him, speak loudly and perhaps not too well of him. In the second aria, the noise becomes greater; and when the din has grown [still louder] with the third, this virtuoso finally perceives an evident insult; and instead of taking himself in hand with greater diligence for his ill-con-ceived swaggering, he curses the depraved taste of that nation which pays no attention to him. He threatens never to come to that place again, and with that the proud fool consoles himself.

69. A good teacher will be amused at those who refuse to perform unless they themselves have chosen the libretto and the composer according to their own taste, and probably also with the proviso that they not sing in the presence of this male singer or without the pre-sence of that female singer.

70. Similarly, he will regard with scorn certain others who, with feigned humility that is worse than pride itself, go from box to box [in the theater] and, under the pretext of humble respect, collect praises from distinguished personages. By the following evening they [these praises] have become more familiar to everyone than the epistles of Cicero. Humility and modesty are the finest virtues of the soul, but if they are not accompanied by a little bit of decorum, they are easily confused with hypocrisy.

71. Of him who is never satisfied with his role and yet has never mastered it; of him who will not sing without being able to insert into all operas an aria which he carries around in his pocket; of him who bribes the composer for an aria that was intended for another singer; of him who learns a great many useless things and thereby misses the important things; of him who, by means of a number of undeserved recommendations, practically forces another person to protect him only to bring disgrace upon himself as well as his patron; of him who, out of distaste for the pathetic style, does not make his voice legato; of him who always wants to gallop to be in style, – in short, all of the bad singers (since these are the ones who pay court to fashion so that they may imitate its weaknesses, since they do not know its strengths) – of all these, I maintain, a good teacher will not have a favorable opinion.

72. In short, he will say of no singer that he has merit, with the exception of that scrupulously correct [lit., rule-following] singer, who with an abundance of special turns, performs that which his insight provides directly from his own invention, knowing full well that the greatest singer could never repeat an aria with the same variations, even if he wanted to. The singer who has given thought to his ornaments has done his homework.

73. After such a master has weeded out various other misuses and errors for the benefit of the singer, he will try to persuade him anew, with even more convincing proof, to take refuge in the fundamentals of music; so that through them he may learn how to work above the bass and how to proceed with secure and well-measured steps from one interval to another without being afraid of falling. But should the singer answer him as follows: **Dear Sir, you are wasting your time. Your knowledge of errors does not suffice for me. I need more instructions than words** [can provide]**, and I do not know from whom I am to obtain them, since the good teachers in Italy seem to me to be so few and far between.** Thereupon the teacher will shrug his shoulders and will answer, more with a sigh than with words, that if the future singer has not already taken in [lit., sucked in] the art of singing with his mother's milk, or at maturity cannot have it grafted onto him, he should seek to imitate the best singers in whatever his further education requires. He should be particularly diligent in his observation of **two women** whose merits cannot be praised enough and who, with combined strength though very different styles, in our time are helping to support the tottering art; so that, following the decline that it has already suffered, its

total destruction does not seem so near at hand. One of these female singers is inimitable in her extraordinary gift for singing. She enchants the world with a remarkable flexibility in execution and with an especially tasteful and brilliant manner, which, whether it comes from nature or from art, is exceedingly pleasing. The other, of a nobly flattering and gentle disposition – being closely joined with the sweetness of an incredibly beautiful voice, a perfectly true intonation, an exact observance of rhythm, and with the remarkable and charming inventions of her fruitful genius – is endowed with gifts as rare as they are difficult to imitate. The pathetic style of the latter and the allegro of the former are the most admirable qualities in each. What a beautiful combination it would make if the best qualities of these two angelic creatures could be united in one person (m)!

(m) Whoever has heard in person both of these excellent singers, Madame **Faustina Hasse**[10] and Madame **Francesca Cuzzoni Santoni**,[11] or at least has read the detailed and unusually favorable descriptions of their musical characters by **Quantz**, who had often heard both at various times in their prime (α), will not have to guess to whom **Tosi** is referring.

(α) Refer to the sketch of Quantz's Life in Marpurg's **Historisch-kritische Beyträge zur Aufnahme der Musik**, vol. I, sec. iii, p. 240. One may also find there descriptions of several other famous singers.

74. But let us not entirely lose track of our teacher. In the meantime, he will not have lost his enthusiasm. He will seek to set forth with infallible proof that the art of a singer is never used at a more propitious time than when it will surprise the listener through pleasant and unexpected novelties. He will thus counsel the singer to seek to assume an innocent demeanor, so that people may believe that this honest simplicity is the soul of all his endeavor.

75. But the moment the members of the audience have no further expectation of hearing anything new and are about to fall asleep, the singer should endeavor to revive them by means of an adroitly applied variation.

76. As soon as the audience is awake again, the singer must return to the previous simplicity, even though doing so makes him seem incapable of again deceiving the audience – since his listeners await a second deception with curious impatience and gradually come to expect several more.

77. Finally, an experienced teacher will not neglect to give the singer a description of the length and necessary characteristics of the

improvised ornaments, thereby enlightening him and providing him with the rules for everything useful to him.

78. It is only fair that I should deplore here the faithlessness of my memory, which has failed to preserve, as it should have, all those precious benefits once revealed to me by a certain good man, concerning the improvised ornaments. To my great sorrow and perhaps to the deprivation of others, my ungrateful memory allows me to make known nothing more than the few (what a paltry residue!) that remain. And that I shall do in the following chapter.

CHAPTER TEN

CONCERNING IMPROVISED VARIATIONS OF MELODIES

1. Since the so-called improvised variations[1] (a) are the most beautiful that a singer can conceive of introducing and the most pleasant that the connoisseur can hear, it is necessary that a singer should consider very seriously how he may learn the art of skillfully inventing them.

(a) An improvised ornamentation, or variation, is called by the Italians, *un passo*.

2. He must know that there are **five essential qualities** that when combined with each other, yield a marvelous perfection. **These are knowledge of harmony, invention, observance of the rhythm, judgment, and taste**.

3. There are also **five non-essential embellishments**, which are always available to further ornament the improvised variations. These are: **the appoggiatura, the various essential graces, the portamento of the voice,[2] the slur, and the drag**.

The essential qualities teach:

4. That no changes may occur but through the application of a thorough **knowledge of harmony**.

5. That a fortuitous **power of invention** should present rare and special thoughts, but at the same time beautiful ones, in that it avoids the familiar and the ordinary.

6. That these variations, since they are ruled by the strict but sound [lit., worthy] rules of **rhythm**, can never leave the ordered boundaries thereof without losing their own integrity.

7. That the improvised ornaments, as introduced with the finest

232

discernment, are placed only in an appropriate location above the bass. Here they cavort playfully and provide unexpected pleasure.

8. That to our great pleasure, only the most exquisite **taste** is free to accompany them at the right time with a pleasant portamento of the voice that charms us.

The non-essential qualities teach:

9. That the improvised variation should give the impression of being easy, so that it will please everyone.

10. That it must be inherently difficult, so that one may admire the ingenuity of the inventor.

11. That the art of execution as well as the expression of the words must not be neglected [lit., must be observed].

12. That it must be slurred and legato[3] in the pathetic style, since this is more effective than detached articulation.

13. That it must not appear studied if it is meant to pass unnoticed.

14. That in the pathetic style it is sometimes made more gentle by being sung softly, becoming thereby all the more pleasing.

15. That in the allegro it must be performed, sometimes loudly and sometimes softly – resulting in a type of *chiaroscuro* .[4]

16. That it is better restricted to a few conjunct notes [lit., notes lying close together] than to many disjunct ones [lit.,widely spread-out ones].

17. That if the rhythm permits the space and the bass accommodates it, it may also be spread over several figures.

18. That it should be applied in an appropriate place, since outside of its proper place it would displease.

19. That it should be distanced from other variations rather than be in close proximity to them where it would not be noticed.

20. That it should be produced more from the heart than from the voice, in order that our innermost beings be touched more easily.

21. That it should not be introduced on a closed **e** or **o** and much less on an **i** or **u**.

22. That it should not be stolen from someone else, so that it becomes insipid [lit., formless].

23. That it should at times consist of notes on which *rubato* is made.

24. That it should never be repeated in the same place, particularly in arias of the pathetic style, since it is to those that the connoisseurs pay the most attention.

25. Most importantly, that it make the prescribed thoughts of the composer better and not worse.

26. Many singers are of the opinion, however, that one should not introduce detached runs in improvised variations unless they are mixed with some of the above-mentioned essential ornaments; but they may occur if they are interrupted with a syncopation or some other pleasing incidental feature (b).

(b) Since not only all inventions but also the delivery of improvised variations must be in accord with the reigning passion, no hard and fast rule may be given concerning slurring or detaching. Tenderness prefers a slurred articulation, while cheerfulness and liveliness prefer the detached notes. In the allegro, one can likewise introduce improvised variations. Here many slurred notes would make just as inappropriate a parade as would many detached notes in the adagio.

27. This may be the time to speak about the embellishment of the **Drag**[5] (*Strascino*), so that, if the pathetic style should again come into fashion in the world, it would not be unknown to the singer. It would be easier to make it comprehensible by musical example than by words, were it not so difficult for the printer to print a few notes (c). Nevertheless, I will seek to make myself as clear as possible.

(c) Now would be a wonderful opportunity to clarify this by means of musical example. Unfortunately, however, we lack written-out musical examples from **Tosi**.[6]

28. If, over a slowly progressing bass consisting entirely of equal eighth notes, a singer makes a crescendo upon a high note and makes a descrescendo on the same, alternating the forte and piano, and descends gently and almost always in stepwise movement as if dragging his voice from the height to the depth, but with uneven movement, holding a few of the middle notes somewhat longer than those which begin and end this dragging – it is obvious to every good musician that, among the most beautiful techniques of singing, no invention or endeavor can more effectively touch the heart than this, provided that it is applied with the proper understanding and in the correct place according to the rhythm and the bass. Whoever has a voice of wide range has a greater advantage [in this technique], since the lower it descends, the more beautiful this delightful ornament is. In the mouth of a skillful soprano who uses it rarely, it becomes nearly a marvel; but though it pleases very greatly in descending, it would displease even more greatly in ascending.

(d) I would like very much to clarify **Tosi's** description if I only could be completely sure of his actual meaning. Meanwhile, my reader must imagine a delivery consisting of many descending slow notes of increasing and decreasing loudness slurred together without interruption. Either the composer must have prescribed these notes, or the singer must select, from a progression whose main notes descend always stepwise and mainly in half steps, only these main notes and perform them in the required manner, letting the passing notes go. The so-called drag is distinguished from the slurring only by its slowness.

It is not necessary to explain in a detailed fashion the reason for introducing the improvised variations or ornaments in a piece; it lies in the concept of the term itself. Ornaments are a matter of either adding several notes to a few, or reducing several notes to fewer, or substituting an equal number for a given number of notes – all in keeping with the rules of harmony. That the tempo should not be disturbed in the least goes without saying. The ornaments either fill out an empty interval of a leap or make a leap out of stepwise progressing notes. Figures wherein both of these things can be done are innumerable. The essential ornaments may occur in improvised variations as well as in melodies that are already written down.

Because I assume that anyone inclined to apply these variations has already heard a great deal of music, and is therefore already adept at combining a few notes in his own head, and is already familiar with the fundamentals of harmony necessary for the realization above which the variation may be applied; and since much depends upon certain fashionable figures and divisions that constantly change over the years, I am loath to deliver by musical example even a small collection of variations that perhaps one or another of my readers might wish to have.[7] I am all the more reluctant, since **Quantz** in his **Versuch einer Anweisung die Flöte traversière zu spielen**, pp. 118 ff., has not only already provided a number of variations for each of the individual intervals, and given instructions in their use, but has also provided variations for [lit., placed above] an entire adagio. From these the singer will be able to acquire an adequate understanding of the ways to go about inventing and sensibly applying these variations. However, one who is already rich in inventions can bring the same into order and maintain them by means of the excellent service that **Quantz's** teaching provides, by means of careful examination of **Tosi's** fundamentals as collected and revealed in this chapter and in the chapter on the arias, and by listening diligently to good singers.

A correct, pure, and expressive performance of a melody, as prescribed by the composer and including the essential small ornaments, is preferable to a performance with variations that are excessive and exaggerated.

Many singers are plagued with an overly zealous desire for variations, which they use ad nauseam. Nothing, however, is more insufferable than their not singing the simple prescribed melody at all, but singing [instead] monotonous, perhaps memorized variations twice.[8] By doing this, they cancel out the actual purpose of the variations: namely, to provide variety by means of the alternation of the simple with the more complex.

29. O, most beloved singers who are still inclined to study, have you understood me? Approximately the foregoing was taught by the school of those whom the ignorant call Ancient. Observe its precepts exactly, examine closely its laws. If you are not blinded by preconceptions, you will see that it teaches the singer to sing in tune, to put forth the voice, to make the words understandable, to sing expressively and to act [lit., recite], to keep to the rhythm, to use adroit variations, to be trained in the fundamentals of harmony, and to study the pathetic style, wherein taste and insight can be displayed to their greatest advantage. Compare this school with your own. If the fundamentals above are insufficient to make you into finished singers, learn the rest from the modern school.

30. However, if these exhortations of mine, which spring from a justifiable zeal, do not make an impression upon you, perhaps because you do not wish to hear the counsel of lesser people, try to imagine that one who has been able to think about this for sixty years might just once have thought of something wise. If you perhaps imagine that I have been too partial to the past, I should seek to persuade you, if your hand is not too shaky, to assess with a just scale your most famous singers (whom you consider to be modern but who are not so in any other place save their cadenzas). You would then be freed from misconceptions and would see instead of affectations, abuses, and errors, that these most famous singers sing according to these binding principles, which fill the innermost soul with pleasure and which my heart will never forget. Ask them for advice, just as I did. They will acknowledge to you openly that they market their wares wherever they are appreciated, that singers of eminence do not hold to fashion, and that nowadays bad singing occurs in many places.

31. We do have now a few very worthy singers, who hopefully, once the heat of their youth has dissipated [lit., gone up in smoke], will teach, out of a feeling of obligation to maintain music in all its splendor and to bequeath to posterity an everlasting and glorious memorial to their efforts. I am in position to point them out with my finger, so that if you find yourselves in error, you will not be lacking either in the means to correct yourselves or in the good fortune of hearing, in every lesson, fundamental pronouncements and decisions. But I have just reason to hope that true good taste in singing will last until the end of the world.

32. He who correctly understands the content of these and many other remarks does not need any further motivation to study. Driven

by his own longing, he is drawn to his beloved instrument; at the same time, he will be aware through diligent attention that he still has no reason to be satisfied with that which he has already learned. He will make new discoveries; he will invent variations among which he will choose the best as the result of mature and closely considered comparisons – these also only as long as he recognizes them to be the best. He will keep on searching until he has found more and more other varieties (of variations) more worthy of his inclination and attention. Finally, he will arrive at an almost endless number of variations and turnings, by means of which he will have developed his insight to such a degree that the most hidden treasures of the art, which were furthest removed from his imagination, will reveal themselves to him voluntarily. If he is not blinded by arrogance, if studying does not make him irritable, and if his memory does not fail him, he will continue, in a way uniquely his own, to enlarge his store of the ornaments of melody and, so to speak, develop a taste of his own. This is the most noble aim of those who strive to win the greatest applause.

33. Hear me now finally for your own sakes, young singers. The abuses, deficiencies, and errors to which I have called attention in these remarks have perhaps been unjustly attributed to the modern style. I myself was possessed of almost all of them, and since they were mine, I could not perceive them so easily in the flowering years of youth when my blind self-love persuaded me with such tyrannical force that I was an excellent man. At a riper age, however, one's error is always recognized too late. I know that I have sung poorly and hope to heaven that I have not written even more poorly. But since my youthful ignorance has already suffered injury and punishment, may it at least serve as a good example for him who would wish to sing well. A student should imitate the wise bee, which sucks its honey from the loveliest flowers. Among the famous Ancients, as well as among the so-called Moderns (as I have said before), there are people from whom one can still learn. He must only seek the flower and know how to distill it [the nectar] properly to gain its essence.

34. The most sincere and useful counsels that I can give you are the following:

35. Never be satisfied with only the mediocre: it is often clouded; greatness, however, has an enduring light.

36. Abhor the example of those who hate punishment. Punishment serves as a bolt of lightning for him who walks in darkness; although it frightens, it lights the way.

237

37. Always study the errors of others. What a great lesson! It costs little but teaches much: one learns from everyone, and the most ignorant is the greatest teacher.

Truth and roses have their thorns, but whoever knows how to break them off from the blossom will not be pricked by them.

THE END

Notes

Introduction : Agricola's treatise

1 Friedrich Wilhelm Marpurg, *Historisch-kritische Beyträge zur Aufnahme der Musik* (5 vols., Berlin, 1754–78), vol. I (1754–55), pt. 4, pp. 326–31. Hereafter referred to as *Beyträge*.

2 *Opinioni de' cantori antichi e moderni, o sieno Osservazioni sopra il canto figurato* (Opinions regarding ancient and modern singers; or Observations on the florid song) (Bologna, 1723). In the present work the references to Tosi's *Opinioni* are taken from the facsimile reprint edition of Erwin R. Jacobi (Celle: Hermann Moeck Verlag, 1966), which was issued as a companion to the facsimile reprint of Johann Friedrich Agricola, *Anleitung zur Singkunst*, ed. Erwin R. Jacobi (Celle: Hermann Moeck Verlag, 1966), with Preface and Appendix. Tosi's work is hereafter referred to as *Opinioni*; and Agricola's as *Anleitung*, usually with reference also to the present translation (hereafter referred to as Baird).

3 *A General History of Music from the Earliest Ages to the Present Period*, ed. Frank Mercer (2 vols., [1789]; New York: Dover Publications, Inc., 1957), vol. II, p. 950. Hereafter cited as *General History*.

4 *The Present State of Music in Germany, The Netherlands, and United Provinces* (2 vols. London, 1775; rpt., New York: Broude Brothers, 1969), vol. II, pp. 91–92. Hereafter cited as *Present State*.

5 The first translation of Tosi on record appeared in Leyden in 1731, the year before Tosi died. Attributed to an anonymous "Mr. J. A.", the *Korte Aanmerkingen over de Zangkonst* (Leiden, 1731) is an abridged Dutch translation of the *Opinioni*, very little known and difficult of access (see Jacobi, ed., *Anleitung*, Preface, pp. xi–xii; xxix–xxx). The rather free Dutch translation (possibly by J. Alençon) omits some of Tosi's information, especially references to Italy and the entire last chapter, "De' Passi." The English translation by John Ernest (or Johann Ernst) Galliard, *Observations on the Florid Song; or Sentiments on the Ancient and Modern Singers* (London, 1742 and 1743; rpt. London: William Reeves Bookseller, 1967), with added notes and musical examples (hereafter referred to as Galliard), appeared about

239

ten years after Tosi's death, and had a mixed reception. *General History*, vol. II, p. 989, refers to the Galliard translation as "admirable," but John Hawkins, *A General History of The Science and Practice of Music* (London, 1776; rpt. Graz, 1969), p. 824a. objects to the rhapsodical expressions that Galliard (a native German by birth) rendered into English from Tosi's Italian, calling them "disgusting"; modern analysts agree that Galliard at times imperfectly renders Tosi's sense (see Ernest C. Harriss, "J. F. Agricola's *Anleitung zur Singkunst*: A Rich Source by a Pupil of J. S. Bach," *Bach* 9/3 [1978], pp. 3–4). The present writer observes that Galliard omits certain phrases from Tosi that must have been puzzling to him. Agricola's translation, the subject of the present study, followed in 1757.

The next confirmed translation is in French, appearing late in the next century: Théodore Lemaire, *L'Art du Chant, opinions sur les chanteurs anciens et modernes ou observations sur le chant figuré* (Paris, 1874), which relies on Galliard for notes and musical examples, but contains also an original preface and authorial notes.

In addition, Tosi's original Italian text has been reissued by Luigi Leonesi as part of the series La Scuola di Canto dell'epoca d'oro (secolo XVII) (Naples, 1904); and by Andrea Della Corte, in *Canto e bel canto*. Biblioteca di cultura musicale, no. 5 (Turin, 1933).

6 In his announcement in *Beyträge*, vol. I (1755), pt. 4, pp. 326–27, Agricola refers to the following basic texts as available but inadequate: Wolfgang Caspar Printz, *Anweisung zur Singe-Kunst oder Bericht wie man einen Knaben ... könne singen lehren* (Guben, 1671); Martin Heinrich Fuhrmann, *Musicalischer Trichter dadurch ein geschickter Informator sienen Informandis die Edle Singe-Kunst nach hertiger Manier ... einbringen kan* (Frankfurt an der Spree, 1706); Johannes Crüger, *Kurtzer und verstendlicher Unterricht recht und leichtlich singen zu lernen* (Berlin, 1625); Johann Peter Gabriel Sperling, *Principia musicae, das ist: gründliche Anweisung zur Music, wie ein Music-Scholar vom Anfang instru-iret und nach der Ordnung zur Kunst oder Wissenschaft der Figural-Music soll geführet ... werden* (Bautzen, 1705); Henricus Baryphonus, *Ars Canendi: apho-rismis succinctis descripta & notis philosophicis, mathematicis, physicis et historicis illustrata* (Leipzig, 1620); Georg Baumgarten, *Rudimenta musices: Kurze, jedoch gründliche Anleitung zur Figuralmusik, fürnehmlich der studirenden Jugend zu Landsberg an der Martha zum Besten vorgeschrieben* (1673).

7 *Beyträge*, vol. I, pt. 4, pp. 326–27 (my translation).

8 Franz Gehring and Alfred Loewenberg, "Frederick II," *Grove's Dictionary*, 5th edn. (1954), vol. III.

9 Johann Christoph Gottsched *et al.*, eds, *Beyträge zur critischen Historie der deutschen Sprache, Poesie une Beredsamkeit*, vol. XXV (1741), p. 16. Translated by Eugene Helm, *Music at the Court of Frederick the Great* (Norman: University of Oklahoma Press, 1960), pp. 92–93.

10 Hermann Wucherpfennig, "Johann Friedrich Agricola (Sein Leben und seine Werke)" (Ph. D. diss., Friedrich Wilhelm University, Berlin, 1922), p. 3.

11 Frederick's court was one of the few musical establishments in Europe

where German composers were sought out in preference to the Italian.

12 A policy echoed by Agricola in the Translator's Preface: "Our purpose is
... to make use of the insights, experiences, and examples of all skillful
people, regardless of the nation to which they belong" (*Anleitung*, p. iv;
Baird, p. 40).

13 R. Batka, "Friedrich II als Musiker," *Der Kunstwart*, vol. 25 (24 January
1912), p. 132. See also Helm, *Music at the Court*, p. 73.

14 *Present State*, vol. II, p. 234.

15 A tasteful ornamentation was one whose character matched the Affekt or
passion of the piece. Burney's definition: "*Taste*, the adding, diminishing,
or changing a melody, or passage, with judgement and propriety, and in
such a manner as to *improve* it." *The Present State of Music in France and Italy*,
2nd edn. (London, 1773; facs. rpt. New York: Broude Brothers, 1969),
p. viii.

16 Eugene Helm, "Johann Friedrich Agricola," *New Grove*, vol. I, p. 165.

17 Frederick Neumann, *Ornamentation in Baroque and Post-Baroque Music*
(Princeton University Press, 1983), p. 183.

18 She was the first of Frederick's *prime donne* at the Berlin opera, making her
début in 1743. Upon news of their marriage, Frederick cut their joint
salary to 1000 thalers, whereas Benedetta alone had made 1500 thalers a
year. According to *Present State*, vol. II, p. 92, Frederick's prejudice against
church music was such that it was his tendency to also discredit all other
works of a composer of church music with the statement: "Oh this smells
of the church."

19 Helm, *"Agricola,"* p. 165.

20 See Galliard, pp. 145–46.

21 *Magazin der Musik*, 2 (1786), p. 809. This description precedes Agricola's
essay, "Beleuchtung von der Frage von dem Vorzuge der Melodie vor der
Harmonie," published several years after his death.

22 Burney, *Present State*, vol. II, p. 91.

23 [Johann Friedrich Agricola], *Schreiben an Herrn ... [sic] in welchem Flavio
Amicio Olibrio sein Schreiben an den critischen Musicus an der Spree vertheidiget*
(Berlin, 6 July 1749).

24 Berlin, 1768. In this landmark treatise, more than eighty German organs
are described, with valuable and detailed descriptions of the cases, the
wind chamber pipes, and the registers; lengthy discussions are given of
tuning and temperament; and methods are suggested for testing new
instruments.

25 See *Anleitung*, ch. 1, pp. 5–17, nn. (d), (e), and (f) (Baird, pp. 54–65).

26 *Anleitung*, p. 9 (Baird, pp. 56–57).

27 *Anleitung*, p. 16 (Baird, p. 64). Agricola presumably is referring to the vowels used in pronouncing the names of the notes in German which yield
"es" and "is," i.e. "Es" (E♭) and "Gis" (g♯), although curiously he does
not mention the vowel "a" as it was pronounced in the note name "As"
(A♭) or "Ha" ("H" or B♮).

28 Johann Adam Hiller, *Anweisung zum musikalisch-zierlichen Gesange* (Leipzig, 1780), trans. Suzanne Julia Beicken, with commentary (Ph. D. diss., Stanford University, 1980), p. 21.

29 Johann Heinrich Buttstedt, *Ut, re, mi, fa, sol, la, tota Musica et Harmonia Aeterna* (Erfurt, 1716).

30 See Marpurg, review of Agricola's *Anleitung* in *Beyträge*, vol. III (1757), pt. 2, p. 167, and pt. 4, pp. 357–67, esp. p. 359.

31 *Anleitung*, pp. 22–47 (Baird, pp. 68–84).

32 "De la formation de la voix de l'homme" in *Mémoires de l'Académie des Sciences*, Paris, 1741), pp. 409–32. He proved that in order to phonate, the lips of the glottis had to come together, that the vibration of the glottal lips was the essential factor because when they were touched the sound ceased, and that the difference in tension of the edges of the glottis caused the change in pitch. He gave the appellation "vocal cords" to the lips of the glottis. Although Agricola credits Ferrein with first discovering the manner in which the vocal cords work, it was actually Marin Mersenne, *Harmonie Universelle* (Paris, 1636), who took the first steps in this direction. Having observed that many singers possess a range of at least two octaves, and that a vibrating column of air has to be doubled in size to produce a sound even an octave lower, he decided that the vast alterations in the size of the various respiratory canals proposed by Agricola and others were impossible; and that the solution was to be found in the edges of the glottis or vocal cords.

33 Kurt Wichmann, *Anleitung zur Singkunst: Einführung und Kommentar* (Leipzig: VEB Deutscher Verlag für Musik, 1966), p. 27.

34 See Translator's Preface, p. vii (Baird, p. 42).

35 *Anleitung*, pp. 22–27 (Baird, pp. 68–71).

36 See Johan Sundberg, "Acoustics" (pt. 5: "The Voice"), *New Grove*, vol. I, pp. 82–86.

37 William Vennard, *Singing: the Mechanism and the Technique* (New York: Fischer, 1967), p. 66, para. 239.

38 *Opinioni*, p. 14. See *Anleitung*, pp. 18, 21–22 (Baird, pp. 65, 67–68); Galliard, pp. 23–24).

39 *Opinioni*, p. 11–12, 13–15; *Anleitung*, pp. 18, 21–22 (Baird, pp. 65, 67–68).

40 *Anleitung*, pp. 36–37 (Baird, pp. 76–77).

41 Giambattista Mancini, *Riflessioni practiche sul canto figurato*, 3rd rev., enlarged edn. (Milan, 1777; rpt. Bologna: Forni Editore, 1970), pp. 135–36. Cf. a translation of this work: Edward Foreman, *Practical Reflections on Figured Singing* (Champaign, Illinois: Pro Musica Press, 1967), pp. 39–40.

42 Hiller, *Anweisung* (1780), pp. 7–8 (Beicken trans., pp. 30–32).

43 In the Western music world of the 1990s, pitch has come much closer to the ideal of the standard, but there is still no universal standardization in practice; for example, certain European orchestras tune to 449 Hz for a′, rather than to 440 Hz.

44 Joseph Sauveur, "Sur la determination d'un son fixe," *Histoire de l'Académie Royale des Sciences, Anneé 1700* (Paris: Imprimerie Royalle, 1703), pp. 131–40.
45 See *Anleitung*, p. 45 (Baird, p. 83).
46 *Opinioni*, p. 16; *Anleitung*, pp. 45–47 (Baird, pp. 83–84).
47 *Anleitung*, p. 46 (Baird, p. 183).
48 *Porpora's Elements of Singing*. Adopted by Righini and all eminent Masters since his time. Extracted from the Archives at Naples. Edited by Marcia Harris (London, 1858). Information and musical examples are found in Franz Haböck, *Die Kastraten und ihre Gesangskunst* (Berlin and Leipzig, 1927), pp. 382–85.
49 Owen Jander, "Messa di voce," *New Grove*, vol. XII, p. 201.
50 *Opinioni*, p. 17; *Anleitung*, p. 47 (Baird, p. 84). A half century after Agricola's *Anleitung*, Mancini, devoting the better part of an article to the *messa di voce*, recommends that ordinarily the *messa di voce* be used "at the beginning of an aria, and on notes with hold signs [fermatas]; and similarly it is necessary at the beginning of a cadenza; but a true and worthy professor will use it on every long note, which are found scattered through every musical cantilena." *Riflessioni* (Foreman trans., p. 44).
51 *Anleitung*, p. 145, (Baird, pp. 167–68).
52 *Anleitung*, p. 166, (Baird, pp. 183–84).
53 *Anleitung*, p. 48 (Baird, pp. 84–85).
54 Many eighteenth-century composers such as Georg Philipp Telemann, *Der Harmonische Gottesdienst* (Hamburg, 1725–26), and Friedrich Wilhelm Marpurg, *Des critischen Musicus an der Spree erster Band* (Berlin, 1750; collected issues of the journal *Der critische Musicus* 1749–50), p. 66, use the word "Akzent" for the appoggiatura.
55 Ch. 2, para. 16; and ch. 7, paras. 5ff. See *Anleitung*, pp. 57–58, 174ff. (Baird, pp. 91, 189ff.).
56 Daniel Gottlob Türk, *Klavierschule, oder Anweisung zum Klavierspielen für Lehrer und Lernende* (Leipzig and Halle, 1789). Translated by Raymond H. Haggh as *School of Clavier Playing* (Lincoln and London: University of Nebraska Press, 1982), p. 195.
57 C. P. E. Bach, *Versuch über die wahre Art das Clavier zu spielen* (Berlin, 1752), p. 63. See also translation and edition by William J. Mitchell, as *Essay on the True Art of Playing Keyboard Instruments* (New York: Norton, 1949), p. 87.
58 *Anleitung*, pp. 60, 67, 68 (Baird pp. 93, 99–100, 101). The longer appoggiaturas occur most often on the strong beats where they can create a dissonance with the bass.
59 Bach, *Versuch*, pp. 62–63 (Mitchell trans., p. 87).
60 *Anleitung*, p. 59 (Baird, pp. 92–93). The fact that these four aims – and in fact much of the chapter on the appoggiatura – are reiterated almost verbatim in Hiller's *Anweisung* (1780) attests to the long-lasting impact of Agricola's work. Both Agricola and Hiller acknowledge their indebtedness to the work of C. P. E. Bach. In addition, Türk in his *Klavierschule* of 1789 quotes numerous passages from Agricola.

61 Bach, *Versuch* (Mitchell trans.), p. 98.
62 The "preferred Lombardian Taste" to which the Berlin writers referred was believed by them to derive ultimately from the Italian violinists Torelli and Corelli. It consists, according to Quantz, of "shortening the note ... on the beat in a group of two or three short notes, and dotting the following unstressed note ... a style which had its beginnings about the year 1722." See Johann Joachim Quantz, *Versuch einer Anweisung die Flöte traversière zu spielen* (Berlin, 1752). See translation and edition by Edward R. Reilly, *On Playing the Flute*, 2nd edn. (New York: Macmillan, 1966), p. 323.
63 The *messa di voce crescente* is an ornament often connected with a special word affect (not necessitating the crescendo decrescendo) in which the singer slides in a glissando fashion imperceptibly up the interval of a half or whole step.
64 Lit., placing of the voice. The *messa di voce* functions both as an expressive ornament and as a technical pedagogical means to strengthen the voice. It exercised the singer in producing a steady tone and in the control of his voice, especially in the crescendo–decrescendo. It is one of the most basic exercises of singing.
65 *Anleitung*, p. 57 (Baird, p. 91). Eighteenth-century symbols for the *messa di voce crescente* are very few and somewhat vague, sometimes consisting of a horizontal wedge-shaped line between the two notes. In Italian seventeenth-century literature, especially the works of Sigismondo d'India, only a slur above the enharmonic change (required by this ornament) indicates its presence, which was common on words rich in Affect such as *lagrime* (tears) and *piangere* (to cry).
66 *Anleitung*, p. 77. (Baird, pp. 109–10). Agricola is less exacting than Bach in that he prohibits only the very noticeable parallel octaves.
67 Quantz, *Versuch* (Reilly trans.), p. 159.
68 *Anleitung*, p. 85 (Baird, p. 117).
69 *Anleitung*, p. 88 (Baird, p. 120).
70 Türk, *Klavierschule* (Haggh trans.), p. 240.
71 Neumann, *Ornamentation*, pp. 235–36. *Anschlagende Tactglieder* refers to strong beats and *durchgehende Tactglieder* to passing or weak beats.
72 Italian *trillo* refers to the oscillation between the notated note (main note) and a note a semitone or a whole tone away. See also p. 18 above and n. 94 below.
73 *Anleitung*, p. 94. (Baird, p. 126).
74 *Opinioni*, p. 24. See also *Anleitung*, p. 94 (Baird, p. 126). Vincenzo Manfredini, *Regole Armoniche* (Venice, 1775; 2nd edn. Venice, 1797), p. 66, says that when the singer cannot improvise a more complicated cadenza, he may instead perform a *messa di voce* and a trill.
75 Burney, *Present State*, vol. I, p. 339, reports that "for the shake, he [Mancini] thinks it ruined ninety-nine times out of a hundred by too much impatience and precipitation, both in the master and scholar; and many who can execute passages, which require the same motion of the

larynx as the shake, have notwithstanding never acquired one. There is no accounting for this, but from the neglect of the master to study nature and avail himself of these passages, which by continuity, would become real shakes."

76 *Anleitung*, pp. 97–99 (Baird, pp. 128–30).

77 *Opinioni*, pp. 25–28; *Anleitung*, pp. 95–103 (Baird, pp. 127–33).

78 Neumann's interpretation of Tosi's *trillo maggiore* is part of his argument in favor of the main-note-dominated trill. See *Ornamentation*, pp. 345–46.

79 Galliard, pp. 45–46, has clearly misunderstood or ignored Tosi's description of this trill, as is shown by the musical example which he provides for it (pp. 192–93). Tosi specifies an "imperceptible rise from comma to comma." Instead, Galliard's musical example is of the ever-popular "chain of trills" (*catena di trilli*), a series of uninterrupted trills of half and whole steps – intervals which, of course, are quite perceptible to the ear and a good deal bigger than a comma. Agricola, *Anleitung* p. 100 (Baird, pp. 130–31), understanding the passage correctly, differentiates the glissando of this trill from the chain of trills (*Trillerkette*).

80 The extra notes that Agricola adds in his interpretation are at the *beginning* and not in the middle as Tosi specifies. See *Anleitung*, pp. 101–02 (Baird, pp. 131–32).

81 Agricola interprets this trill as a mordent. See *Anleitung*, pp. 102–03 (Baird, pp. 131–32).

82 Neumann, *Ornamentation*, p. 345.

83 *Opinioni*, p. 25; *Anleitung*, p. 95 (Baird, p.126).

84 If the trill were not beaten (*battuto*), it often resulted in the goat bleat or *caprino* described elsewhere in Tosi's chapter.

85 *Korte Aanmerkingen*, p. 12. The Dutch translator uses the phrase *wel aangeslaagen*.

86 *Anleitung*, p. 95 (Baird, pp. 126–27).

87 *Anleitung*, p. 104, note (n) (Baird, p. 135).

88 *Anleitung*, p. 98 and pp. 105–06 (Baird, pp. 129 and 135–36).

89 This motion, one of three mechanisms that effect a change in voice frequency, consists of an elevation or depression of the larynx, perceptible by placing the fingers on the Adam's apple.

90 See for example, Mancini, *Riflessioni*, p. 173 (my translation).

91 *General History*, pp. 879, 883, 898.

92 It must be mentioned here that the *caprino* (or *Bockstriller*, to use Agricola's term) is discussed only as a defect and is not intended to indicate the *trillo*, an ornament (used in the music of Monteverdi and Caccini) which also consisted of the reiteration of one note. The *trillo* is a tone repetition which can be the distinct (almost staccato) articulation of one note or can be a more legato pulsing on the same note. The seventeenth-century writer Christoph Bernhard, "Von der Singekunst oder Manier" (*ca.* 1649), when describing the *trillo*, specifies that "one should take great care not to change the quality of the voice in striking the trillo, lest a bleating sound

result." See translation by Walter Hilse, "The treatises of Christoph Bernhard: On the Art of Singing; or, Manier," *The Music Forum* 3 (1973), pp. 13–29, esp. p. 15.

93 *Cassell's Italian Dictionary* (New York, 1958), s.v. "granire". We are enlightened as to the meaning of *granito* by Quantz, whose description of Faustina Hasse includes the expression and a clarification thereof. See "Herrn Johann Joachim Quantzens Lebenslauf, von ihm selbst entworfen" in *Beyträge*, vol. I, pt. 3, p. 240.

94 See, for example, Quantz, *Versuch*, pp. 84–85 (Reilly trans., p. 102). Quantz's method of determining the speed of the moderately fast trill by coordinating finger strokes on an instrument to coincide with the pulse beat yields a metronome indication of ($\downarrow$ = 160). Quantz permits this quicker trill only upon short notes and when there are several short notes in succession.

95 *General History*, vol. II, p. 879.

96 *Anleitung*, p. 101 (Baird, pp. 131–32).

97 Quantz, *Versuch* (Reilly trans.), pp. 102–03.

98 *Anleitung*, p. 101 (Baird, pp. 131–32).

99 *Anleitung*, p. 101 (Baird, pp. 131–32).

100 Quantz, *Versuch*, p. 86 (Reilly trans., p. 103).

101 Johann Mattheson, *Der Vollkommene Capellmeister* (Hamburg, 1739), pt. 2, ch. 3, para. 33, p. 115 (my translation): "the Italians, by contrast to the French, render their regular trills very fast, strong and short, almost like *trillettos* except when they first hold either of the two tones, which [holding] they call a tenuta."

102 *Anleitung*, p. 98. (Baird, p. 129).

103 Agricola suggests the impulse of the breath (*Anstoss des Athems*) only for the trill that begins on the auxiliary, indicating that he wants that note stressed, probably so that its dissonant quality is more easily perceived.

104 A *gruppo* is an ornament related to both the trill and the turn, starting with either the upper note or the main note and ending with a turn. The oscillations are usually slower than those of the trill and sometimes, unlike those of the trill, are rhythmically measured.

105 Giulio Caccini, *Le Nuove Musiche* (Florence, 1602), ed. H. Wiley Hitchcock. Recent Researches in the Music of the Baroque Era, vol. IX (Madison, Wisconsin: A-R Editions, Inc., 1970), p. 51.

106 Mattheson, *Capellmeister*, pt. 2, ch. 3, para. 47, p. 276.

107 *Anleitung*, p. 100 (Baird, pp. 130–31).

108 Bach, *Versuch*, p. 73 (Mitchell trans., p. 101).

109 *Anleitung*, pp. 114–16 (Baird, pp. 142–44). The terminations of trills must occur without pause, and must be executed in the speed of the trill itself, and must be immediately connected to the following note. In his discussion of the termination of two notes occurring after fairly long trills, he draws the reader's attention to chapter 2, where he had specified that the termination should be slurred to the preceding note and that it is

only rarely indicated in notation.

110 *Critischer Musicus*, pp. 57–58ff. Marpurg's terms for the ornaments were *Der gezogene oder geschleifte Triller* or *cadence coulé ou portée*. Cited from Neumann, *Ornamentation*, p. 408.

111 Agricola, *Schreiben an Herrn*, p. 49. Agricola rejected Marpurg's ornaments 2 and 3 as offensive, charging that they "would hardly be used by any person of good taste."

112 Friedrich Wilhelm Marpurg, *Anleitung zum Clavierspielen* (Berlin, 1755; facs. rpt., New York: Broude Brothers 1966), pp. 53–58.

113 *Anleitung*, p. 113 (Baird, pp. 141–42).

114 *Anleitung*, p. 103 (Baird, pp. 133–34).

115 Although there are several mechanisms in the human voice for producing the vibrato, one of these occurs in the same manner as the trill (i.e. by the up-and-down movement of the larynx in the human throat, although usually less exaggerated than the trill); hence its inclusion by Agricola in the chapter on trills.

116 *Anleitung*, p. 121 (Baird, pp. 148–49).

117 The divisions were also an extremely important measuring stick for determining the style of a piece of music in the eighteenth century. Charles Burney, for example, judged the vocal works of his era and several generations preceding him (1680–1770) largely on the style of the divisions themselves, finding those that are derived from the trill, for example, to be antiquated and trite (*General History*, vol. II, p. 683).

118 Tosi does not ignore the issue since there are references to extempore variations in several chapters including the chapter on the arias. But he disapproves of the use of excessive virtuosity as the singer's primary tool to gain acclaim.

119 *Opinioni*, p. 35. See *Anleitung*, p. 133 (Baird, p. 158).

120 Quantz, *Versuch*, pp. 118–35 (Reilly trans., pp. 136–61).

121 Bach, *Versuch*, "Vom Vortrage," pp. 115–35 (Mitchell trans., pp. 147–66).

122 Friedrich Wilhelm Marpurg, *Anleitung zur Musik überhaupt, und zur Singkunst besonders* (Berlin, 1763), p. 144. Marpurg also includes all repetitions and transpositions of some principal musical ideas, particularly of a certain liveliness, which are derived from certain mechanical motives.

123 This was, however, not the case with Frederick himself or with Frederick's teacher Quantz, as the student's written-out ornamentations (such as his elaboration of an aria from Hasse's *Cleofide*), and the teacher's lengthy chapters on extempore ornamentation prove. See Quantz, *Versuch*, chs. 8, 13, 15, 18.

124 *Anleitung*, pp. 124–26, 141–42 (Baird, pp. 151–52, 164–65).

125 *Opinioni*, p. 31 (Baird, p. 153).

126 *Anleitung*, p. 135 (Baird, pp. 160–61).

127 Also very commonly found in string parts, this effect is achieved by moving the bow on the string in an undulating fashion. One example in

Handel's cantata for tenor and strings *Look down Harmonious Saint* occurs in the tenor part quite fittingly over the words "every trembling string."

128 *Anleitung*, pp. 124–26 (Baird, pp. 151–53). Agricola's "certain great female singer who for many years delighted audiences in Italy, England, and Germany but retired from the theatre six years ago, and who was admired for the extraordinary clarity and speed with which she executed all sorts of fast notes," and who used this glottal articulation, can be none other than Faustina, whose last stage appearance was on 23 February 1751 in Dresden in Hasse's opera *Ciro riconosciuto*, six years before the 1757 publication of Agricola's *Anleitung*.

129 *General History*, vol. II, pp. 745–46.

130 *Anleitung*, p. 125 (Baird, p. 152).

131 *Opinioni*, pp. 105–06 (Baird, pp. 227–28). Called the *dispositione della voce*, this very prevalent type of extremely rapid glottal articulation was necessary to the singer's art of the late sixteenth and early seventeenth centuries. See Robert Greenlee, "*Dispositione di voce*: Passage to Florid Singing," *Early Music*, 15/1 (February, 1987), pp. 47–55.

132 *Opinioni*, pp. 114–15 (Baird, p. 234).

133 *Anleitung*, p. 128 (Baird, p. 154). The drag also is distinguishable from the *messa di voce crescente* (referred to in ch. 2) only by the fact that the compass of the latter is restricted to a half step. Both involve an imperceptible alteration of the pitch.

134 Johann Adam Hiller, *Anweisung zum musikalisch-richtigen Gesange* (Leipzig, 1774), as translated by Cornelius L. Reid, *Bel Canto: Principles and Practice* (1950; New York: The Joseph Patelson Music House, 1972), p. 117.

135 Hiller, *Anweisung* (1780), p. 83 (my translation).

136 *Anleitung*, pp. 141–43 (Baird, pp. 164–66). Agricola also sanctions breathing in the middle of a word.

137 *General History*, vol. II, p. 738.

138 Burney, *The Present State of Music in France and Italy*, pp. 213–14, reports that "during the run of an opera, there was a struggle every night between him [Farinelli] and a famous player on the trumpet, in a song accompanied by that instrument: this, at first, seemed amicable and merely sportive, till the audience began to interest themselves in the contest, and to take different sides: after severally swelling out a note, in which each manifested the power of his lungs, and tried to rival the other in brilliancy and force, they had both a swell and shake together, by thirds, which was continued so long, while the audience eagerly waited the event, that both seemed to be exhausted; and, in fact, the trumpeter, wholly spent, gave it up, thinking, however, his antagonist as much tired as himself, and that it would be a drawn battle; when Farinelli, with a smile on his countenance, showing he had only been sporting with him all that time, broke out all at once in the same breath, with fresh vigor, and not only swelled and shook the note, but ran the most rapid and difficult divisions, and was at last silenced only by the

acclamations of the audience. From this period may be dated that superiority which he ever maintained over all his contemporaries [sic]."

139 *Anleitung*, p. 142 (Baird, p. 165).

140 See *Opinioni*, p. 34, *Anleitung*, p. 131 (Baird, pp. 156–57). Agricola supports Tosi's comments in this matter without any mention of the practices of other contemporary German composers. Composers such as Buxtehude, Telemann, and Johann Sebastian Bach (Agricola's teacher) wrote divisions on every conceivable vowel.

141 *Anleitung*, p. 131 (Baird, pp. 156–57). Diphthongs on the *a* vowel occur in such words as "laut," "leise"; diphthongs beginning with the *e* vowel occur in such words as "Ewigkeit" or "elende."

142 *Anleitung*, p. 137 (Baird, p. 162).

143 *Anleitung*, p. 137 (Baird, p. 162). See Bérard, *L'Art du Chant* (Paris, 1755; facs. rpt., New York: Broude Brothers, 1967), pp. 52–53. Bérard lists faults such as pronouncing *Bérouger* for *Berger, Chadore* instead of *J'adore*.

144 According to De Brosses, in Italy "they beat time in church for Latin music but never at the opera, no matter how large the orchestra is or how complicated the score that is being played. Unlike ourselves [i.e. the French], these people have exactness and precision. Consequently they are even more critical of our playing than of our music." See Charles De Brosses, *Letter on Italian Music*, trans. and annotated by Donald Schier (printed by Donald S. Schier, 1978), p. 34.

145 *Anleitung*, p. 153 (Baird, pp. 173–74). The term *recitativo accompagnato* meaning accompanied recitative is also called *recitativo obbligato* because the recitative calls for scoring of part or all of the orchestra. Agricola refers to this as *Accompagnement*.

146 The appoggiatura was also a dramatic tool to help the singer in his individual interpretation of the declamation, and as such it was felt to be the prerogative of the singer and not to be mandated by the composer. Since the appoggiatura is usually dissonant with the harmony, one of the effects in introducing it in the recitative was to give stress, or emphasis, to the syllable or word which bore it. Certain writers such as Telemann, Mattheson, and Marpurg use the terminology "Akzent" for the appoggiatura. This is particularly effective when a series of notes on the same pitch occur, so that one word or syllable can be discernible from the pattern of notes on the same pitch.

147 *Anleitung*, pp. 151, 154–55 (Baird, pp. 172, 174–75).

148 *Anleitung*, p. 154 (Baird, p. 174).

149 Agricola suggests that arbitrarily performing some of the cadential notes of a church recitative as *langsam gezogene Noten* (lit., long spun-out notes) is often appropriate should the singer not want to add more.

150 *Anleitung*, pp. 151–52 (Baird, pp. 172–73).

151 For a complete discussion of this issue see Sven Hansell, "The Cadence in 18th-Century Recitative," *Musical Quarterly*, 54/2 (April, 1968), pp. 228–48, esp. pp. 233ff.

152 *Opinioni*, p. 47; *Anleitung*, p. 162 (Baird, pp. 180–81).
153 *Opinioni*, p. 47; *Anleitung*, p. 162 (Baird, pp. 180–81).
154 A German musical movement of which Carl Philipp Emanuel Bach is considered the prime exponent and the clavichord the prime instrument. It sought to move the passions.
155 Another kind of intensity fluctuation was notated by the Berlin school for the voice by eighth notes on the same pitch marked by individual dots over which a slur occurs. See *Anleitung*, p. 135 (Baird, pp. 160–61).
156 They were patterned after the following general form. After the opening instrumental ritornello (which ends with an authentic cadence) is presented the first vocal entry (set to the first stanza of the poem). This section then closes with a cadence in the secondary key (either dominant or minor, depending on the initial key of the piece). A ritornello then follows in that key; and the subsequent second entry by the voice cadences on the tonic, the final line of the first stanza of the A section text often being set as a coloratura passage. The ensuing instrumental ritornello brings the A (first) section to an end. The text for the B (second) section is usually given only once, although the last line or couplet is often repeated. Consequently, the music of the B section is in a subsidiary key (usually the mediant, subdominant, or submediant) and is typically quite short in comparison with the A section. The repetition of the A (da capo) section follows, and here it was considered appropriate (in fact essential) for the singer to ornament. Cadenzas were often inserted at the ends of the statements of both stanzas, and thus it was important that the librettist choose words containing proper vowels for divisions (*a* and open *o*), for these cadenzas consisted largely of such passages.
157 According to Galliard, p. 116, note, the unison aria was developed in Venice: "The *Airs*, sung in Unison with the Instruments, were invented in the *Venetian* Opera's to please the *Barcaroles*, who are their Watermen: and very often their Applause supports an Opera."
158 According to Agricola, *Anleitung*, p. 183, note (k) (Baird, p. 196), "the term 'pathetic,' as it is generally understood, means that which is filled with strong passion. Thus, some of the fast, even furioso, arias, in a certain sense, can be called pathetic ... the slow arias – which are generally expressions of a high degree of tender, sad, or otherwise nobly serious emotions" were in Tosi's time designated as "pathetic arias," and their character is "usually recognized ... by means of the terms *adagio, largo, lento mesto, grave*, etc ..."
159 *Anleitung*, p. 172, note (a) (Baird, p. 188).
160 Agricola's reputation suffered on account of his sharp opposition to Gluck's reforms. Agricola attacked Gluck in his articles published in C. Friedrich Nicolai's *Allgemeine deutsche Bibliothek* (Berlin, Kiel, and Stettin, 1766–96).
161 These sounds are found in the Italian words *casa, oggi*, and *ecco*.
162 Charles Burney, *Memoirs of the Life and Writings of the Abate Metastasio* (3 vols.,

London, 1796; rpt., New York: Da Capo Press, 1971), vol. II, pp. 135–36.

163 Tosi recommends to the aspiring singer three methods for gaining confidence. First, he should attend as many performances of the best singers as he can, taking along the score in order to best realize what ornamentations are being added. Secondly, to avoid errors in a public performance he should repeat the arias over again and again alone. Thirdly, upon performing the arias for the first time in public, he should add only the most essential ornaments, but resolving to reflect "at the same time where one might add improvised ornaments the next [lit., second] time." *Opinioni*, pp. 58–62; *Anleitung*, pp. 172–76 (Baird, pp. 188–92).

164 Angus Heriot, *The Castrati in Opera* (London, 1956; rpt , New York: Da Capo Press, 1975), pp. 149–50.

165 John Spitzer, "Improvised Ornamentation in a Handel Aria with Obbligato Wind Accompaniment," *Early Music*, 16 (1988), pp. 514–22.

166 *Anleitung*, pp. 58–59, note (i) (Baird, p. 92).

167 *Opinioni*, pp. 59–60, 88; *Anleitung*, pp. 174, 202 (Baird, pp. 189–90, 200–10).

168 Other eighteenth-century Italian writers such as Manfredini use *cadenza libera* or *cadenza fiorita* to distinguish the cadenza from the cadence.

169 In Agricola this passage reads *ohne Aufhaltung der Tactbewegung* (without delaying the tempo) even though Tosi's original is *senza offesa del tempo* (without giving offense to the time).

170 In a subsequent discussion of *tempo rubato*, Tosi refer to it as "an especially praiseworthy robbery, especially in the pathetic, enabling one singer to sing better than another provided that he has the insight and wit to replace that which has been taken away." See *Opinioni*, p. 99; *Anleitung*, p. 220 (Baird, p. 223).

171 *Anleitung*, pp. 195–96 (Baird, p. 205).

172 *Anleitung*, pp. 202–03 (Baird, pp. 210–11).

173 *Opinioni*, p. 80; *Anleitung*, p. 194 (Baird, p. 204).

174 *Opinioni*, p. 80; *Anleitung*, p. 195 (Baird, p. 205). Quantz gives a more probable reason for the popularity of these bass cadences: "To remove the opportunity for unskilled singers to make cadenzas, the composers concluded most of their arias with bass-like passages in unison." *Versuch*, p. 152 (Reilly trans., p. 180).

175 *Anleitung*, p. 199 (Baird, p. 207–08).

176 De Brosses, *Letter*, p. 37, for example, writes of the breath capacity of a certain castrato singer as encompassing seven and one-half minutes: "I want to laugh when I see a fat castrato puff himself up like a balloon so as to go from the top to the bottom of his voice for half of a quarter of an hour."

177 *Anleitung*, p. 143 (Baird, p. 166).

178 *Anleitung*, p. 204 (Baird, p. 211).

179 Hiller, *Anweisung* (1780), p. 111 (Beicken trans., p. 127).

180 De Brosses, *Letter*, pp. 36–37, felt that the cadenzas of the castrati were

not only too frequent, but "they are always the same."

181 *Anleitung*, p. 204 (Baird, p. 211).

182 Quantz, *Versuch*, p. 154 (Reilly trans., p. 182).

183 Hiller, *Anweisung* (1780), pp. 113–14 (Beicken trans., pp. 129–30).

184 *Anleitung*, p. 204 (Baird, p. 211).

185 *Anleitung*, pp. 203–4 (Baird, pp. 210–11).

186 *Anleitung*, p. 204 (Baird, p. 211).

187 *Anleitung*, p. 206 (Baird, p. 212).

188 Despite its literal meaning, *tempo rubato* (lit., stolen time) in its eighteenth-century sense actually signifies a *borrowing* (rhythmic alteration) of the notated rhythm, in which the time was made up before the measure was over. The altered part was often juxtaposed to a regularly moving part such as, for example, the walking bass in an andante.

189 *Opinioni*, p. 99; *Anleitung*, p. 219 (Baird, pp. 222–23).

190 *Opinioni*, p. 65; *Anleitung*, p. 178 (Baird, pp. 192–93).

191 *Opinioni*, p. 81; *Anleitung*, p. 196 (Baird, pp. 205–06).

192 *Present State*, vol. II, p. 189.

193 Two different phrases are used by Tosi to express this. In ch. 8 he uses *sul moto di bassi* (over the motion of the bass) and in ch. 7, *senza offendere le misure del Tempo* (without going against the observance of the time).

194 De Brosses, *Letter*, p. 36, reveals that "a singer, of whom you request a song in a private house [in Italy] will not sing without going to the harpsichord to accompany herself, playing the bass with her left hand, and the tune, not the chords, with her right. All singers can play well enough for that."

195 *Opinioni*, p. 53; *Anleitung*, pp. 167–68 (Baird, pp. 184–85).

196 *Opinioni*, p. 105; *Anleitung*, p. 225 (Baird, p. 227). The latter, according to Tosi, is the "ingenious invention of those who understand the art of composition and possess the best taste."

197 Some writers such as Sandra P. Rosenblum, *Performance Practices in Classic Piano Music* (Bloomington: Indiana University Press, 1988), p. 377, have used the term "displaced."

198 Leopold Mozart translated the term *tempo rubato* with the German *gestohlenes Tempo* (stolen time) in *Versuch einer gründlicher Violinschule* (Augsburg, 1756, 1787), p. 267, note e; trans. Editha Knocker, *A Treatise on the Fundamental Principles of Violin Playing* (London: Oxford University Press, 1948), p. 224, note 1.

199 Marpurg, *Anleitung zum Clavierspielen*, p. 83.

200 Marpurg, *Anleitung zur Singkunst*, p. 149 (my translation). See also pp. 147–49.

201 Marpurg, *Anleitung zum Clavierspielen*, pp. 147–48. In addition to *Vorausnehmen* and *Aufhalten*, Marpurg's other terms are *Rückungen* (syncopations), *Bindungen* (tied syncopations), and *Tonverbeissung* (a hocket-like effect).

202 *Anleitung*, p. 219 (Baird, pp. 222–23).

203 Some writers such as Kamiénski have sought to interpret Agricola's musical examples in conjunction with Tosi's description of the two types of *tempo rubato*, but this relationship seems hardly likely in view of the fact that they are taken from Marpurg, *Anleitung zum Clavierspielen*, pp. 147–48. See Lucian Kamiénski, "Zum 'Tempo rubato,'" *Archiv für Musikwissenschaft*, 1 (1918–19), p. 115.

204 *Anleitung*, pp. 219–20 (Baird, pp. 222–23).

205 See the review of Agricola's *Anleitung* in *Beyträge*, vol. III (1757), pt. 4, pp. 357–67.

206 G. E. Lessing and F. Nicolai, eds., *Bibliothek der schönen Wissenschaften und der freyen Kunst*, vol. II (1758), pt. 2, p. 421 (my translation). For further laudatory reviews, see Jacobi, ed., *Anleitung*, Preface, pp. xxi–xxv.

207 Bernhard Ulrich, *Die altitalienische Gesangsmethode: Die Schule des Belcanto* (Leipzig, 1933), p. 5.

208 Christoph Willibald Gluck, Preface to *Alceste* (Paris, 1769).

209 *Allgemeine deutsche Bibliothek*, vol. XIV, no. 1 (Berlin, 1771).

210 To Gluck's disdain for excessive passages, for example, Agricola countered with a spirited defense of many related repetitions of words and phrases.

211 *Magazin der Musik*, 2 (Hamburg 1784), p. 450, para. 57; Wucherpfennig, "Agricola," p. 28.

212 W. A. Mozart, 4th edn. (Leipzig, 1905), pt. 1, p. 521, para. 76.

213 Wucherpfennig, "Agricola," pp. 28–29.

214 See Garcia's "Preface to the First Edition" in *A Complete Treatise on the Art of Singing: Part One* by Manuel Garcia II, edited and translated by Donald V. Paschke (New York: Da Capo Press, 1984), p. xvii. For a brief summary of Garcia's life and work, see Paschke's "Translator's Preface," pp. ii–xl.

215 *Traité complet sur l'Art du Chant* (Paris, 1840, 3/1851; Eng. trans., enlarged, 1894).

216 Hugo Goldschmidt, *Die italienische Gesangsmethode des XVII Jahrhunderts und ihre Bedeutung für die Gegenwart* (Breslau: S. Schottlaender, 1892), pp. 49, 115ff., 136. In *Die Lehre von der Vokal-Ornamentik* (Charlottenburg, 1907), Goldschmidt makes various references to Tosi and Agricola, occasionally taking issue, as for example on p. 106, where he opposes Agricola's teaching that every appoggiatura, whether long or short, variable or invariable, must always be stronger than the following main note.

217 Kurt Wichmann, *Der Ziergesang und die Ausführung der Appoggiatura; Ein Beitrag zur Gesangspädagogik* (Leipzig: VEB Deutscher Verlag für Musik, 1966).

218 *The Interpretation of Early Music* (London: Faber & Faber, 1963).

219 "Agricola,", p. 165.

Translator's preface

1 Bologna, 1723. In the present work the references to Tosi's *Opinioni* are taken from the facsimile reprint edition of Erwin R. Jacobi (Celle: Hermann Moeck Verlag, 1966), which was issued as a companion to Johann Friedrich Agricola, *Anleitung zur Singkunst*, ed. E. R. Jacobi (Celle: Hermann Moeck Verlag, 1966), with Preface and Appendix.

2 The Accademia Filarmonica (Philharmonic Academy) of Bologna, of which Tosi was a member, was founded on 26 May 1666 by fifty musicians – composers, singers and instrumentalists – who discussed theoretical matters and analyzed and performed new musical works.

3 Agricola's rebuke to his native land must certainly include his own employer, Frederick II, at whose Berlin court only Italian singers were paid well. Karl Heinrich Graun, Royal Capellmeister for Frederick, often travelled to Italy for the express purpose of hiring Italian singers for operatic roles. In a letter printed by Johann Mattheson, an anonymous Berliner commented: "Because of such circumstances, our best performers leave the country in shocking numbers, while wretched Italians are accorded great honour." See Johann Christoph Gottsched *et al.*, eds., *Beyträge zur critischen Historie der deutschen Sprache, Poesie und Beredsamkeit*, vol. 25, p. 16, as translated by Eugene Helm, *Music at the Court of Frederick the Great* (Norman: University of Oklahoma Press, 1960), p. 93.

4 No stranger himself to such controversies, Agricola (under the pseudonym Flavio Amicio Olibrio) had previously published two pamphlets on French and Italian style, in support of the latter: *Schreiben eines reisenden Liebhabers* (Berlin, 1749) and *Schreiben an Herrn … in welchem Flavio Amicio Olibrio sein Schreiben an den critischen Musicus an der Spree vertheidiget* (Berlin, 1749).

5 On Tosi's career as castrato, see Franz Haböck, *Die Kastraten und ihre Gesangskunst* (Berlin and Leipzig, 1927), pp. 341–55.

6 Agricola's friend is surely Johann Joachim Quantz, who in 1719 was a member of the Polish royal orchestra at Dresden and Warsaw. In Quantz's autobiographical essay, "Herrn Johann Joachim Quantzens Lebenslauf, von ihm selbst entworfen" in *Beyträge*, vol. I (Berlin, 1754–55), pt. 3, p. 242, he indicates that he had met the "old castrato" Tosi in London in 1727. On the other hand, Galliard, in the Prefatory Discourse of his translation of Tosi, pp. vii–viii, *praises* Tosi's voice: "Pier Francesco Tosi, the Author of the following Treatise, was an *Italian*, and a Singer of great Esteem and Reputation … His manner of Singing was full of Expression and Passion; chiefly in the Stile of Chamber-Musick."

7 Johann Gottlob Krüger (1715–59) became a doctor of medicine in 1742 and from 1751 pursued a career as professor of medicine and philosophy at Helmstadt. The largest and best known work of this prolific writer is *Naturlehre* (Halle, 1740–49).

8 Denis Dodart (1634–1707) was a doctor of practical (experimental) medicine and physician ordinary to Louis XIV, as well as a member of the

Académie des Sciences in Paris from the year 1673 and a writer on vocal science.

9 Antoine Ferrein (1693–1769) is responsible for making the first acoustical experiments on the natural larynx and advancing the knowledge of the human voice more than had any researcher up to his time. See Julianne C. Baird, "Commentary on Agricola's *Anleitung zur Singkunst*" (Ph.D. diss., Stanford University, 1991), pt. 2, pp. 30–32.

10 Johann Joachim Quantz (1697–1773), German flutist, composer, and author of a classic treatise on flute playing, which is mentioned variously throughout the present work. Agricola uses the variant "Quanz."

11 Carl Philipp Emanuel Bach (1714–88), German keyboardist, composer, and author of a classic treatise on keyboard playing, which is later referred to in the present work.

12 The present translation observes and reproduces Agricola's differentiation in type size.

13 Georg Heinrich Bümmler (also Bümler, or Bimmler), German singer, keyboard player and composer. He sang alto in the chapel at Ansbach and in 1717 was named Capellmeister there. He was noted for the beauty of his voice, his manner of singing and acting, and his religious compositions. He also studied mathematics and optics, publishing a treatise on telescopes (*Ferngläser*) and sundials. See Ernst Ludwig Gerber, *Historisch-Biographisches Lexikon der Tonkünstler* (2 vols., Leipzig, 1790–92), ed. Othmar Wessely (Graz: Akademische Druck- und Verlagsanstalt, 1966), vol. I; and Johann Mattheson, *Mithridat wider den Gift einer Welschen Satyr* (Hamburg, 1749), p. 47.

14 Gottfried Grünewald (1675–1739), German composer, bass singer and pantaleonist (the pantaleon is a large dulcimer). He first came to attention in Hamburg, where in 1706 his opera Germanicus was performed with Grünewald singing the title role. He later was employed as vice-Capellmeister in Darmstadt. All or most of his compositions have been lost. See *MGG*, vol. V, and *New Grove*, vol. VII.

15 Johann Gottfried Riemschneider (fl. 1720–40), German baritone and composer, employed by Handel as the lowest paid member of his London troupe in 1729. His voice was described by Rolli as "more of a natural contralto than a bass. He sings sweetly in his nose and throat, pronounces Italian in the Teutonic manner, acts like a sucking pig, and looks more like a valet than anything." See *New Grove*. vol. XVI, p. 6.

16 Conrad Friedrich Hürlebusch (*ca.* 1696–1765), German harpsichord virtuoso, theorist, and composer of organ music and operas (mostly lost). He was associated with musical affairs in various cities in Germany and Austria (especially Hamburg and Vienna), in Sweden, and in Italy. He was an organist in Amsterdam (1743–65). His *150 Psalmen Davids* seem to have been in wide use in the Reformed Church, according to *New Grove*, vol. VIII.

17 Anton Raaff (1714–97), German tenor (in fact, the principal tenor in

Naples and Florence for a decade), and a student of Bernacchi. Schubart praised his extensive range, but Mozart found his range narrow and his technique limited. (Nevertheless, in return for a favor, Mozart composed the title role of Idomeneo for the sixty-seven-year-old tenor.) Michael Kelly, Reminiscences of Michael Kelly (2 vols., London, 1826; rpt. New York: Da Capo Press, 1968), vol. I, p. 278, regards "Raff" as "by far the greatest singer of his day," and reports that he retained much of his ability past the age of seventy. He is considered "one of the last and greatest representatives of the legato technique and *portamento* brought to perfection by Bernacchi and his school." See *New Grove*, vol. XV, and Häbock, *Kastraten*, pp. 364–65.

18 Kayserinn (Madame Kayser, or perhaps Keiser) is a shadowy figure almost unknown in music literature. Perhaps she is that Elisabeth Kayser mentioned by John Sainsbury, as a singer "not less celebrated for her beauty and fecundity, than for her talents as a singer. At the age of fifteen, she sang with great success at the opera, in Dresden. She afterwards was married to a tenor singer of the same theatre, and became the mother of twenty-three children, having, four times, twins. From Dresden she went to Stockholm, where her charms were still such as to captivate Frederick, King of Sweden, whose mistress she became, and by whom she had her twenty-fourth child. It was to Madame Kayser that the king owed the preservation of his life, in the fire at the Opera-house in Stockholm. Already was the machinery at the end of the stage in flames, without the audience knowing of it, when Madame Kayser, observing the fire to spread, had sufficient presence of mind to approach the royal box without interrupting her singing and action. At first she made signs to the king, who did not understand her; she then, seizing a favourable moment, said to him in a low voice, 'Leave the theatre, sire, it is on fire.' The King instantly quitted the house; when, after giving him time to escape the crowd, she vociferated *fire!* and gaining her box, threw herself and royal son, who was then about four years old, out of a window, which not being very high from the ground, she escaped without injury." See Sainsbury, ed., *A Dictionary of Musicians from the Earliest Times* (London, 1825; rpt., New York: Da Capo Press, 1966), vol. II, pp. 4–5. F. J. Fétis, *Biographie universelle des musiciens*, 2nd edn. (Paris, 1875), vol IV, "Kaiser (Elisabeth)," adds that her husband's name was Charles, a "tenor d'un mediocre talent," with whom she produced twenty-three children, and that her twenty-fourth child by Frederick was named Hesenstein.

19 Giambattista Mancini tells us that the Viennese-born Teresa de Reüther [later Holzhauser] (fl. 1728–40) was a chamber virtuoso (*virtuosa da camera*) at the Imperial court of Austria in Vienna and "a singer celebrated for her agility, her sostenuto, and her expressiveness – a vivacity [in singing] to which she joined her excellent talents as an actress" (my translation). See *Riflessioni pratiche sul canto figurato*, 3rd rev., enlarged edn. (Milan, 1777; rpt., Bologna: Forni Editore, 1970), p. 37, and Margarete Högg, *Die*

Gesangskunst der Faustina Hasse und das Sängerinnenwesen ihrer Zeit in Deutschland (Berlin, 1931), p. 53.

20 Johanna Elisabeth Döbricht Hesse (*ca.* 1690–1774), from the province of Braunschweig, was an excellent and celebrated singer, about whose youth information is sketchy. The daughter of a musician from Altenburg, she was one of several musically gifted siblings. She held a position in the Hamburg Opera and was employed in 1709 in the Leipzig opera theater together with her sister, the renowned Simonetti (see below) and her brother Ludwig. After a guest engagement in Darmstadt in 1711, she married Ernst Christian Hesse. She soon triumphed over her rivals, and with every concert tour her reputation increased, so that she was in league with such famous Italian singers as Tesi and Durastanti. Telemann noted that "although she was indeed a German, she was almost equally appreciated by everyone." See *MGG*, vol. VI, "Hesse, Ernst Christian," esp. col. 318.

21 Simonettin (usually Simonetti) was a famous singer and apparently the wife or sister (probably the wife) of a famous violinist by the same name, who was concertmaster in the Ducal Chapel of Braunschweig about 1730. During the same time Simonettin was active in the Duke of Braunschweig's opera theater during Graun's directorship. Graun considered her the best singer of her day in that theater. She was the sister of Johanna Elisabeth Hesse (see above). See Gustav Schilling, *Encyclopädie der gesammten musikalischen Wissenschaften, oder Universal-Lexikon der Tonkunst* (Stuttgart, 1838), vol. VI, "Simonetti" (2); and Högg, *Gesangskunst*, p. 56.

22 Marianne Pirker (née von Geyerseck) (1717–82) was born in Eschenau, near Heilbronn, Germany. In 1737, she married the Austrian violinist Franz Joseph Karl Pirker. She sang in Italy (1744–47) and London (1747). She was in Mingotti's troupe in Hamburg and Copenhagen (1748–50) and in Stuttgart (1750). She was imprisoned between 1756 and 1764 because she remained loyal to the Duchess of Württemberg, who at that time was separated from her husband. After her release, she lived in Heilbronn where she was a teacher of singing (1765). Burney includes Pirker in the 1746 London opera season, describing her as a "German woman of small abilities" – but adds in the next paragraph that "*Se spuntan vezzose*, sung by Pirker ... pleased much." See *General History*, vol. II, p. 846; and Riemann, *Musik-Lexicon* (Mainz: B. Schott's, 1961). Compare Högg, *Gesangskunst*, pp. 51–52, and see also pp. 25 and 34.

23 These two Capellmeisters are without doubt Carl Heinrich Graun (1704–55) and Johann Adolph Hasse (1699–1783). Both were German tenors and composers. The former served in the role of Royal Capellmeister for the court of Frederick II and as composer of operas. The latter was regarded as the best opera composer in Europe during his lifetime.

Introduction of the author

1 The use of numbered paragraphs enables the reader to make comparisons with Galliard, which contains certain inaccuracies and, of course, rather archaic language. Tosi's and Agricola's chapters themselves are unnumbered.

2 Palestina, an alternative spelling of Palestrina, is given in both Tosi and Agricola. The fact that this composer is so venerated by Tosi is a further witness to his musical conservatism.

3 Zarlino (1517–90) is the only source which Tosi mentions having consulted before writing his *Opinioni*. The relevant passage follows: "Matters for the singer to observe are these: First of all he must aim diligently to perform what the composer has written. He must not be like those who, wishing to be thought worthier and wiser than their colleagues, indulge in certain divisions (*diminutioni*) that are so savage and so inappropriate that they not only annoy the hearer but are ridden with thousands of errors, such as many dissonances, consecutive unisons, octaves, fifths, and other similar progressions absolutely intolerable in composition. Then there are singers who substitute higher or lower tones for those intended by the composer, singing for instance, a whole tone instead of a semitone, or vice versa, leading to countless errors as well as offense to the ear. Singers should aim to render faithfully what is written to express the composer's intent, intoning the correct steps in the right places. They should seek to adjust to the consonances and to sing in accord with the nature of the words of the composition; happy words will be sung happily and at a lively pace whereas sad texts call for the opposite. Above all, in order that the words may be understood, they should take care not to fall into the common error of changing the vowel sounds, singing *a* in place of *e*, *i* in place of *o*, or *u* in place of one of these; they should form each vowel in accord with its true pronunciation. It is truly reprehensible and shameful for certain oafs in choirs and public chapels as well as in private chambers to corrupt the words when they should be rendering them clearly, easily, and accurately. For example, of we hear singers shrieking certain songs – I cannot call it singing – with such crude tones and grotesque gestures that they appear to be apes, pronouncing the words 'Aspro core, e selvaggio e cruda voglia,' so that we hear 'Aspra cara, e salvaggia e croda vaglia,' are we not compelled to laugh? Or more truthfully who would not become enraged upon hearing such horrible, ugly counterfeits?

A singer should also not force the voice into a raucous, bestial tone. He should strive to moderate his tone and blend it with the other singers' so that no voice is heard above the others. Such pushed singing produces more noise than harmony. For harmony results only when many things are tempered so that no one exceeds the other. The singer should know too that in church and in public chapels he should sing with full voice, moderated of course as I have just said, while in private chambers he should use a subdued and sweet voice and avoid clamor. Singers in such places should use good taste, so as not to leave themselves open to rightful censure. Further, they should refrain from bodily movements and gestures that will incite the audience to laughter as some do who move – and this is also true of certain instrumentalists – as if they were dancing.

But to leave these matters, I shall conclude by saying that if the composer and singer observe those things that pertain to their respective offices, there is no doubt that every composition will be sweet, soft, and harmonious, and the listeners will be pleased and grateful." See Gioseffo Zarlino, *Le Istituzioni harmoniche* (Venice, 1558), translated by Guy A. Marco and Claude V. Palisca, under the title *The Art of Counterpoint* (New Haven: Yale University Press, 1968; rpt. New York: W. W. Norton, 1976), ch. 45, pp. 110–11.

4 A fairly literal translation of the Spanish proverb is "accusations return to the accuser." Tosi's version is *che le satire tornano a casa*, which Galliard translates as "Calumny recoils back on the Author."

1 Observations for the use of the singing teacher

1 Agricola renders the title of Tosi's first chapter, "Osservazioni per chi insegna ad un Soprano" (Observations for teaching a soprano), as the more general "Anmerkungen zum Gebrauche des Sangmeisters" (Observations for the use of the singing teacher). A note by Galliard (p. 10) would explain this: "The Author directs this for the Instruction of a *Soprano*, or a treble Voice, because Youth possesses that Voice mostly, and that is the Age when they should begin to study Musick."

2 Tosi's term *mediocre* is translated by Agricola as *mittelmässig* (average, indifferent, mediocre, fair, tolerable). When it is clear from his context that Tosi uses the word pejoratively, the present translator renders the term as "mediocre"; when the context suggests average or tolerable competence (as opposed to the brilliance of a virtuoso), the term "competent" is used.

3 The phrase *reine Harmonie* literally means "pure harmony."

4 Galliard, p. 13, provides Virgil's verses, introduced thus: "Hos ego Versiculos feci, tulit alter Honores" (These verses I made, but another has taken the applause of them):

> *Sic vos non vobis nidificatis aves.*
> *Sic vos non vobis vellera fertis oves.*
> *Sic vos non vobis mellificatis apes.*
> *Sic vos non vobis fertis aratra boves.*

> (So ye Birds build not your Nests
>   For yourselves.
> So ye Sheep bear not your Wool
>   For yourselves.

> So ye Bees make not your Honey
> For yourselves.
> So ye Oxen submit to the Plow
> Not for yourselves.)

Virgil's verses were occasioned by an incident in which a certain poetaster Bathyllus took credit for a distich in praise of Augustus written anonymously by Virgil, who by these verses put the imposter to public disgrace (Galliard, pp. 12–13). The context makes it clear that Tosi's concern is that the teacher gets some appropriate award, if not psychological, at least monetary, for his dedication and difficult work.

5 The Italian proverb, "Rincresce a chi ha sete di portar il vino agli altri, e non poter bere" (*Opinioni*, p. 8) is translated literally as follows: "One's thirst is increased, when, unable to drink himself, he must serve wine to others."

6 In certain parts of Italy it was common practice for a successful singer to give his voice teacher a percentage of his earnings from the stage. In his satire of opera, *Il Teatro alla Moda* (Venice, c. 1720), Benedetto Marcello writes: "He [the music teacher] should, out of pure generosity, give free lessons to poor boys and girls–but of course he will have it in writing that he is to receive a mere two-thirds of their pay from the first twenty-four performances, one-half from the next twenty-four and one-third for the rest of their lives. The English translation is that of Reinhard G. Pauly, "Il Teatro alla Moda," pt. 1, *Musical Quarterly* 34/3 (1948), pp. 393–403; pt. 2, 35/1 (1949), pp. 85–105. The passage above is found in pt. 2, p. 103.

7 Galliard defines the golden age of the "ancients" to which Tosi (and here Agricola) refer: "By the *Ancient*, our Author means those who liv'd about thirty or forty years ago; and by the *Modern* the late and present Singers" (title page verso). By "ancients" he is thus referring to singers whose careers were flourishing around 1700–10. Agricola clarifies this elsewhere (in his advertisement of the publication of his *Anleitung*) in *Beyträge*, vol. I, p. 328: "He [Tosi] lived at the time in which Italy was more fruitful with regard to good singers and well trained composers than nowadays – namely at the end of the previous and into the first thirty years of the present century" (my translation).

8 In other words, a pretty face is insufficient to insure a successful career, but it might be useful in other ways. For further information on the social position of eighteenth-century female singers, see Marcello's opinions in *Il Teatro alla Moda* (Pauly trans., pt. 1), and Högg, *Gesangskunst*, pp. 28–38.

9 This seems to be a veiled reference to the castration of young boys to preserve the high voice.

10 As Tosi indicates, soprano singers of this time were accustomed to singing in C clefs. The difficulty in distinguishing the "**mi** from the **fa**" simply refers to the location of the half steps, which (in the same key) are different in each of the clefs.

11 This is a reference to the need for the student to also understand *musica ficta*, described by Galliard, p. 17, as *"Alla Capella* Church-Musick, where the Flats and Sharps are not mark'd." Agricola finds Tosi highly conservative in his support of the Guidonian system, but in the *Anleitung* he faithfully elucidates it and the rather complicated method of mutation involved.

12 The seven French names are do, re, mi, fa, sol, la, si. The French system with seven instead of six names simplifies solmization for the tonal system since each name of the scale is assigned to only one pitch, thereby saving the student the trouble of learning to mutate between hexachords. Despite its obvious drawbacks, the hexachord system, which required mutation, was still in use in Italy in the late eighteenth century in vocal pedagogy.

13 In German terminology B is B♭ and H is B♮.

14 Johann Mattheson, *Das Neu-eröffnete Orchestre* (Hamburg, 1713).

15 Johann Mattheson, "Die Orchester-Kanzeley," *Critica Musica* 2/7 (Hamburg, 1724–25), p. 185. Not all musicians and theorists were in agreement, and not all accepted Mattheson immediately. Fux, for example, felt that Mattheson's ridicule of Guido was "atrocious" and that Mattheson failed to appreciate properly Guido's contributions to music. For Fux's defense of Guido with translation, see Beekman C. Cannon, *Johann Mattheson: Spectator in Music.* Yale Studies in the History of Music, vol. I (New Haven: Yale University Press, 1947; Hamden, Conn.: Archon Books, 1968), pp. 139–40.

16 After the 1713 appearance of *Das Neu-eröffnete Orchestre,* in which Mattheson championed a new style of secular music together with a new pedagogy, a debate on the matter raged in Germany, so that several other solmization systems designed to replace the antiquated Guidonian format had been proposed by the time of Agricola's *Anleitung* (1757). However, Johann Heinrich Buttstedt, among others, defended the traditional Guidonian method of solmization and teaching in his book *Ut, re, mi, fa, sol, la, tota Musica et Harmonia Aeterna* (Erfurt, 1716), from which Agricola adopts his explanation of the modes. Agricola dutifully explains the complicated Guidonian system and its history even though he was determined to bring vocal pedagogy and the science of vocal physiology up to date in his own time.

17 Agricola refers to him here as Guido Aretinus and thereafter as Aretinus.

18 Agricola's expression is *die gebräuchlichen Töne* (lit., the customary tones).

19 St. John the Baptist was considered a patron saint of music along with St. Cecilia.

20 Translation: "So that thy servants may freely sing forth the wonders of thy deeds, remove all stain of guilt from their unclean lips, O Saint John."

21 Otto Gibelius, *Kurtzer, jedoch gründlicher Bericht von den Vocibus musicalibus* (Bremen, 1659) is excerpted by Lorenz Mizler von Kolof, *Neu eröffnete musikalische Bibliothek* (4 vols., Leipzig, 1739–54), vol. I, pt. 3, pp. 1–79.

22 Agricola's chart has been faithfully reproduced. But the modern reader should note the German usage of B for B♭ and H for B♮, as well as the Greek gamma for G.

23 The citation is Mattheson, "Orchester-Kanzeley," p. 186.
24 Agricola's note (g) on terminology indicates that both the terms "solfeging" and "solmizing" were employed.
25 "Guidonian" is the recognized English equivalent of Agricola's *aretinisch.*
26 *Modulata Pallas* (Milan, 1599).
27 Daniel Hitzler, *Extract aus der neuen Musica oder Singkunst* (Nuremberg, 1623).
28 Marin Mersenne, *Harmonie Universelle* (Paris, 1636–37).
29 Seth Calvisius, *Compendium Musicae* (Leipzig, 1594).
30 In the term *Pontacgläser,* Agricola indicates that the wine is Pontac, a white Burgundy.
31 In this discussion of the distinction between the major and the minor semitone, Tosi is clearly referring to mean-tone temperament, in which the D$\sharp$ is considerably lower in pitch than E$\flat$.
32 Georg Philipp Telemann, "Neues musikalisches System" in Mizler, *Neu eröffnete musikalische Bibliothek,* vol. III, pt. 4 (1752), pp. 713–19. Marpurg, *Beyträge,* vol. I, pt. 2, p. 150, says in his biographical sketch of Agricola that Telemann's and Handel's works had long been a pleasant preoccupation of Agricola's. Telemann was so enthusiastic about the *Anleitung* that he made advance payment to Agricola for thirty copies.
33 Georg Andreas Sorge's work was published in Lobenstein in 1749.
34 Agricola thus identifies a secondary function of this ornament as a sight-singing aid used by Italian singers to find the notes of a leap. One of the first theorists to describe this ornament is Giovanni Battista Bovicelli, *Regole, passaggi di musica* (Venice, 1594; rpt. Kassel and Basel: Bärenreiter, 1957), p. 11: "beginning from the third or fourth below the main note depending on the harmony of the other parts" (my translation). Christoph Bernhard in "Von der Singekunst oder Manier" (*ca.* 1649), in *Die Kompositionslehre Heinrich Schützens in der Fassung seines Schülers Christoph Bernhard,* ed. Joseph Maria Müller-Blattau (Kassel: Bärenreiter, 1963), p. 35, specifies that it is the "note directly below the initial note" employed either at the beginning or during the course of a phrase and performed in a gliding manner very imperceptibly to the initial note. Johann Adam Hiller, *Anweisung zum musikalisch-zierlichen Gesange* (Leipzig, 1780), pp. 49–55, advocates the *cercar della nota* except when excessively used, although he does not mention its portamento-like "gliding" or indistinct quality. Besides its function as an ornament, the *cercar della nota* is also a vocal technique used in the twentieth century to enable the singer to reach a high note more easily.
35 Tosi's word is *solfeggi.* Many famous composers and teachers of singing were composers of their own *solfeggi,* among whom may be numbered Mozart, Leo, and Porpora.
36 For Tosi and most Italians there were only two registers: the natural (or chest) and the head (or falsetto).
37 This claim may seem exaggerated, but the sad fate of the castrato Luca Fabbris tells us otherwise. Fabbris died on stage in 1765, attempting to perform notes that were overly high, written for him by the composer

Guglielmi. See Angus Heriot, *The Castrati in Opera* (London, 1956; rpt., New York: Da Capo Press, 1975), pp. 47–48.

38 Tosi is referring to the soprano C-clef, thus c″ and d″.

39 Agricola discusses these as three classifications of vocal registers, whereas Tosi and most of the Italians recognized two: "head" (or falsetto) and "chest" (or natural) voices.

40 Actually, air moves in a spherical rather than in a circular motion.

41 The German words *stark* (strong) and *schwach* (weak) are used consistently by Agricola to refer to loud and soft.

42 Kurt Wichmann, *Anleitung zur Singkunst: Einführung und Kommentar* (Leipzig: VEB Deutscher Verlag für Musik, 1966), p. 26, notes that Agricola's essay on sound is physiologically correct. In this section the small numbers refer to Agricola's numbered comments directly above.

43 Agricola uses *Linien* (lines) to mean the tenth part of an inch. In this translation his measurements will be given in inches or parts of inches.

44 Interspersed among Agricola's many accurate observations, which largely have their basis in empirical observation, are many outmoded scientific ideas derived from the writings of Galen, Krüger, and Dodart. For a review of the sources on vocal physiology before and during Agricola's time, see Philip A. Duey, *Bel Canto in its Golden Age* (New York, 1951; rpt., New York: Da Capo Press, 1980), pp. 13–18 and 126–38.

45 The gland referred to here is actually a series of mucus-producing glands contained in the appendix of the laryngeal ventricle.

46 The nineteenth-and twentieth-century term for this voice range is "mezzo soprano."

47 Farinelli, or Carlo Broschi (1705–82), was perhaps the most famous of the castrati. A student of Porpora, he was praised for the width of his range, the beauty of his sound, and his technical prowess, especially his extraordinary breath control and agility. See Haböck *Kastraten*, p. 386 and Heriot *Castrati*, pp. 95–110, *et passim*.

48 Possibly Madame Mara (née Mademoiselle Gertrud Elisabeth Schmeling), a German soprano who was well-known in Leipzig and Berlin for her exceptional range. Charles Burney marveled over this aspect of her singing on his trip through the Berlin court. In *Present State*, vol. II, p. 109, Burney gives her range as "G to E in *altissimo*" [g to e‴].

49 Caspar Förster the Younger (1616–73) was a German composer, bass singer, and choir director. He served as Hofcapellmeister in Copenhagen (1655–57) and took over his father's job at the Marienkirche in Danzig. After 1661 he was active in Hamburg. In his *Grundlage einer Ehren-Pforte* (Hamburg, 1740), p. 21, Mattheson writes: "Förster played continuo and sang bass at the same time. In the hall his voice was like hearing a quiet, pleasant sub-bass. Outside of the hall, however, it sounded like a trombone. He sang from a′ to Contra A three octaves lower" (my translation).

50 Antonio Montagnana was a bass singer in Handel's London opera company (1731–33 and 1737–38) and in the Opera of the Nobility (1733–37).

Burney, *General History*, vol. II, p. 773, describes his voice as displaying "depth, power, mellowness, and peculiar accuracy of intonation in hitting distant intervals." Among the Handel roles that he created is Polyphemus in the masque *Acis and Galatea*. The Handel cantata *Nell'Africane selve*, written for him, has a range of C to a′.

51   d. 1760. He was a first-rate Italian soprano castrato who performed alongside the famous Farinelli in the theater of Madrid. In 1742 he went to St. Petersburg, where he was highly respected. When he departed from that city in 1755, he received from the Queen the sum of about 1000 ducats as well as a golden box. See Schilling, *Encyclopädie*, vol. VI.

52   There are many exceptions to this, as Wichmann, *Anleitung*, points out (p. 27).

53   Agricola is referring to the Italian language, which was and continues to be regarded as the best language for singing, because of the purity of vowels and the absence of guttural consonant combinations. For ease of singing, eighteenth-century librettists avoided all but *a* and *o* for the divisions. The closest approximation in the English language to the Italian *a* of *casa* occurs in the first vowel of the diphthong of a word such as "mine" (the *a* in "father" being too dark). Basic Italian has two sounds for the letter *o*, as in *voce* and *oggi*.

54   The passage is quite complicated in the original German: "Denn es ist der Luft, in Ansehung der Geschwindigkeit, gleichgültig, ob sich mehr Luft an die so viel erweitere **Glottis**, als zum Durchgange dieser Menge Luft, mit eben der Geschwindigkeit, als zuvor, bey dem Uebergange vom Schwachen zum Starken, nötig ist, stellet; oder ob sich die **Glottis** eben so viel enger machet, als zu Erhaltung eben desselben Grades der Geschwindigkeit, bey einer kleinen Menge Luft, und dem Uebergange vom Starken zum Schwachen, nöthig ist" (*Anleitung*, p. 31). Agricola has provided a detailed explanation of the fact that the tone undergoing a crescendo or decrescendo remains the same pitch because the speed of vibration, which determines the pitch, stays the same. This passage has been rendered rather freely.

55   The following information is provided by Quantz, "Lebenslauf," p. 218, as translated by Burney, *Present State*, vol. II, p. 180. "*Gaetano Orsini* was one of the greatest singers that ever existed; he had a powerful, even, affecting *contralto* voice, of a considerable compass; his shake was perfect, and his *portamento*, excellent. In *allegros* he articulated divisions, particularly in triplets, most admirably, and always from the breast. In *adagios*, he was so perfect a master of every thing which pleases and affects, that he took entire possession of the hearts of all that heard him; he was many years in the imperial service, and though he lived to an advanced age, he preserved his fine voice to the last."

56   Giovanni Carestini (*ca.* 1705 – *ca.* 1760), an Italian alto castrato, was one of Handel's star castrati in London for two seasons (1733–35), creating principal male roles in *Ariodante, Ottone, Parnasso in Festa*, and many other

operas. In the very early stages of his career, Carestini was a soprano with the range b to c‴, according to Quantz, "Lebenslauf," pp. 234–35. A survey of the roles composed for him by Handel reveals the lowering of his range – a to a″ – and an examination of Hasse's *Demofoonte* (1748) reveals his range as e♭ to g″. This evidence supports Quantz's statement that "little by little, his strong and full soprano voice changed into the strongest, deepest and most beautiful contralto" (my translation). On his life and career, see Haböck, *Kastraten*, pp. 358–59.

57 From Latin *fistula* (reed pipe), referring perhaps to the reedy sound of some falsettos.

58 *Gesichte,* perhaps a metonym for "head."

59 See Sergio Panconcelli-Calzia, *Die Phonetik des Aristoteles* (Hamburg, 1942) for Aristotle's theories concerning the formation of sound, particularly the social aspects of speech.

60 Galen (*ca.* 130 – *ca.* 200) was a Greek physician and founder of experimental physiology.

61 As late as 1706 we find Dodart presenting a monograph based on the erroneous theories of Galen about the human voice.

62 Georg Heuermann (1722–68) was born in Oldesloe in Holstein. He studied at the University of Copenhagen and dedicated his life's work to surgery. His published dissertation, *De lingua humana* (Copenhagen, 1749) earned him his doctorate. His major publication is his *Physiologie* (Copenhagen and Leipzig, 1751–55). In this latter work, see especially pt. 2, ch. 18, which deals with the larynx, voice, and related matters. The anatomical drawings at the end of this chapter in the section, "Erklärung derer Figuren," present surprisingly detailed and accurate representations of the larynx.

63 Mattheson, *Der Volkommene Capellmeister* (Hamburg, 1739), pt. 2, pp. 98–99: "An exception may be made with regard to breath support while in a sitting position. One can save breath by sitting straight and supporting the arms and by not leaning back too comfortably. Because the body is at rest it wastes less movement in sitting than standing. As a result a tone can be sustained for a much longer period of time. However, the arms must be supported with the hands and not the elbows, much as a coachman sits on the carriage box. This has been tried with success" (my translation).

64 Joseph Sauveur, "Sur la determination d'un son fixe," *Histoire de l'Académie Royale des Sciences, Anneé 1700* (Paris: Imprimerie Royalle, 1703), pp. 131–40.

65 In the following passage, Tosi, *Opinioni,* p. 52, gives this pedagogical method the name *fermar la voce:* "Non tralasci di tempo in tempo di mettere, e di fermar la voce, affinchè sia sempre disposta per servirsene in tutte due le forme" (He should not fail from time to time to practice the steadying of the voice and the *messa di voce* [lit., di mettere...la voce] so that the voice always remains adaptable to the one and to the other [my translation]). He thus specifies two types of sustaining of the voice. The

function of the *fermar* is to steady the voice on a long sustained note without crescendo and make it capable of singing sustained tones evenly and without vibrato; whereas, performance of the *messa di voce* entails a crescendo–decrescendo and often the introduction of vibrato at the highest point of the crescendo.

66 Agricola's term is *Herausziehen der Stimme* (drawing out of the voice). The Italian term *messa di voce* is familiar to the twentieth-century singer and has therefore been retained in this translation.

67 Agricola's term is *Aushaltung*. In the course of the *Anleitung* he uses a number of different terms to translate Tosi's term *messa di voce*. Tosi's passage is difficult to render with the proper clarity and emphasis. See Galliard, p. 28, and Agricola, p. 48 (Baird, p. 84).

68 This is an example of Tosi's pointed sarcasm directed at the moderns. Since classical times the nightingale has been recognized for its beautiful singing, eminently worthy of imitation by humans.

69 London, 1753.

70 Here Agricola's term for *messa di voce* is *Aushaltung* (sustaining).

71 Tosi, para. 33, and Agricola are referring to the *portamento*. Eighteenth-century Italian voice teachers felt the *portamento* was to be developed only after the basics of reading music were mastered, defects in singing (such as singing through the nose or in the throat) had been eliminated, and the blending of the registers was achieved.

2 Concerning appoggiaturas

1 The term *Vorschlag* (lit., forebeat) is used by Agricola and other eighteenth-century German writers (such as Quantz, C. P. E. Bach, and Leopold Mozart), but not by all (Marpurg and Mattheson use *accent*). The term does not imply any rhythmic anticipation of the main note, but rather is simply descriptive of the ornament's location *before* the main note; and for this reason the slide *(Schleifer)* and compound appoggiatura *(Anschlag)* are included in this chapter. Frederick Neumann, *Ornamentation in Baroque and Post-Baroque Music* (Princeton University Press, 1978), p. 591, defines the *Vorschlag* as "a generic term for a single ornamental note that belongs either exclusively or predominantly to the following parent note."

2 Agricola does not observe Tosi's paragraph divisions (which are maintained here), in that he combines paragraphs three through five and paragraphs six through ten.

3 See Agricola's note (d) below (p. 56 [Baird, p. 90]) and Galliard's explanation as given in n. 4 below.

4 Galliard, pp. 32–33, n. 2, explains: "A *Semitone Major* changes Name, Line, and Space: A *Semitone Minor* changes neither…To a *Semitone Major* one can go with a Rise or a Fall distinctly; to a *Semitone Minor* one cannot." In mean-tone temperament, which was widely used in the eighteenth century, B♭ is distinctly sharper that A♯. To simplify Tosi's rule, therefore,

A♯ to B is possible whereas B♭ to B is not.

5 Galliard, p. 191, plate 3, provides additional musical examples of deceptive leaps that do not permit an appoggiatura.

6 A *messa di voce crescente* is simply a long sustained note with a crescendo–decrescendo that rises imperceptibly in pitch. While there are many instances of it in the madrigals of Claudio Monteverdi and Sigismondo d'India, one of the clearest examples occurs in Michel Pignolet de Montéclair's cantata *Pan et Sirinx*, Archivum Musicum: La cantata barocca, no. 9 (Florence: Studio per Edizioni Scelte, 1981), pp. 33–52.

7 Tosi, p. 23, uses the expression *Virtuosi alla Moda*.

8 Frederick forbade his singers to introduce improvised ornamentation. Composers thus wrote out more for the performer.

9 See Introduction, p. 28 above, on Mara, who wrote out the ornaments for arias ahead of time.

10 Most German and even many of the Italian composers were already indicating the appoggiatura by the mid eighteenth century. Agricola concurs with C. P. E. Bach (and not with Quantz) in favoring the systematic indication of exact note values for the appoggiatura.

11 In contrast to the earlier practices of Tosi, the Berlin writers tended to regularize the performance of appoggiaturas, both by making them on the beat and by indicating their exact rhythmic value. A few instances of on-the-beat performance, however, were allowed (by Quantz, for example), such as between falling thirds.

12 Agricola's rule referring to on-beat appoggiatura performance must be understood by reference to the earlier Baroque term, "anticipatione della syllaba," which referred to a situation in which an appoggiatura (or a one-note grace similar to it) preceded the beat and bore the syllable.

13 See Carl Philipp Emanuel Bach, *Versuch über die wahre Art das Clavier zu spielen* (Berlin, 1752), trans. and ed. William J. Mitchell (New York: Norton, 1949), pp. 87–99.

14 In most instances, the reader may substitute the word "long" for variable and "short" for invariable.

15 Flattery is one of the Affects or passions. It refers to that which charms, cajoles, or beguiles the senses. Quantz describes the musical attributes of a flattering style: "Flattery is expressed with slurred notes, that ascend or descend by step, and also with syncopated notes, in which the first half of the note must be sounded softly, and the second reinforced by chest and lip action." See *Versuch einer Anweisung die Flöte traversière zu spielen* (Berlin, 1752), trans. and ed. Edward R. Reilly (New York: Macmillan, 1966), p. 134.

16 In this translation *Affekt* (emotional state) is rendered as "Affect," a noun used in modern psychology to mean "an emotion, feeling, or mood" (*Webster's New World Dictionary*). The capitalized form has been retained. The five Affects (or passions) to which the Berlin writers frequently refer

are flattery, boldness, gaiety, majesty, and melancholy.

17 The final bass note of the following example (last section) has been altered to match the previous example over the word *cader*.

18 Cf. Quantz, *Versuch* (Reilly trans.), pp. 93–94, 159–60. Here Agricola is apparently referring to ideas of his teacher and mentor.

19 Agricola is referring to Bach, *Versuch*. See Mitchell trans., p. 98.

20 See also Quantz, *Versuch* (Reilly trans.), p. 82, for another example of this feature.

21 The first two notes in the treble clef of the second of the following examples have been made an anacrusis. The print is flawed on this point.

22 Agricola's term is *gute Tacttheile*, by which he is referring to the accented and unaccented parts of a measure, For example, in 4/4 time, the first and third beats are strong or accented; and the second and fourth beats are unaccented, weak, or passing *(schlimm* or *durchgehend)*. The concept of *quantitas intrinsica* is implied in Agricola's terminology. *Quantitas intrinsica*, as explained by Wolfgang Caspar Printz, *Phrynis Mytilenaeus oder Satyrischer Componist* (Quedlinburg, 1676–77), is "The apparent different length of notes that are equal according to their time or value." The translation is by George Houle in his *Meter in Music, 1600–1800: Performance, Perception, and Notation* (Bloomington and Indianapolis: Indiana University Press, 1987), p. 81.

23 Agricola's term is *Tactglied*. See n. 24 below.

24 The terminology here seems to have been coined by Agricola. His term *Tacttheil*, here translated as "pulse," represents the primary subdivision of the measure, below which is the secondary subdivision or *Tactglied*. Thus in 4/4 time the *Tacttheil* is two half notes, and the *Tactglied* is a quarter note. *Anschlagend* (strong) designates the first and the third; and *durchgehend* (passing), the second and the fourth. The same classification extends to all the smaller subdivisions as well.

25 The *Anschlag* (compound appoggiatura) consists of two ornamental notes that straddle the main note – most commonly, first the lower note, followed by the upper neighbor, and ending with the main note. Friedrich Wilhelm Marpurg, *Anleitung zum Clavierspielen* (Berlin, 1755; facs. rpt. New York: Broude Brothers, 1966), calls this ornament by the name *Doppelvorschlag*. Agricola adopts the term *Anschlag* used in Bach, *Versuch*.

26 Agricola's term *Nachschlag* can have two meanings: it refers either to a single ornamental note that is connected directly to the main note that precedes it, or to a two-note termination.

27 Agricola's term *Überwurf* (overthrow) refers to an ascending termination.

28 *Rückfall* (backfall) refers to a descending termination that goes either to the pitch of the note that follows it, or to the step above that pitch to soften the sharpness of the large descending leap.

29 Agricola's discussion of this matter shows his unique understanding of it. The second type of slide is clearly not a slide of the Lombard type. Daniel Gottlob Türk, *Klavierschule, oder Anweisung zum Klavierspielen für Lehrer und*

Lernende (Leipzig and Halle, 1789), trans. Raymond H. Haggh (Lincoln and London: University of Nebraska Press, 1982), ch. 4, sec. 2, para 20 (p. 240), misunderstood Agricola. Agricola's intention was not to limit the slide that fills a leap only to the weak beat, but merely to differentiate the dynamic level between it and the slide preceding the strong beat, and is thus in keeping with Agricola's understanding of *anschlagende* and *durchgehende Tactglieder*. For more information, see Neumann, *Ornamentation*, p. 235.

30 Agricola has made a error in the bass notes of the following example under the word *mai*, which Hiller corrects in his *Anweisung* (1780), p. 59. The second note in the bass of each section of this example has been modified from a B, which was incorrect in the print.

31 In the second of the following three musical examples, the values of the first two notes in the bass have been reversed and the final dot in the soprano has been moved to match the example above.

3 Concerning trills

1 This is, of course, most evident in the improvised cadenza, where attention is focused on the singer, and where the trill serves the very necessary function of alerting the orchestra that the final ritornello is imminent.

2 Both Galliard and Agricola translate only four of Tosi's five adjectives describing the qualities of the trill. Agricola has combined Tosi's two adjectives *eguale* and *battuto* in the phrase *gleich schlagend*, not realizing that *battuto* referred to the vertical movement of the larynx, necessary to the eighteenth-century Italian trill. Galliard combines the second and third adjectives *battuto* and *granito* in the phrase "distinctly marked." See Introduction, pp. 17ff.

3 Tosi's phrase *con più padronanza* (with more forcefulness or propriety) has served as a point of departure for Neumann's argument (*Ornamentation*, p. 345) in favor of the main-note trill.

4 An inferior cadence is one from below, for example B♮ to C. See below in Agricola's note (d) for further explanation.

5 The term "discant" refers to the treble or the melodic part.

6 The manner of performance of the *Schneller* (Agricola's term for the snap) must be similar to that indicated by Bach (*Versuch*, Mitchell trans., p. 101). For keyboard instruments this was accomplished by abruptly removing the finger from the key.

7 Tosi seems to be describing a trill performed in the course of a *glissando*.

8 Galliard illustrates the ascending and descending trills incorrectly, notating them as though they were a chains of trills *(catena di trilli)*, thereby ignoring Tosi's description. Tosi's term *impercettibilmente* (imperceptibly) implies a sort of glissando effect. Agricola correctly differentiates between the two types.

9 According to Quantz, a moderate speed which was not so fast as to become

a flutter was the preferred speed for the trill (*Versuch,* Reilly trans., p. 101).

10 Thus Tosi's implication is that when one unites the slow trill with the first or second types, the former eventually is meant to achieve the speed of the trill of a half step or whole step.

11 Agricola here expands on Quantz's statement (*Versuch,* Reilly trans., p. 102) that a faster trill served better for a more lively expression.

12 Mattheson, *Capellmeister,* pt. 2, ch. 3, para. 33, describes the trill of French singers as "a rather slow trill, which sounds distinct and clean, though slightly dull" (my translation).

13 Agricola's demonstration of Tosi's double trill is confusing. In the first examples he gives, he ignores Tosi's description in order to present contemporary Berlin practice. Agricola's second series of examples under letter (k) more closely illustrate Tosi's description of notes inserted "in the middle," but they differ somewhat from Galliard's illustration of the same (Pl. IV, No. 8).

14 Here Agricola uses the German term *mordent* for Tosi's *trillo mordente* (biting trill). In note (l) he expresses the opinion that the Italians confuse the mordent proper *(eigentlich Mordent)* with the short trill *(Pralltriller).* He specifies that the mordent consists of the alternation of a note and the half step or (more rarely) whole step below.

15 Tosi's phrase is *mal a proposito* (ill-timed, out of place).

16 Agricola's term is *Bockstriller.* In Italian this defect was called *il caprino* (little goat) or *il cavallino* (little horse) by eighteenth-century vocal pedagogues.

17 Agricola is referring to the vertical movement of the larnyx in the neck, the depression and elevation of which manipulates the vocal folds and changes the pitch.

18 Bach, *Versuch* (Mitchell trans.), p. 103, like Agricola, makes the same exception and specifies that the termination and the following ascending note must be able to be heard as two separate elements, with the length being dependent on the tempo.

19 Both Agricola and C. P. E. Bach disapprove of either an anticipation or a pause as an anacrusis to the the main note. Marpurg, however, in *Des critischen Musicus an der Spree erster Band* (Berlin, 1750; collected issues of the journal *Der critische Musicus* 1749–50), designates it as the *point d'arrêt.*

20 Bach, *Versuch* (Mitchell trans.), p. 112.

21 Agricola's term *geschnellter Doppelschlag* involves a turn starting with the main note.

4 Concerning divisions

1 Tosi's title "Del Passaggio" (Concerning the passages) refers to the rapid runs or divisions that were fashioned by the composer according to the singer's capabilities to fit such divisions into the rhythmic framework of the aria, but that could be changed in the course of the da capo.

2 The drag *(das Ziehen)* is a heavily slurred chromatic glissando. This special ornament is discussed more thoroughly in ch. 10. To Germans the term *Ziehen* implied a chromatic ascent or descent (perhaps performed in a glissando fashion). J. S. Bach set the word chromatically in the *St. John Passion* (see p. 23 above). Because no good English equivalent exists, Galliard's term "drag" is retained in this translation.

3 The mezzo soprano Faustina Bordoni Hasse (see below, n. 5 and p. 278, n. 10) and the castrato soprano Farinelli (Carlo Broschi) are two famous singers known for their excellence in performing reiterations of the same tone.

4 Although this onomatopœic term does not actually appear in his Italian text, Tosi later clearly describes the effect (p. 106): "Più forte impulso però lo sforzerà a detestar l'invenzione di rider cantando, o di cantar come le galline quando han fatto l'uovo" (For even stronger reasons he will abhor the invention of laughing in a singing manner or singing in the manner of hens that have just laid an egg). See *Anleitung*, p. 226 (Baird, pp. 227–28).

5 The singer to whom Agricola refers is obviously Faustina, the wife of the celebrated composer Johann Adolph Hasse. Agricola praises her by name below *(Anleitung*, pp. 138, 229, note m [Baird, pp. 163, 230]).

6 Both Agricola and Tosi discuss the drag further in ch. 10. The drag may be distinguished from the *messa di voce crescente* (see Introduction, p. 14 above) in that the latter involves only the interval of a half step, while the drag has a more extended compass.

7 This erroneous notion is based on the principles of Galen and Leonardo Da Vinci, who held that the windpipe functions like a wind instrument, shortening and elongating to vary the pitch.

8 The vowel *i* as in English "beet" and *u* as in English "food." Some Italian writers, for example, Camillo Maffei, "Lettere" (Naples, 1562) translated in Carol McClintock, *Readings in the History of Music in Performance* (Bloomington and London: Indiana University Press, 1979), felt that the *u* vowel sounded like howling, especially since the Italian word for howling is *ululando*. See Introduction, p. 24.

9 The vowel *e* as in English "hay" and *o* as in English "go."

10 Agricola is in disagreement not only with Tosi but also with Quantz, who writes in his *Versuch*: "An *alla Siciliana* in twelve-eight time, with dotted notes interspersed, must be played very simply, not too slowly, and with almost no shakes. Since it is an imitation of a Sicilian shepherd's dance, few graces may be introduced other than some slurred semiquavers and appoggiaturas" (Reilly trans., p. 168).

11 Agricola added the adjective *rund* (round) to the description of the divisions.

12 Neumann *Ornamentation*, p. 603, calls this phenomenon "vocal intensity pulsations". Among many examples in the literature in which this phenomenon occurs may be included Handel's cantata for tenor, *Look down harmonious Saint*, and Hasse's cantata *Quel vago Seno* for flute, soprano, and continuo.

13 The soprano member of the so-called "serpent" family of instruments, made of a curved piece of wood covered in leather and played with a cupped mouthpiece.

14 See Introduction, p. 25.

15 Printz's *Musica modulatoria vocalis* (Schweidnitz, 1678), essentially a book for choirboys, includes the basics of music, enunciation, and ornamentation, as well as practice exercises.

16 This refers to the well-documented stylized use of specific body and hand positions to represent certain passions.

17 By *Figur der Rede*, Agricola is obviously referring to declamatory devices.

18 Leipzig, 1736.

19 Paris, 1707. This is a treatise concerned with all sorts of declamation, including public speaking, declamation in the theater, and gesture.

20 See Quantz, *Versuch* (Reilly trans.), pp. 169–78, for information on dynamics, the crescendo and decrescendo, slurrings, tempo rubato, etc.

21 *Ripienists*, or supporting singers in the choir, were not expected to perform solos, that being the duty of the *concertists*. Agricola's comments indicate that the *ripienists'* voices were of a lower technical ability than the *concertists'*.

22 Printz's term *das Maul* is a pejorative for "mouth."

23 Agricola's adjective *gebunden* perhaps has the meaning of "fugal."

24 A veiled reference to menstruation.

25 Agricola's term *Herablassung* suggests "accommodation" in the sense that the teacher condescends to the level of the student.

5 *Concerning recitative*

1 Here Agricola's translation for Tosi's *messa di voce* is *eine lange Aushaltung*. In ch. 1, he uses *Herausziehen der Stimme* (spinning out the voice) and in ch. 5, *Schwellung*. This variability perhaps indicates that no readily identifiable German equivalent existed, or perhaps that Agricola interpreted the concept to encompass a wider range of possibilities than did Tosi.

2 Agricola's term *Tact* in eighteenth-century German musical documents has many meanings. It may mean "measure," or "beat," or even the more generalized "time."

3 The *Accompagnament* or *recitativo accompagnato* (recitative accompanied with orchestral instruments) as a compositional style was one which came to be associated with the Berlin *Empfindsamer Stil*. The *accompagnato* (a favored form of musical composition) accomplished the programmatic portrayal of strong feelings both through instrumental expression and through empassioned dramatic utterance from the singer, often in soliloquy.

4 Both Quantz, *Versuch* (Reilly trans.), p. 265 and Bach, *Versuch* (Mitchell trans.), pp. 423–24, advocate special assistance to the singer performing from memory, such as note assistance in the recitatives from the continuo keyboard player. Thus, Agricola's statement is a reminder that in passages marked *a tempo* the singer performing from memory can expect no special

dispensation.

5 Agricola's term *bellen* onomatopœically suggests the howling of a dog.

6 Agricola's term *recitiren* also means "to act."

7 The original English of Agricola's source, Joseph Addison, *The Spectator*, no. 13, appears in *General History*, vol. II, pp. 665–66.

8 The opera being performed was Francesco Mancini's *l'Idaspe fedele*.

9 Agricola's *Singspiel* here must be understood in the more general sense of a stage work that includes vocal music as opposed to its twentieth-century designation of an opera in which spoken dialogue replaces recitative.

10 Agricola starts a new paragraph here, whereas Tosi and Galliard do not.

11 Ger., *abgebrochene Cadenzen* or It., *cadenze tronche*. For a thorough discussion of this type of cadence, see Sven Hansell, "The Cadence in 18th-century Recitative," *Musical Quarterly*, 54/2 (April, 1968), pp. 228–48.

12 Agricola has misunderstood Tosi's term *cadenze tronche*. Instead of the over-lapped telescoped cadences in which the penultimate and final chords of the continuo are played *under* the singer's final notes, Agricola seems to understand an incomplete (broken-off) or deceptive cadence.

6 *Remarks intended especially for the music student*

1 As Agricola explains in ch. 7, "pathetic" indicates that which was filled with strong passion, especially the sad, tender or nobly serious. See *Anleitung*, p. 183 (Baird, p. 196).

2 Agricola's phrase is *lange schwellende Aushaltung* (a long swelled sustaining [of the voice]).

3 Tosi, p. 52. "Non tralasci di tempo in tempo di mettere [la voce], e di fer-mar la voce, affinchè sia sempre disposta per servirsene in tutte due le forme" (He should not fail from time to time to practice both the *messa di voce* and the steadying of the voice *(fermar la voce)* so that he is proficient in both [my translation]). Both Agricola and Galliard misunderstood Tosi's sense here. By contrast, Mancini, another Italian writer, also differentiates the *fermare* from the *mettere la voce*. The former – the "steadying of the voice" – consists of holding long, full-voice tones with no fluctuation of pitch or volume. The *messa di voce*, on the other hand, involves a long crescendo–decrescendo and, according to some writers, the introduction of a vibrato at the height of the crescendo. Agricola, who did not make a distinction between the two, omits the *fermar la voce* and allows *dem einem* (to the one) in the second clause of para. 9 to refer back to the agility discussed in para. 8.

4 See Introduction, p. 32.

5 Simply put, Tosi is warning the singer against spending too much of his time on composition, and not balancing this with the physical exercise of the voice, which he considers necessary to maintain it.

6 Here Agricola translates *messa di voce* as *die Aushaltung* (sustaining).

7 Concerning arias

1 Galliard, p. 91, note, gives a very clear explanation of what Tosi means: "Suppose the first Part expressed Anger, and the second relented, and was to express Pity or Compassion, he must be angry again in the Da Capo." De Brosses, *Letter*, p. 37 says: "I also do not like the invariable custom, as in our cantatas, of having every aria divided into two parts of which the first is repeated after the other. That is indeed disturbing because of the way the words are put together, for the verses consist of two quatrains of which the second has the stronger idea, but is weakened by the repetition of the first" (Schier trans.).

2 Agricola is probably referring to Metastasio, a renowned Italian librettist, who was court poet in Vienna.

3 Tosi's phrase is *soave portamento di voce*. He first describes the *portamento* without identifying it by name in ch. 1, p. 18: "Thereupon he should teach him the art of slurring and dragging the voice smoothly in a pleasant manner on the vowels while proceeding from high to low" (my translation) and advocates saving it (as Mancini, *Riflessioni*, p. 110, also suggests) until the singer has accomplished the blending of the registers. Agricola translates the term in this chapter as the more general *Vortrag der Stimme* (lit., delivery, good use, or deportment of the voice), whereas he employs below (chs. 9–10) the more usual eighteenth-century term *Tragen der Stimme* (which refers to the legato connection of tones). The phrase *portamento di voce* is thus used both generally and specifically by Tosi, Agricola, and other eighteenth-century writers. In keeping with its literal meaning (carriage of the voice) it is used in a general sense to refer simply to the physical process of "singing well," or "good use of the voice." In its more specific sense it refers to a blending achieved by the "smooth and rapid sliding between two pitches executed continuously without distinguishing the intervening tones or semitones" (*New Grove*, vol. XV, p. 134).

4 Here Agricola's translation of Tosi's *le messe di voce* is *wohl gezogene Aushaltungen*.

5 For interesting accounts of the custom of imitating the ornamentation of other singers to discredit them, see Heriot, *Castrati*, pp. 88–89.

6 Eighteenth-century arias usually are tripartite with sections in both the tonic and the dominant keys. Tosi is referring to the intervals created by the first of two notes of the normal discant or tenor cadence (discussed in ch. 1) in the dominant and in the tonic keys. For example, in C major the two varieties of V–I cadences would yield D–C and B–C in the melodic part with the cadenzas being performed on the D and B that are the second and seventh scale degrees above C. Likewise, in the dominant V/V–V or (D major to G major), the two varieties of perfect cadences include A–B and F♯–G, the A and F♯ of which are the sixth and the fourth.

7 Francesco Antonio Pistocchi (1659–1726) began his singing career as a

soprano castrato, but after having lost his voice owing to a dissolute life style, developed his compositional skills. After a ten-year hiatus in his singing career, he recovered his voice, which had then become a contralto. He was responsible for the training of many famous castrati (Bernacchi among them) and thus is associated with helping to establish the traditions of the Bolognese school of singing, with its emphasis on the pathetic style and the understanding of the *tempo rubato*. See Häbock, *Kastraten*, pp. 330–41; Heriot, *Castrati*, pp. 171–75; Galliard, pp. 101–02, note; and Agricola, p. 180, note (d) (Baird, p. 194).

8 Giovanni Francesco Grossi (1653–97), a Tuscan soprano castrato, was nicknamed "Siface" after his highly sucessful role in Cavalli's *Scipione affricano* in Venice in 1678. He enjoyed tremendous success in his stage career in the major cities of Italy and became a member of the theatrical retinue of Christina of Sweden. He also performed in Paris and London. Heriot, *Castrati*, p. 129, says of him that "with Cortona and Matteuccio [Siface] formed a kind of musical trinity..." On the colorful life and career of Siface, see Heriot, *Castrati*, pp. 129–35; and Galliard, pp. 102–03, note. He enjoyed success in England, being praised for the high standard of singing which he introduced there. He was assassinated in Bologna by agents of the Marsili family because of his fatuous boasting of his affair with Countess Elena Forni, a member of this family.

9 Buzzoleni or Bussoleni (fl. 1701)was born in Brescia in the second half of the seventeenth century. He was a tenor singer who was first employed in the service of the Duke of Mantua, and then by the emperor. See Fétis, *Biographie*, vol. II, p. 135; and Francesco Algarotti, *Saggio sopra l'opera in musica* (Livorno, 1763; Venice, 1755; rpt., Lucca: Libreria musicale Italiana, *ca.* 1989), pp. 20 and 49.

10 Luigino (d. 1707) was a student of Pistocchi and a highly reputable singer in the Vienna court chapel of the Emperor Joseph. John Hawkins, *A General History of the Science and Practice of Music*, ed. Othmar Wessely (5 vols., London 1776; rpt., Graz: Akademische Druck- und. Verlagsanstalt, 1969), vol. II, p. 808b, says that "by the introduction of a chaste, elegant, and pathetic style, [Luigino] greatly improved the practice of vocal music among the Italians..."

11 Francesca Vanini Boschi (d. 1744) was a contralto at the court of Mantua, who also performed in London and other major cities in Europe. According to Hawkins, *History*, vol. II, p. 809b, Signora Boschi could be ranked "in the first degree of eminence" at the turn of the century, but by 1710, when she sang in Handel's *Rinaldo* in London, her voice was already in decline. Her husband, Giuseppe Maria Boschi, was a bass singer. See also Galliard, p. 103, note.

12 Santa Scarabelli Stella (fl. 1710, d. 1759), a soprano also known as Santini, is referred to here as Signora Lotti because she was the wife of Antonio Lotti, a renowned *maestro di cappella* of St. Mark's in Venice. A native of Bologna, this prima donna gained a considerable reputation in

several German courts, including Dresden, where her husband was also employed as court composer. See Hawkins, pp. 775b, 809b. Both Santini and her sister Chiara were highly paid as singers. She was described by Burney (his source was Quantz, "Lebenslauf," pp. 213–14), *Present State*, vol. II, p. 176, as follows: "*Santa Stella Lotti* had a full, strong, *soprano* voice, a true intonation, and a good shake; high tones gave her little trouble; her principal excellence was in singing *adagios*. It was from her that Quantz first heard what professors call *tempo rubato:* her figure on the stage was full of dignity, and her action, particularly in elevated parts, could not be surpassed." See also *New Grove*, vol. XI, "Antonio Lotti," p. 250b; and Agricola, note (i) below (Baird, p. 195).

13 Tosi is referring to a contemporary practice of which he disapproves: that of having the orchestra, and more specifically the continuo, cease playing entirely to allow the singer to perform the cadenza. In many earlier eighteenth-century arias, cadenzas were improvised by the singer at the cadence points (often marked adagio or andante) over a slow but continually moving bass, more or less in time.

14 Hawkins, *History*, vol. II, p. 809a, identifies this publication as follows: "There is extant of Pistocchi's composition, a collection of cantatas, duets, and songs, entitled 'Scherzi-Musicali,' dedicated to Frederic III., Margrave of Brandenburg Anspach, published by Estienne Roger of Amsterdam; at the end are two airs, one with French the other with German words; in the former he professes to have imitated the style of Lully, in the latter that of the German composers."

15 Antonio Maria Bernacchi (1685–1756) began as a soprano castrato, but his voice later lowered in pitch to alto range. A student of Pistocchi, he was nevertheless known for an instrumentally conceived style of singing, for which Pistocchi chided him. Although possessed of an excellent technique, for which he was famous all over Europe, he was faulted for lacking expression, and for lacking a voice of inherent beauty. See Haböck, *Kastraten*, pp. 355–63; *General History*, pp. 698–99; and *New Grove*, vol. II.

16 Antonio Lotti (*ca.* 1667–1740) was *primo maestro di cappella* of St. Mark's in Venice, from 1736 until his death. His career as an opera composer took him to Dresden and Austria, but most of his operas were produced for Venice. He was married to the famous Santa or Santini, who caused a monument to be erected to his honor in the church of San Geminiano in Venice. See *New Grove*, vol. XI.

17 Tosi does not use the term but his text presents the idea.

18 Felice Salinbeni, also Salimbeni (*ca.* 1712–51), a castrato who studied with Porpora and made his debut in Hasse's *Cajo Fabrizio*. He was in the service of the Emperor in Vienna (1733–39), and of Frederick the Great at Berlin/Potsdam (1743–50), realizing many roles in Hasse's operas while in his service. He had a reputation for very cold acting, the perfection of his singing being the only advantage over a concert performance. He was one of the teachers of Agricola's wife, Benedetta Emilia Molteni.

19 See ch. 1, n. 57, p. 265.

20 See Translator's Introduction, p. 7, n. 23 and p. 241.

21 Agricola breaks Tosi's long para. 24 up into several paragraphs with inter-spersed notes.

22 Pietro Simone Agostini (*ca.* 1635–80), Italian composer, primarily of cantatas (his most inspired form) and operas. On his rather erratic lifestyle and career, see *New Grove*, vol. I; and Galliard, p. 112, note.

23 Alessandro Stradella (1644–82), a leading Italian composer of his day, was often paired by contemporaries with Agostini because their careers were in many ways parallel. While Agostini was primarily a vocal composer, the versatile Stradella composed works in all major categories. See *New Grove*, vol. XVIII and vol. I, as above; and Galliard, pp. 112–14, note.

24 The full title is *Der General-bass in der Composition, oder Neue und gründliche Anweisung* (Dresden, 1728).

25 Tosi's concluding sentence at the end of para. 24 is "Ma giacche sono entrato in ballo si danzi" (But since we have entered the ballroom, let us dance [my translation]).

8 Concerning cadenzas

1 Agricola's misunderstanding of Tosi's term *cadenze tronche* (telescoped cadences) is explained above in ch. 5, n. 12.

2 Tosi's image is different but no less colorful: "Nel replicar poi l'ultima dell'Intercalare si da fuoco alla girandola di Castel Sant'Angelo, e l'Orchestra tarocca." (Upon repetition of the last cadenza [lit., interpolation] he sets fire to the weathercock of Castel Sant'Angelo and the orchestra grumbles [my translation]).

3 Agricola's provides Tosi's term *rubamento di tempo* in the text and translates it as *Verziehungen der Geltung der Noten,* meaning literally "distortion of the values of the notes."

4 Since in the mid eighteenth century the improvised cadenza (over the held bass note) consisted mostly of divisions, it was expected of the librettist that he would craft the text so that acceptable vowel sounds for singing divisions (of which there were really only two – *a* and *o*) occurred at the ends of the quatrains. Tosi is fairly liberal – forbidding only the *i, u,* and the closed *e* and *a* (thus, open *a, o,* and open *e* were among those which he deemed acceptable). As the century progressed, it would seem that fewer and fewer vowels were considered acceptable for the divisions and for cadenzas.

5 Tosi's word is *cantabile* (singing or melodious).

6 Agricola's phrase is *ohne Aufhaltung der Tactbewegung.* Tosi's expression (p. 88) is *senza offesa del tempo* (without giving offense to the tempo).

7 The issue is probably not copyright, but the exigencies of printing.

8 Although Agricola gives the symbol (ζ), there is no relevant musical example.

9 *Remarks for the use of the professional singer*

1 Because of Tosi's allusion to the stultifying power of monarchs over artistic freedom and the inference that Frederick (Agricola's patron) might have been able to draw, Agricola omits this paragraph of Tosi. For an English translation of the missing paragraph see Galliard, pp. 145–46: "My long and repeated Travels have given me an Opportunity of being acquainted with most of the Courts of *Europe* and Examples, more than my Words, should persuade every able Singer to see them also; but without yielding up his Liberty to their Allurements. For Chains, though of Gold, are still chains; and they are not all of that precious Metal. Besides, [there may be] the several inconveniences of Disgrace, Mortifications, Uncertainty, and above all, Hindrance of Study."

2 Paris, 1750. François Riccoboni was the son of the famous Luigi Riccoboni, and was a French actor, playwright, and director. His book was translated into German and Italian.

3 Paris, 1738. The title page lists him as Louis Riccoboni.

4 Paris, 1747. The author was a dramaturge whose work was translated into Dutch, English, and partly into German.

5 Agricola's note indicated here by (d) is missing.

6 Agricola's phrase is *Die Noten verziehen*.

7 Agricola uses a second term, *Zeitraub*, to mean *tempo rubato*.

8 See *Anleitung*, p. 176 (Baird, p. 191).

9 Agricola thus provides an exercise for achieving the portamento. The crescendo–decrescendo is not always implied by *portamento* in music literature.

10 Faustina Bordoni Hasse (1700–81), Italian mezzo-soprano known for the penetrating quality of voice, excellent acting ability, the flexibility to sing divisions with extreme rapidity and distinctness, and skill at artfully disguising the taking of the breath. See Quantz, "Lebenslauf" (p. 240) or trans. in Paul Nettl, *Forgotten Musicians* (New York: Philosophical Library, 1951), p. 312. See also ch. 4, n. 3, p. 271 above.

11 Francesca Cuzzoni (*ca.* 1698–1770) was an Italian soprano known for the beauty of her voice, especially in the *cantabile*, or "pathetic," style; the perfection of her trill, and her technical control of the shades of dynamics. She was praised as well for the clarity of her high notes, the intonation of her voice in general, and for excellence in applying the *tempo rubato*. See Quantz, "Lebenslauf," p. 240, or trans. in Nettl, *Musicians*, p. 312; *General History*, pp. 736–37, et passim; Hawkins, *History*, vol. II, pp. 872b–74a; *MGG*, vol. II; and *New Grove*, vol. V: "Francesca Cuzzoni."

10 Concerning improvised variations of melodies

1 Tosi's word *passo* [lit., step] in the title of this chapter, "De' Passi." should be differentiated from *passaggio* [lit., passage]. *Passo* was used to indicate the small ornaments of the aria, and is here translated by Agricola by the more lengthy "improvised variations of melodies". See ch. 4, n.1, p. 271 above.

2 See ch. 4, n. 3.

3 Agricola's term *gezogen* in this context means "legato" or "spun-out."

4 De Brosses' *Letter*, p. 35, contains a fascinating description of *chiaroscuro:* "They [the Italian orchestras] have one accompaniment technique which we do not use, which it would be easy to introduce into our [French] playing, and which does much to heighten the effect of their music; this is the art of increasing or reducing the volume of sound, which I might call the art of shading or of *chiaroscuro*. This can be done imperceptibly by degrees or all at once. Besides the loud and the soft, the very loud and the very soft, they also produce a *mezzo piano* and a *mezzo forte* more or less sustained. These are reflections or half-tints that give an incredible attractiveness to the tone colors...Sometimes when the orchestra is accompanying *piano*, all the instruments begin a *crescendo* at once for one or two beats, to the point of covering the voice entirely; then they suddenly play very softly. This is an excellent effect."

5 Agricola's term for *lo Strascino* is *das Ziehen der Stimme* (the dragging of the voice). The "drag" (a term adopted from Galliard) receives treatment on two occasions in the course of the text. Besides its description here it is also discussed in ch. 4 as a type of articulation consisting of an extreme slur or *portamento,* which is distinguishable from the slur primarily by its slowness and imperceptibility. Hiller, *Anweisung* (1780), p. 83, distinguishes between the *portamento* and the drag in the following manner: "The slur [*Tragen der Stimme*] consists in there being no gap or pause in passing from one note to another, nor any unpleasant slipping or dragging through smaller intervals..." On the other hand, the drag [*Das Ziehen*] for Hiller implies a chromatic passage: "When divisions proceed in a chromatic fashion, one finds slurring the only means of performance. Should one wish to call it by another name, the term dragging [*Das Ziehen*] can be used" (my translation).

6 Galliard, however, provides two musical examples. See p. 197, nos. 8–9.

7 Hiller, however, was not loath to do so. His *Anweisung* (1780), p. 91, provides a list of interchangeable figures to help the singer learn how to fashion da capo ornamentation.

8 Agricola is referring to the contemporary Italian habit of singing the ornamentation for the da capo in the first section of an aria.

Bibiliography

Primary sources

Works by Agricola

Agricola, Johann Friedrich. *Anleitung zur Singkunst.* A translation (with additions) of P. F. Tosi's *Opinioni de' cantori antichi e moderni.* Berlin, 1757. Facsimile reprint edition by Erwin R. Jacobi with Preface and Appendix. Celle: Hermann Moeck Verlag, 1966.

"Beleuchtung von der Frage von dem Vorzuge der Melodie vor der Harmonie." Edited with introduction by Carl Friedrich Cramer. *Magazin der Musik,* 2 (Berlin, 1786), pp. 809–29.

Agricola, Johann Friedrich and Jakob Adlung. *Musica mechanica organoedi.* Berlin, 1768.

Olibrio, Flavio Amicio [Johann Friedrich Agricola]. *Schreiben an Herrn...in welchem Flavio Amicio Olibrio sein Schreiben an den critischen Musicus an der Spree vertheidiget.* Berlin, 1749.

Schreiben eines reisenden Liebhabers. Berlin, 1749.

Works by Tosi and translations of Tosi

Tosi, Pier Francesco. *Opinioni de' cantori antichi e moderni, o sieno Osservazioni sopra il canto figurato.* Bologna, 1723. Facsimile reprint edition by Erwin R. Jacobi. Celle: Hermann Moeck Verlag, 1966.

Opinioni de' cantori antichi e moderni de Pier Francesco Tosi, con note ed esempi di Luigi Leonesi. La scuola di canto dell'epoca d'oro (secolo xvii). Naples, 1904.

Agricola, J. F. *Anleitung zur Singkunst.* See above.

A[lençon], J. *Korte Aanmerkingen over de Zangkonst.* Leyden, 1731.

Della Corte, Andrea. *Canto e bel canto.* Biblioteca di cultura musicale, no. 5. Turin, 1933.

Galliard, Mr. [John Ernest]. *Observations on the Florid Song; or, Sentiments on the Ancient and Modern Singers.* London, 1743. Reprint. London: William Reeves Bookseller, 1967.

Observations on the Florid Song. Edited with additional notes by Michael Pilkington. London: Stainer & Bell, 1987.

Lemaire, Theodore. *L'Art du Chant, opinions sur les chanteurs anciens et modernes ou observations sur le chant figuré.* Paris, 1874.

Secondary sources

Addison, Joseph. *The Spectator*, no. 13. London, 1711–12.

Algarotti, Francesco. *Saggio sopra l'opera in musica.* Livorno, 1763; Venice, 1755. Reprint. Lucca: Libreria musicale Italiana, 1989.

Anthony, James R. "Preface" and "Appendix." In Michel Pignolet de Montéclair. *Cantatas for One and Two Voices.* Edited by James R. Anthony and Diran Akmajian. Recent Researches in the Music of the Baroque Era, vols. XXIX, XXX. Madison, Wis.: A-R Editions, Inc., 1978.

Aristotle, *Historia animalium.* English translation by A. L. Peck. The Loeb Classical Library: Greek Authors. 3 vols. Cambridge: Harvard University Press, 1965.

Bach, Carl Philipp Emanuel. *Versuch über die wahre Art das Clavier zu spielen.* Berlin, 1752. Translated and edited by William J. Mitchell under the title *Essay on the True Art of Playing Keyboard Instruments.* New York: Norton, 1949.

Badura-Skoda, Eva. "Cadenza." *New Grove*, vol. III, pp. 586–93.

Baryphonus, Henricus. *Ars Canendi: aphorismis succinctis discripta & notis philosophicis, mathematicis, physicis et historicis illustrata.* Leipzig, 1620.

Batka, R. "Friedrich II als Musiker." *Der Kunstwart* 25 (24 January 1912), pp. 131–34.

Baumgarten, Georg. *Rudimenta musices: Kurze, jedoch gründliche Anleitung zur Figuralmusik fürnehmlich der studirenden Jugen zu Landsberg an der Martha zum Besten vorgeschrieben.* 1673.

Bérard, Jean Antoine. *L'Art du Chant.* Paris, 1755. Facsimile reprint. New York: Broude Brothers, 1967.

Bernhard, Christoph. "Von der Singekunst oder Manier." *ca.* 1649. In *Die Kompositionslehre Heinrich Schützens in der Fassung seine Schülers Christoph Bernhard.* Edited by Joseph Maria Müller-Blattau. Kassel: Bärenreiter, 1963. Pp. 31–39.

"Von der Singekunst oder Manier." Translated by Walter Hilse, "On the Art of Singing: or, Manier." *The Music Forum* 3 (1973), pp. 13–29.

Blom, Eric, ed. *Grove's Dictionary of Music and Musicians.* 5th edn. 9 vols., and supplement. London and New York, 1954.

Blume, Friedrich, ed. *Die Musik in Geschichte und Gegenwart: Allgemeine Enzyklopädie der Musik.* 17 vols., including 2-vol. supplement and index. Kassel and Basel: Bärenreiter-Verlag, 1949–79.

Bontempi, Giovanni. *Storia della musica.* 1695.

Bovicelli, Giovanni Battista. *Regole, passaggi di musica.* Venice, 1594. Reprint. Kassel and Basel: Bärenreiter, 1957.

Bowman, Horace D. "The Castrati Singers and their Music." Ph.D. dissertation, Indiana University, 1951.

Boyden, David D. "Portamento." *New Grove,* vol. XV, p. 134.

Brosses, Charles de. *Letter on Italian Music* (*ca.* 1740). Edited by Donald S. Schier. Donald S. Schier, 1978.

Browne, Lennox, and Emil Behnke. *Voice, Song, and Speech.* 13th edn. New York, 1891.

Buelow, George J. "Gottfried Grünewald." *New Grove,* vol. VII, p. 763.

Burney, Charles. *A General History of Music from the Earliest Ages to the Present Period* (1789). Edited with critical and historical notes by Frank Mercer. 2 vols. New York: Dover Publications, Inc., 1957.

Memoirs of the Life and Writings of the Abate Metastasio. 3 vols. London, 1796. Reprint. New York: Da Capo Press, 1971.

The Present State of Music in France and Italy. London, 1773. Reprint. New York: Broude Brothers, 1969.

The Present State of Music in Germany, the Netherlands, and United Provinces. 2 vols. London, 1775. Reprint. New York: Broude Brothers, 1969.

Buttstedt, Johann Heinrich. *Ut, re, mi fa, sol, la, tota Musica Aeterna.* Erfurt, 1716.

Caccini, Giulio. *Le Nuove Musiche.* Florence, 1602. Edited by H. Wiley Hitchcock. Recent Researches in the Music of the Baroque Era, vol. IX. Madison, Wis.: A-R Editions, Inc., 1970.

Calvisius, Seth. *Compendium Musicae.* Leipzig, 1594.

Cannon, Beekman C. *Johann Mattheson: Spectator in Music.* Yale Studies in the History of Music, vol. I. New Haven: Yale University Press, 1947. Hamden, Conn.: Archon Books, 1968.

Cobbett, W. W. and R. J. Pascall. "Conrad Friedrich Hurlebusch." *New Grove,* vol. VIII, pp. 819–20.

Corri, Domenico. *The Singer's Preceptor.* London, 1810.

Crüger, Johannes. *Kurtzer und verständlicher Unterricht recht und leichtlich singen zu lernen.* Berlin, 1625.

Dean, Winton. "Antonio Maria Bernacchi." *New Grove,* vol. II, pp. 613–14.

"Faustina Bordoni [Hasse]." *New Grove* vol. III, pp. 46–47.

"Francesca Cuzzoni." *New Grove* vol. V, pp. 109–10.

"Johann Gottfried Riemschneider." *New Grove,* vol. XVI, p. 6.

Donington, Robert. *The Interpretation of Early Music.* London: Faber & Faber, 1963.

Duey, Philip A. *Bel Canto in its Golden Age.* New York, 1951. Reprint. New York: Da Capo Press, 1980.

Ferrein, Antoine. "De la formation de la voix de l'homme." In *Mémoires de l'Académie des Sciences.* Paris, 1741. Pp. 409–32.

Fétis, F. J. *Biographie universelle des musiciens et bibliographie générale de la musique.* 2nd edn. Paris, 1860-80. Reprint. 10 vols. including a 2-vol. supplement. Brussels: Culture et Civilisation, 1972.

Fuhrmann, Martin Heinrich. *Musicalischer Trichter dadurch ein geschichter Informator seinen Informandis die Edle Singe-Kunst nach heutiger Manier...einbringen kan.* Frankfurt an der Spree, 1706.

Galen. *On the Usefulness of the Parts of the Body.* Translated by Margaret Tallmadge May. 2 vols. Ithaca, New York: Cornell University Press,1968.

Garcia, Manuel. *A Complete Treatise on the Art of Singing: Part One.* Edited and translated by Donald V. Paschke. New York, 1984.

Traité complet sur l'Art du Chant. Paris, 1840, 3/1851.

Gehring, Franz and Alfred Loewenberg. "Frederick II." *Grove's Dictionary,* vol. III.

Gerber, Ernst Ludwig. *Historisch-biographisches Lexikon der Tonkünstler* (1790–92) and *Neues Historisch-biographisches Lexikon der Tonkünstler* (1812–14). Leipzig, 1790–1814. Edited by Othmar Wessely. Reprint. Graz, Austria: Akademische Druck- und. Verlagsanstalt, 1966–77.

Gianturco, Carolyn M. "Alessandro Stradella." *New Grove,* vol. XVIII, pp. 188–93.

Gibelius, Otto. *Kurtzer, jedoch gründlicher Bericht von den Vocibus musicalibus.* Bremen, 1659.

Gluck, Christoph Willibald. Preface to *Alceste.* Paris, 1769.

Gottsched, Johann Christoph. *Ausführliche Redekunst.* Leipzig, 1736.

Gottsched, Johann Christoph et al., eds. *Beyträge zur critischen Historie der deutschen Sprache, Poesie und Beredsamkeit.* Leipzig, 1732–44.

Greenlee, Robert. "Dispositione di voce: Passage to Florid Singing." *Early Music* 15/1 (February, 1987), pp. 47–55.

Grimarest, Jean Léonard le Gallois de. *Traité du récitatif.* Paris, 1707.

Goldschmidt, Hugo. *Die italienische Gesangsmethode des XVII Jahrhunderts und ihre Bedeutung für die Gegenwart.* Breslau, 1892.

Die Lehre von der Vokal-Ornamentik. Charlottenburg, 1907.

Gümmer, Paul. "Francesca Cuzzoni." *MGG,* vol. II, cols. 1830–31.

Haböck, Franz. *Die Gesangskunst der Kastraten.* Vienna, 1923.

Die Kastraten und ihre Gesangskunst. Berlin and Leipzig, 1927.

Hanley, Theodore D. and Wayne L. Thurman. *Developing Vocal Skills.* 2nd edn. New York: Holt Rinehart and Winston, 1970.

Hansell, Sven. "Antonio Lotti." *New Grove,* vol. XI, pp. 249–52.

"The Cadence in 18th-Century Recitative." *Musical Quarterly* 54/2 (April, 1968), pp. 228–48.

Harris, Marcia, ed. *Porpora's Elements of Singing.* London, 1858.

Harriss, Ernest C. "J. F. Agricola's *Anleitung zur Singkunst:* A Rich Source by a Pupil of J. S. Bach." *Bach* 9/3 (1978), pp. 2–8.

Hawkins, John. *A General History of the Science and Practice of Music.* Edited by Othmar Wessely. 5 vols. London, 1776. Reprint (5 vols. in 1). Graz: Akademische Druck- und. Verlagsanstalt, 1969.

Heartz, Daniel. "Anton Raaff." *New Grove,* vol. XV, pp. 520–21.

Heinichen, Johann David. *Der General-bass in der Composition, oder; Neue und gründliche Anweisung.* Dresden, 1728.

Helm, Eugene. "Johann Friedrich Agricola." *New Grove*, I, pp. 164–66.
Music at the Court of Frederick the Great. Norman: University of Oklahoma Press, 1960.

Heriot, Angus. *The Castrati in Opera.* London, 1956. Reprint. New York: Da Capo Press, 1975.

Heuermann, Georg. *De lingua humana.* Copenhagen, 1749.
Physiologie. Copenhagen and Leipzig, 1751–55.

Hiller, Johann Adam. *Anweisung zum musikalisch-richtigen Gesange.* Leipzig, 1774.
Anweisung zum musikalisch-zierlichen Gesange. Leipzig, 1780.
Anweisung zum musikalisch-zierlichen Gesange. Translated by Suzanne Julia Beicken under the title "Johann Adam Hiller's *Anweisung zum musikalisch-zierlichen Gesange,* 1780: A Translation and Commentary." Ph.D. dissertation, Stanford University, 1980.

Hitzler, Daniel. *Extract aus neuen Musica oder Singkunst.* Nuremberg, 1623.

Hogarth, William. *The Analysis of Beauty.* London, 1753.

Högg, Margarete. *Die Gesangskunst der Faustina Hasse und das Sängerinnenwesen ihrer Zeit in Deutschland.* Berlin, 1931.

Holmes, Gordon. *The Science of Voice Production and Preservation.* New York, 1880.
A Treatise on Vocal Physiology and Hygiene. London, 1879.

Houle, George. *Meter in Music, 1600-1800: Performance, Perception, and Notation.* Bloomington and Indianapolis: Indiana University Press, 1987.

Jander, Owen. "Pietro Simone Agostini." *New Grove*, I, p. 160.
"Messa di voce." *New Grove*, vol. XII, p. 201.

Jahn, Otto. *W. A. Mozart.* Leipzig, 1905.

Kamiénski, Lucian. "Zum 'tempo rubato.'" *Archiv für Musikwissenschaft* 1 (1918-19), pp. 108–25.

Kelly, Michael. *Reminiscences of Michael Kelly.* 2 vols. London, 1826. Reprint. New York: Da Capo Press, 1968.

Klein, Joseph. *Singing Technique.* Princeton, N. J.: D. Van Nostrand Co., [1967].

Krüger, Johann Gottlob. *Naturlehre.* Halle, 1740–49.

Lanza, Gesualdo. *Lanza's Elements of Singing in the Italian and English Styles.* London, 1813.

Lessing, Gotthold Ephraim. *Theatralische Bibliothek.* 4 vols. Berlin, 1754–58.

Lessing, Gotthold Ephraim, and F. Nicolai, eds. *Bibliothek der schönen Wissenschaften und der freyen Künste.* 2 vols. Leipzig, 1757–65.

Lindley, Mark, and Klaus Wachsmann. "Pitch: 1." *New Grove*, vol. XIV, p. 780.

MacCurdy, Edward, trans. *The Notebooks of Leonardo da Vinci.* New York: George Braziller, 1956.

McClintock, Carol. *Readings in the History of Music in Performance.* Bloomington and London: Indiana University Press, 1979.

Maffei, Camillo. "Lettere." Naples, 1562. Translated in McClintock, *Readings in the History of Music in Performance,* pp. 38–61.

Mancini, Giambattista. *Riflessioni practiche sul canto figurato.* 3rd rev., enlarged edn. Milan, 1777. Reprint. Bologna: Forni Editore, 1970.

Riflessioni practiche sul canto figurato. Translated by Edward Foreman under the title *Practical Reflections on Figured Singing:* The Editions of 1774 and 1777 Compared, Translated and Edited. Champaign, Illinois: Pro Musica Press, 1967.

Manfredini, Vincenzo. *Regole Armoniche.* Venice, 1775. Reprint. New York: Broude Brothers, 1966.

Regole Armoniche...seconda edizione. Venice, 1797.

Marcello, Benedetto. *Il Teatro alla Moda.* Venice, *ca.* 1720. Translated by Reinhard G. Pauly, *Musical Quarterly* 34/3 (1948), pp. 393–403; 35/1 (1949), pp. 85–105.

Marpurg, Friedrich Wilhelm. *Anleitung zum Clavierspielen.* Berlin, 1765. Facsimile reprint. New York: Broude Brothers, 1966.

*Anleitung zur Musik überhaupt und zur Singkunst besonders...*Berlin, 1763.

Des critischen Musicus an der Spree erster Band. Berlin, 1750.

Historisch-kritische Beyträge zur Aufnahme der Music. 5 vols. Berlin, 1754–78. Reprint. Hildesheim and New York: Georg Olms Verlag, 1970–.

Kritische Briefe über die Tonkunst. Vol. II. Berlin, 1761–63.

Mattheson, Johann. *Grundlage einer Ehren-Pforte.* Hamburg, 1740.

Mithridat wider den Gift einer Welschen Satyr. Hamburg, 1749.

Das Neu-eröffnete Orchestre. Hamburg, 1713.

Mattheson, Johann. "Die Orchester-Kanzeley," *Critica Musica* 2/7 (Hamburg, 1724–25).

Der Vollkommene Capellmeister. Hamburg, 1739. Translated by Ernest C. Harriss. Ann Arbor, Mich.: UMI Research Press, 1981.

Mengozzi, Bernardo. *Méthode de chant du Conservatoire de Musique.* Paris, 1803.

Mersenne, Marin. *Harmonie universelle.* Paris, 1636–37.

Miller, Richard. *The Structure of Singing.* New York: Schirmer Books, 1986.

Mizler von Kolof, Lorenz. *Neu eröffnete musikalische Bibliothek.* 4 vols. Leipzig, 1739-54.

Montéclair, Michel Pignolet de. *Nouvelle méthode pour apprendre la musique.* Paris, 1709.

Mori, Rachele Maragliano. *Coscienza della voce nella scuola italiana di canto.* Milan: Edizioni Curci, 1970.

Mozart, Leopold. *Versuch einer gründlichen Violinschule.* Augspurg [Augsburg], 1756. Translated by Edith Knocker under the title *A Treatise on the Fundamental Principles of Violin Playing.* London: Oxford University Press, 1975.

Negus, V. E., and Owen Jander. "Falsetto." *New Grove,* vol. VI, p. 375.

Nettl, Paul. *Forgotten Musicians.* New York: Philosophical Library, 1951.

Neumann, Frederick. *Ornamentation in Baroque and Post-Baroque Music.* Princeton University Press, 1978. Paperback reprint, 1983.

Nicolai, Christoph Friedrich. *Allgemeine deutsche Bibliothek.* Berlin, Stettin and Kiel, 1765–1806.

Bibliothek der schönen Wissenschaften und der freyen Künste. See under Lessing and Nicolai, eds.

Panconcelli-Calzia, Sergio. *Die Phonetik des Aristoteles.* Hamburg, 1942.

Pauls, Karlheinz. "Ernst Christian Hesse." *MGG*, vol. VI, cols. 317–19.

Printz, Wolfgang Caspar. *Anweisung zur Singe-Kunst oder Bericht wie man einen knaben...könne singen lehren.* Guben, 1671.
Musica modulatoria vocalis. Schweidnitz, 1678.
Phrynis Mytilenaeus oder satyrischer Componist. Quedlinburg, 1676–77. 2nd edn. Dresden and Leipzig, 1696.

Puteanus, Erycius. *Modulata Pallas.* Milan, 1599.

Quantz, Johan Joachim. "Herrn Johann Joachim Quantzens Lebenslauf, von ihm selbst entworfen." In Friedrich Wilhelm Marpurg, *Historisch-kritische Beyträge* 1/3 (Berlin, 1755). English translation by Paul Nettl, *Forgotten Musicians*, pp. 197–265.
Versuch einer Anweisung die Flöte traversiere zu spielen. Berlin, 1752. Translated and edited by Edward R. Reilly under the title *On Playing the Flute.* New York: Macmillan, 1966.

Reid, Cornelius. *Bel Canto: Principles and Practice.* New York: The Joseph Patelson Music House, 1972.

Rhodes, J. J. K., and W. R. Thomas. "Pitch: 2." *New Grove*, vol. XIV, pp. 781–82.

Riccoboni, François. *L'Art du théâtre.* Paris, 1750.

Riccoboni, Luigi [Louis]. *Pensées sur la déclamation.* Paris, 1738.

Riemann, Hugo. *Dictionary of Music.* Translated by J. S. Shedlock. 4th edn. London, 1908. Reprint (2 vols. from l). New York: Da Capo Press, 1970.
Musik Lexicon Mainz: B. Schott's, 1961.

Rosenblum, Sandra P. *Performance Practices in Classic Piano Music.* Bloomington: Indiana University Press, 1988.

Rubin, Henry J. "The Falsetto, a High Speed Cinematographic Study." *The Laryngoscope* (September, 1960).

Sadie, Stanley, ed. *The New Grove Dictionary of Music and Musicians.* 20 vols. London: Macmillan Publishers, Ltd., 1980.

Sainsbury, John S. *A Dictionary of Musicians from the Earliest Ages to the Present Times.* 2 vols. London, 1825. Reprint. New York: Da Capo Press, 1966.

Sainte Albine, Rémond von. *Le comédien.* Paris, 1747.

Sauveur, Joseph. "Sur la determination d'un son fixe." In *Histoire de l'Académie Royale des Sciences, Année 1700.* Paris: Imprimerie Royale, 1703. Pp. 131–40.

Schilling, Gustav. *Encyclopädie der gesammten musikalischen Wissenschaft, oder Universal-Lexikon der Tonkunst.* 6 vols. Stuttgart, 1835–38.

Sorge, Georg Andreas. *Ausführliche und deutliche Anweisung zur Rational-Rechnung.* Lobenstein, 1749.

Sperling, Johann Peter Gabriel. *Principia musicae, das ist: gründliche Anweisung zur Music, wie ein Music-Scholar vom Anfang instruiret und nach der Ordnung zur Kunst oder Wissenschaft der Figural-Music soll geführet...werden.* Bautzen, 1705.

Spitzer, John. "Improvised Ornamentation in a Handel Aria with Obbligato Wind Accompaniment." *Early Music* 16 (1988), pp. 514–22.

Stanley, Douglas. *The Science of Voice.* 5th edn. New York: Fisher, 1958.

Steele, Richard. *The Tatler.* 3 January 1709.

Sundberg, Johan. "Acoustics: 5. The Voice." *New Grove*, I, pp. 82–86.

Tagliavini, Luigi Ferdinando. "Pier Francesco Tosi." *MGG*, vol. XIII, cols. 58–82.

Telemann, Georg Philipp. *Der Harmonische Gottes-Dienst.* Hamburg, 1725–26.

"Neues musikalisches System." In Mizler, *Neu eröffnete musikalische Bibliothek* 3/4 (Leipzig, 1752).

Türk, Daniel Gottlob. *Klavierschule, oder Anweisung zum Klavierspielen für Lehrer und Lernende...nebst 12 Handstücken.* Leipzig and Halle, 1789.

*Klavierschule, oder Anweisung zum Klavierspielen...*Translated by Raymond H. Haggh under the title *School of Clavier Playing.* Lincoln and London: University of Nebraska Press, 1982.

Uberti, Mauro. "Vocal Techniques in the Second Half of the 16th Century." Translated by Mark Lindley. *Early Music* 9/4 (October, 1981), pp. 486–95.

Ulrich, Bernard. *Die altitalienische Gesangsmethode: Die Schule des Belcanto.* Leipzig 1933.

Vennard, William. *Singing: the Mechanism and the Technique.* New York: Fischer, 1967.

Walker, Thomas. "Aria: 4. 18th Century." *New Grove*, vol. I, pp. 576–78.

Walther, Johann Gottfried. *Musikalisches Lexikon, oder musikalische Bibliothek.* Leipzig, 1732. Facsimile reprint by Richard Schaal. Kassel and Basel: Bärenreiter-Verlag, 1953.

Wichmann, Kurt. *Anleitung zur Singkunst: Einführung und Kommentar.* Leipzig: VEB Deutscher Verlag für Musik, 1966.

Der Ziergesang und die Ausführung der Appoggiatura: Ein Beitrag zur Gesangspädagogik. Leipzig: VEB Deutscher Verlag für Musik, 1966.

Wilcox, John. *The Living Voice.* New York: Carl Fischer, 1945.

Wucherpfennig, Hermann. "Johann Friedrich Agricola (Sein Leben und sein Werke)." Ph.D. dissertation, Friedrich Wilhelm University. Berlin,1922.

Zarlino, Gioseffo. *Le Istituzioni harmoniche.* Venice, 1558. Translated by Guy A. Marco and Claude V. Palisca under the title *The Art of Counterpoint.* New Haven: Yale University Press, 1968. Reprint. New York: W. W. Norton, 1976.

Zemlin, F. W. R. *Speech and Hearing Science: Anatomy and Physiology.* 2nd edn. Englewood Cliffs, N.J.: Prentice Hall, 1981.

Index

accent (beat/stress), *see* stress
accent (term for appoggiatura), 12 (n. 54),
   25 (n. 146), 88 (n. l)
  see also appoggiaturas
accompaniment, 92, 199, 204–05
  self-accompaniment, 32, 86, 92, 185
  stopping, 193–4 (+ n. 13)
  in teaching, 51
acoustics, 18
acting, 177–78 (+ n. 6), 198, 220–21
adagios, 198
Addison, Joseph, 178
Adlung, Jacob, 7, 36
Affect(s), 94 (n. 16), 163–64,
  and appoggiaturas, 94, 96–97, 108, 109,
   110
  and compound appoggiaturas, 118–19
  and cadenzas, 30, 31, 211
  and divisions, 21
  and dynamics, 168
  and slides, 120
  and trills, 18
  and turns, 147–48
  see also pathetic style
agility (of voice), 131, 147, 151, 184
  register and, 74–75
  as requirement in teaching, 51–52
  see also flexibility
Agostini, Pietro Simone, 198 (+ nn. 22, 23)
Agricola, Benedetta Emilia, 6, 197 (n. 18)
Agricola, Johann Christoph, 4
Agricola, Johann Friedrich, 4–7
  Anleitung, 1–3 (+ n. 2)
  additions in, 7–34
  announcement, 1, 2 (n. 6)
  differentiation of Agricola's

   contribution from Tosi's, 42
  omissions in, 6, 217 (n. l)
  reception and influence, 34–35, 36–38
  compositions, 5, 6, 7
  Frederick the Great and, 4, 5, 6, 7
  opinions, 2–3
  as organist, 7
  as polemicist, 7, 20, 27 (n. 160), 35–36,
   40 (n. 4)
  reputation, 6–7
  as singer, 7
  as theorist, 7 (+ n. 21)
Agricola, Maria Magdalena, 4
Alençon, J., 2 (n. 5)
Allgemeine deutsche Bibliothek, 7, 27 (n. 160)
amateurs, 52–53, 193
Amphion, 45
anapests, 15–16
"Ancient"/"Modern" style, 21, 195–203,
  206–07, 208–10, 226–27
  learning from, 186, 210, 236, 237
  periods concerned, 52, 260 (n. 7)
Anleitung, see under Agricola
Anschlag, 15–16, 268 (n. 25)
  see also appoggiaturas, compound
appearance, 82, 187
appoggiaturas, 12–16, 88–125, 134
  before cadences, 208–09
  breathing and, 165–66
  chromaticism and, 88–91
  compound, 14, 15–16, 108, 110–12, 113,
   117–19, 124, 142, 145
   see also slides
  dissonance/consonance and, 13, 99,
   102–03, 104, 108–09
  dynamics, 97, 102, 103

288

erroneous, 107–10
filling in thirds, 93 (n. 11), 99, 101–02
in improvised variations, 232
invariable, 13, 93 (+ n. 14)
length, 13–14, 93–97, 102, 104, 106, 107, 109–10
major/minor semitones and, 88, 89–90
mordents and, 110, 114, 133–34, 156
notation and its interpretation, 12, 13, 92–97 (+ n. 10), 99–102, 107
notation to prevent, 13
and other ornamentation, 110, 113, 114, 133–34, 142, 147–48
see also trills
placement on/before beat, see stress
placing, 88–92, 99–101, 107–09, 110–13
practicing, 86
preparing, 90–91
in recitative, 25 (+n. 146), 26, 171, 174–75, 176
responsibility for, 91–92, 107
slurring, 97, 161
and stress, 14, 15, 92–93 (+ nn. 11, 12), 101–02, 104, 106
terms used for, 12 (+ n. 54), 25 (n. 146), 88 (n. 1)
and trills, 19, 97, 110, 111–12, 129, 130, 135, 136, 138, 140, 141
and triplets, 102, 109–10
uses/purposes, 13, 14, 25 (n. 146), 92, 94, 96–97, 99, 107, 108, 109, 113
variable, 13, 93 (+ n. 14)
arias, 26–28, 188–91, 195–201
accompaniments, 27 (+ n. 156), 29, 199
church, 181
form, 27 (+ n. 156), 188 (+ n. 1), 235 (n. 8)
ornamentation in, 28, 30–31, 189–91
pathetic, 195–97
need to vary performance, 226, 229
ariosos, 174
Aristotle, 9, 78 (+ n. 59)
articulation, 22, 38, 151–53, 161
glottal, 22–23, 152, 153, 157
in improvised variations, 233
following slides, 122–23
in trills, 17, 18
in triplets, 160
varying, in divisions, 156
aytenoid cartilage, 79–80

Bach, Carl Philipp Emanuel, 5, 6, 12, 42 (n. 11)
Agricola and, 4, 42
and *Empfindsamkeit*, 26 (n. 154)
and ornamentation, 13 (+ nn. 57, 60), 14, 19, 20, 130 (n. 6), 138 (n. 18), 139 (n. 19), 143, 149

appoggiaturas, 88 (n. 1), 92 (n. 10), 93, 102 (n. 19)
divisions, 21
on performance from memory, 174 (n. 4)
on rubato, 33
Bach, Johann Sebastian, 4, 23, 24 (n. 140), 151 (n. 2)
backfalls, 115 (+ n. 28)
see also terminations
Baird, Julianne, 1 (n. 2)
balance, 219
Banti, Brigida, 28
Baryphonus, Henricus, 2 (n. 6)
Baumgarten, Georg, 2 (n. 6)
beat(s), strong/weak, see stress
beating time, 157
"beating" of trills, 17–18, 126 (+ n. 2)
Bérard, Jean Antoine, 25, 162
Berlin, 4, 30–31
see also Frederick the Great
Berlin School, 6, 12, 13, 14, 15, 25, 26
and *recitativo accompagnato*, 173 (n. 3)
Bernacchi, Antonio Maria, 42 (n. 17), 193 (n. 7), 194 (+ n. 15)
Bernardi, Francesco, 177–78
Bernhard, Christoph, 3, 18 (n. 92), 67 (n. 34)
Bimmler, Georg Heinrich, 42 (+ n. 13), 87
"bleating", 18, 75, 152
body movements, 82, 157, 187
see also gesture
Boethius, Anicius Manlius Severinus, 45
Bolognese pronunciation, 81
Bononcini, Giovanni, 27
Boschi, Francesca Vanini, 193 (+ n. 11), 194
Boschi, Giuseppe Maria, 193 (n. 11)
Bovicelli, Giovanni Battista, 67 (n. 34)
break between vocal registers, 9, 11, 76
breaking voices, 72, 80, 170
breathing, 22, 23–24, 164–66
articulation and, 157
and cadenzas, 30, 211, 212
controlling, 84, 166
impulse of breath
in detached slurring, 22
in trills, 19, 129, 130
in triplets, 160
and performance nerves, 167
physiology of, 9, 70
and pronunciation of vowels/consonants, 162
and register, 74, 75
and rhythm, 166
standing/sitting and, 82
stress and, 165
words and, 164, 166
bribery, 229

Broschi, Carlo, *see* Farinelli
Brosses, Charles de, 25 (n. 144), 30 (n. 176),
    31 (n. 180), 32 (n. 194), 188 (n. 1),
    233 (n. 4)
Bümmler, Georg Heinrich, 42 (+ n. 13), 87
Burmeister, Joachim, 8
Burney, Charles, 5 (+ n. 15), 18, 21 (n. 117)
    on Agricola, 7 (n. 22)
    on Galliard, 2 (n. 5)
    on Metastasio, 27–28
    on singers, 23, 24 (+ n. 138), 32, 42
        (n. 22), 72 (n. 50), 75 (n. 55), 193
        (n. 12)
Buttstedt, Johann Heinrich, 8, 54 (n. 16)
Buxtehude, Dietrich, 24 (n. 140)
Buzzoleni, 193 (+ n. 9), 194

Caccini, Giulio, 18 (n. 92), 19
cadences, 29, 127, 128, 192 (n. 6), 204–05,
    207–08
    half (imperfect), 212–13
    trills on, 138–39
    ornamented, 212–14
    see also cadenzas
    in recitative, 25, 26, 174, 180–81
        (+ nn. 11, 12)
    singers changing, 207–08, 209
    truncated, 26, 180–81 (+ nn. 11, 12), 204
cadenzas, 28–29, 30–32, 38, 205–07,
    209–12, 236
    accompaniment and, 193–94 (+ n. 13)
    and Affect, 211
    breathing and, 24, 166
    double, 32, 211–12, 220
    invention of, 210–11, 212
    opportunities for, and placing, 27
        (+ n. 156), 30
    and rhythm/tempo, 205, 209, 210
    thematic material in, 31, 211
    trills in, 16, 20, 139, 141
Caffarelli (Gaetano Majorano), 28
Calvisius, Seth, 64
cantatas, 181
Carestini, Giovanni, 75 (+ n. 56), 197
castrati, 2, 53 (+ n. 9), 72–73, 80
cercar la nota, 16, 67 (+ n. 34)
chamber pitch, 83
chamber recitative, 171–72, 173
chest voice, 10, 67 (+ n. 36), 68 (+ n. 39),
    73–75, 76–77, 80
chiaroscuro, 233 (+ n. 4)
choir pitch, 83
choirs/choral singing, 169
chromaticism, 179, 226
    appoggiaturas and, 88–91
    in cadenzas, 31
    drag and, 234 (n. 5)

and dynamics, 168
    in ornamentation, 21
    solmization and, 60, 62
church modes, 198–99, 201
church music, 200, 227
church recitative, 171, 172
Ciecolino, 192–93, 194
clefs, 53 (+ n. 10)
composers, 107, 200–03
    indication of ornaments, *see*
        ornamentation, responsibility for
    and recitative, 179–80
    singers and, 228, 229
composition, need for singers/teachers to
    understand, 185–86, 191, 225, 227,
    229
confidence, 28 (n. 163), 167
consecutives, *see* parallel octaves/fifths
consonance
    appoggiaturas and, 13, 14, 102–03
    stress and, 14
consonants, 161, 162–63
    and divisions, 157
continuo playing, 86, 174 (n. 4)
contrapuntal music, 169–70
copying, *see* imitation
Corelli, Arcangelo, 14 (n. 62)
cornetto, voice compared to, 161
counterpoint, 179, 200, 203
    in double cadenzas, 211
Cramer, Carl Friedrich, 7, 36
criticism, 220
    see also punishment
Crüger, Johannes, 2 (n. 6)
Cuzzoni, Francesca, 230 (+ n. 11)

da capo arias, 27 (+ n. 156), 188 (+ n. 1),
    235 (n. 8)
Davies, Cecilia, 18
De Brosses, Charles, 25 (n. 144), 30 (n. 176),
    31 (n. 180), 32 (n. 194), 188 (n. 1),
    233 (n. 4)
declamation, 163, 177
Della Corte, Andrea, 2 (n. 5)
detached divisions/runs, 151–53, 234
diet, 37, 86–87
Dionysius, 45
diphthongs, 81, 85, 157
dissonance
    appoggiaturas and, 13, 14, 99, 102, 104,
        108–09
    dynamics/stress and, 14, 102
divisions, 21–25, 151–61, 225–26
    exercises for practicing, 155
    placing, 158
    recitative and, 172
    rhythm, 157

speed, 152, 155
stress in, 155
written-out, 28
see also improvised variations
Dodart, Denis, 9, 41 (+ n. 8), 70 (n. 44), 78
  (+ n. 61)
Donington, Robert, 38
dotted rhythms
appoggiaturas and, 94–97, 110
in compound appoggiaturas, 15, 119
double-dotting, 158–59
dynamics, 159, 168
in slides, 119, 120–23
trills and, 138 (+ n. 18)
double-dotting, 158–59
drag (ornament), 23, 86, 151 (+ n. 2),
  154–55, 158, 234–35 (+ nn. 5, 6)
in improvised variations, 232
see also portamento
Dresden orchestra, 4
duets, 219–20
dynamics, 97, 102, 167–69, 199, 214, 233
  (n. 4)
appoggiaturas and, 97, 102, 103
in divisions, 155, 156
in dotted rhythms, 159, 168
in drag, 154, 234
in improvised variations, 233
intonation and, 80
notated, 169
physical basis, 69, 73–74
in portamento, 223 (+ n. 9), 234
practicing, 167, 168–69
in slides, 120
in trills, 138
see also stress

ears, defects of, 187
echoes, 158
elasticity, 69, 70, 75
embellishments, *see* ornamentation
Empfindsamer Stil/Empfindsamkeit, 26, 173 (n. 3)
emphasis, *see* stress
Enlightenment, 9, 12
ensemble singing, 219–20
enunciation, 38, 71, 161–63
see also pronunciation
epiglottis, 70
errors
age and, 184
studying, 238
ethics, 183, 217
exaggeration, 163–64, 177
exercises, 67
for trills, *see under* trills
expression, 163–64, 223–24
appoggiaturas and, 109, 110

in choral singing, 169
da capo arias and, 188 (+ n. 1)
in improvised variations, 233, 234
in recitative, 171–72, 177, 179–80
trills and, 18, 131
see also Affect(s) *and* facial expression

Fabbris, Luca, 67 (n. 37)
facial expression/movements, 82, 157, 187
falsettists, 76
falsetto, 10, 67, 68 (+ n. 39), 75–77
development of, 76
low notes in, 77
words and, 77
Farinelli (Carlo Broschi), 24, 72 (+ n. 47),
  87, 152 (n. 3)
fashion, 186, 195–203, 226–27
and improvised variations, 235
Faustina, *see* Hasse, Faustina Bordoni
fermar la voce, 84 (+ n. 65), 184 (n. 3)
fermatas, 212–14
ornamentation and, 20, 141, 142,
  172–73, 214
Ferrein, Antoine, 9 (+ n. 32), 10, 41
  (+ n. 9), 78–80
figured bass, *see* continuo
flats, 53–54
flattering Affect, 94 (+ n. 15)
flexibility, 152, 153
see also agility
flute, tonguing, 152
food, 37, 86–87
Förster/Forstern, Caspar, 72 (+ n. 49)
Frederick II of Prussia (Frederick the Great),
  4–6, 28, 217 (n. 1)
and Agricola, 4, 5, 6, 7
artistic control, 5, 6, 13, 22
court, 3, 4 (n. 11)
and musical training, 2
and opera, 4–5, 7
and ornamentation, 2, 22 (+ n. 123)
and singers, 40 (n. 3), 197 (n. 18)
tastes, Agricola and, 1
Frederick, King of Sweden, 42 (n. 18)
French language, pronunciation, 25, 162
French style, 101, 131, 208
Fuhrmann, Martin Heinrich, 2 (n. 6)
Fux, Johann Joseph, 54 (n. 15)

Galen, 9, 10, 70 (n. 44), 78 (+ n. 60)
Galliard, John Ernest
on da capo arias, 188 (n. 1)
on major/minor semitones, 89 (n. 4)
on Tosi, 41 (n. 6)
translation of Tosi, 2 (n. 5), 45 (n. 1), 16
  (n. 79), 17, 27 (n. 157), 51 (n. 1),
  184 (n. 3)

on treatment of cadences in recitative, 26
gamut, *see* solmization
Garcia, Manuel, 36–37
Gasparini, Francesco, 27, 170
Gazzaniga, Giuseppe, 28
German language, 7
　regional variations, 81
　vowels in, 24, 81, 85, 157
Germany
　education in, 2
　pitch in, 83
　singers in, 3, 40 (n. 3), 42
gesture, 47 (n. 3), 163, 179
Gibelius, Otto, 55, 64
glissando
　trills in course of, 130–31 (+ nn. 7, 8)
　see also portamento
glottis, 70, 73, 74, 75
　and articulation, 152, 153
　and falsetto singing, 76
Gluck, Christoph Willibald, 27 (+ n. 160),
　35–36
"goat trill", 135
Goldschmidt, Hugo, 37
Gottsched, Johann Christoph, 163
graces, *see* ornamentation
Graun, Carl Heinrich, 2, 5, 42 (n. 23)
　compositions, 26, 197
　and Frederick the Great, 40 (n. 3)
　as singer, 197
　on singers, 42 (n. 21)
Graun, Johann Gottlieb, 5
grimaces, 82, 187
Grimaldi, Nicola (Nicolini), 177, 178
Grimarest, Jean Léonor le Gallois de, 163
Grossi, Giovanni Francesco (Siface), 193
　(+ n. 8), 194
Grünewald, Gottfried, 42 (+ n. 14)
gruppo, 19 (+ n. 104)
Guido of Arezzo, 54 (+ nn. 15, 17), 55

Handel, George Frideric, 3, 72 (n. 50)
　Agricola and, 4, 66 (n. 32)
　singers, 72 (n. 50), 75 (n. 56), 193 (n. 11),
　194
　use of detached slurring, 22 (n. 127), 160
　(n. 12)
hard hexachord, *see under* hexachords
harmony, need for singers to understand,
　86, 109, 232–33, 235
　see also composition
harpsichord, *see* keyboard instruments
Harriss, Ernest C., 2 (n. 5)
Hasse, Faustina Bordoni, 22–23, 24, 25, 32,
　152–53 (+ nn. 3, 5), 163, 178, 230
　(+ n. 10)
Hasse, Johann Adolph, 3, 26, 27, 35, 42

(n. 23), 75 (n. 56), 152 (n. 5), 197
　(+ n. 18)
Agricola and, 4
Frederick the Great and, 5
use of detached slurring, 160 (n. 12)
Hawkins, John, 2 (n. 5), 193 (nn. 10, 11,
　12), 194 (n. 14)
head voice, 10, 67 (+ n. 36), 68 (+ n. 39),
　73–77, 80
health, 67, 73, 85, 86–87, 218
Heinichen, Johann David, 199
Helm, Eugene, 6, 38
Heriot, Angus, 28
Hesse, Ernst Christian, 42 (n. 20)
Hesse, Johanna Elisabeth Döbricht, 42
　(+ n. 20)
Heuermann, Georg, 9, 78 (+ n. 62)
hexachords, 54–55
　hard/natural/soft, 55, 57–60
　see also solmization
Hiller, Johann Adam, 16
　and Agricola's *Anleitung*, 13 (n. 60), 14,
　34, 35
　on cadenzas, 30, 31
　examples for improvised variations, 235
　(n. 7)
　on ornamentation, 14, 21–22, 23, 67
　(n. 34), 234 (n. 5)
　on solmization, 8
　on voice production, 10
Hitzler, Daniel, 64
hocket effects, 33
Hogarth, William, 85
Holzhauser, Teresa, 42 (n. 19)
"howling", 157, 177
Hürlebusch, Conrad Friedrich, 42 (+ n. 16)

illness, 73, 87, 218
imitation (contrapuntal) in cadenzas, 211
imitation (copying others), 185, 191–92
　(+ n. 5), 221–22, 233
improvised variations, 30, 232–35
India, Sigismondo d', 14 (n. 65), 90 (n. 6)
instrumentalists
　dynamics, 199
　ornamentation, 120, 124
　as singing teachers, 223–25
　see also keyboard instruments, stringed
　　instruments *and* wind instruments
intensity fluctuations/pulsations, 22
　(+ n. 127), 26 (+ n. 155), 160
　(+ n. 12)
intonation, 65–66, 80
　in divisions, 157
　in trills, 129, 135
　see also semitones
invention, 232

see also composition *and* improvised variations

Italian language, 73 (n. 53), 164
  dialects, 81
  Frederick the Great and, 4
  vowels, 24, 27, 73 (+ n. 53), 85, 157 (+ nn. 8, 9)
    successive, 16
Italy, pitch in, 83

Jacobi, Erwin R., 38
Jahn, Otto, 36
John the Baptist, 55 (+ n. 19)
Jubal, 45

Kamiénski, Lucian, 34 (n. 203)
Kayserinn (?Elisabeth Kayser), 42 (+ n. 18)
Kelly, Michael, 42 (n. 17)
key signatures, 54
keyboard instruments
  ornamentation on, 20–21, 120, 132, 133, 134, 143
  pitch, 83
  split keys on, 65, 66
  tuning, 66 (+ n. 31)
  use in teaching singing and for self-accompaniment, 19–20, 32, 51, 86, 129, 185
keys, 11
  learning, solmization and, 53–54
  major/minor, 27, 198, 201
Krüger, Johann Gottlob, 9, 41 (+ n. 7), 70 (n. 44), 78

languages, 4, 73 (+ n. 53), 184
  see also French, German *and* Italian
laryngoscope, 36
larynx, checking movement of, 17 (n. 89), 18, 135 (+ n. 17)
Latin, 184
leaps, 66–7
  compound appoggiaturas and, 119
  deceptive, appoggiaturas and, 90, 108
  divisions and, 155
  dynamics and, 168
  and legato, 86
  in terminations, 116–17
learning
  necessity of, 216, 217, 219, 224, 236–37
  from other students, 166–67
legato, 86, 233
  appoggiaturas and, 97
Lemaire, Théodore, 2 (n. 5)
Leo, Leonardo, 67 (n. 35)
Leonesi, Luigi, 2 (n. 5)
Lessing, Gotthold Ephraim, 221
librettists, 73 (+ n. 53), 188

life-style, 86–87, 183, 187, 217
listening, 184–85, 189, 191, 212, 238
Lombardian pitch, 11, 82, 83
Lombardian style, 14 (+ n. 62), 15, 101–02, 120 (+ n. 29)
London, 217–18
long notes
  dynamics, 97, 168
  practice on, 84–86
Lotti, Antonio, 170, 193 (n. 12), 195 (+ n. 16)
Lotti, Signora, *see* Stella, Santa Scarabelli
loudness, *see* dynamics
Luigino, 193 (+ n. 10), 194
lung capacity, 165

madrigals, 170
Maffei, Giovanni Camillo, 24
Mairus, 64
major keys, 27, 198, 201
Mancini, Francesco, 178 (n. 8)
Mancini, Giambattista, 10
  on divisions, 21–22
  on *messa di voce*, 11 (n. 50), 184 (n. 3)
  on portamento, 191 (n. 3)
  on trills, 16 (+ n. 75), 17 (n. 90), 18
Manfredini, Vincenzo, 16 (n. 74), 29 (n. 168)
mannerisms, 82, 157, 187
Mara, Gertrud Elisabeth, 28, 72 (n. 48), 92 (n. 9)
Marcello, Benedetto, 52 (n. 6), 53 (n. 8)
marking time, 157
Marpurg, Friedrich, Wilhelm
  and Agricola's *Anleitung*, 1 (+ n. 1), 2 (n. 6), 8 (+ n. 30), 34
  Agricola's controversy with, 7, 20
  and ornamentation, 14, 20, 21, 139 (n. 19)
  terminology, 12 (n. 54), 25 (n. 146), 88 (n. 1)
  on Quantz, 230
  on rubato, 33–34
  and taste, 6
Martini, Johann Paul, 4
Mattheson, Johann, 16
  on breathing while sitting, 82 (+ n. 63)
  on cadenzas, 31
  on care of the voice, 87
  and ornamentation, 16, 17, 19, 131 (n. 12)
  terminology, 25 (n. 146), 88 (n. 1)
  on singers, 72 (+ n. 49)
  and solmization, 8, 54 (+ nn. 15, 16), 62 (n. 23)
mean-tone tuning, 66 (n. 31), 89 (n. 4)
mediocrity, 216–17, 237

Meissner, 81
memorization, 170, 179
    of divisions, 28
    of recitatives, 174 (+ n. 4)
Mersenne, Marin, 9 (n. 32), 64
messa di voce, 11, 14 (+ n. 64), 84–85
    (+ n. 65), 168, 184 (+ n. 3), 191
    in recitative, 171
    terms used for, 11, 84 (+ nn. 66, 67), 85
        (n. 70), 171 (n. 1), 184 (n. 2), 187
        (n. 6), 191 (n. 4)
messa di voce crescente, 14 (+ nn. 63, 65), 90
        (+ n. 6), 91, 154 (n. 6)
    drag and, 23 (n. 133)
Metastasio, Pietro, 4, 27, 178, 188 (n. 2)
metre, 106
Milanese pronunciation, 81
Mingotti, Pietro, 42 (n. 22)
minor keys, 27, 198, 201
mirror, use in practice, 82, 187
Mizler von Kolof, Lorenz, 55, 66
"Modern" style, *see under* "Ancient" style
modes, 198–99, 201
modulations, 179
Molteni, Benedetta Emilia, 6, 197 (n. 18)
Montagnana, Antonio, 72 (+ n. 50)
Montéclair, Michel Pignolet de, 90 (n. 6)
Monteverdi, Claudio, 18 (n. 92), 90 (n. 6)
mordents, 16, 20–21, 133–34, 142, 214, 227
    appoggiaturas and, 110, 114, 133–34, 156
    in divisions, 156
    in recitative, 25, 26, 176
    turns and, 143
motets, 181
mouth cavities, 71, 76, 85–86
Mozart, Leopold, 33 (n. 198), 34, 67 (n. 35),
        88 (n. 1)
Mozart, Wolfgang Amadé, 12, 42 (n. 17)
mucus, 87
music reading, 53, 216
musica ficta, 53 (n. 11)
mutation (in solmization), 8, 9, 57

Naples, pitch in, 83
national taste, 40
natural hexachord, *see under* hexachords
nerves, 167
    see also confidence
Neumann, Frederick, 6, 15–16, 17, 88
        (n. 1), 127 (n. 3), 160 (n. 12)
Nicolini (Nicola Grimaldi), 177, 178
nose, 71
    defects of, 51–52, 67, 73, 187
notation
    of dynamics, 169
    of ornaments, *see under* ornamentation *and*
        under appoggiaturas

notes, names/naming, 8 (n. 27), 54, 56
        (n. 22), 64
    see also solmization

oboe, voice compared to, 161
"Olibrio, Flavio Amicio," 40 (n. 4)
opera(s), 4, 178
    attending with scores, 189
    audience behavior at, 30–31, 167, 207
Opinioni, see under Tosi
orchestras, 4
ornamentation, 5–6, 19, 149–50, 225–26,
        232
    in arias, 28, 30–31, 189–91
    of cadences, 212–14
        see also cadenzas
    essential, 149
    notation, 14 (n. 65), 15, 20, 28
    notation to prevent, 13
    preparation of, 28 (+ n. 163), 31, 92
    in recitative, 25–26, 171, 172–73, 174–76
    register and, 75
    responsibility for, 2–3, 5–6, 12–13, 28,
        31, 91–92, 107, 138, 156, 187
    and rhythm, 15, 192–94
    in sicilianos, 158 (+ n. 10)
    uses/purposes, 166, 235
    see also appoggiaturas, cadenzas, divisions,
        improvised variations *and* trills
Orsini, Gaetano, 75 (+ n. 55)
overthrows, 115 (+ n. 27)
    see also terminations

palate, and articulation, 152, 153
Palestrina, Giovanni Pierluigi da, 45, 46
parallel octaves/fifths, 14, 29, 109, 199,
        207–08
passing notes, 106
pathetic style, 27 (+ n. 158), 184 (+ n. 1),
        195–97, 202, 223, 233, 234
pauses, *see* fermatas
performance(s), 46
    audience behaviour, 30–31, 167, 207
    need for variety in, 226, 229, 230
    nerves in, 167
    practicing/preparation for, 28 (n. 163),
        167, 182, 190–91
    requirement for self-accompaniment in,
        32 (+ n. 194), 185
    spaces and situations, 18, 162–63, 167,
        219
Pergolesi, Giovanni Battista, 27
phonation, *see* voice production *and* vowels
phrasing
    appoggiaturas and, 108–09
    see also words
physical mannerisms, 82, 157, 187

physiology, 9–10 (+ n. 32), 36–37, 41,
    68–71, 78–80
  of articulation, 152–53
  and trills, 17–18 (+ n. 89), 130, 135
    (+ n. 17)
Pirker, Franz Joseph Karl, 42 (n. 22)
Pirker, Marianne, 42 (+ n. 22)
Pistocchi, Francesco Antonio, 32, 193
    (+ nn. 7, 10), 194 (+ nn. 14, 15)
pitch, 10–11, 82–83
  dynamics and, 73–74 (+ n. 54)
  physical aspects, 69, 70, 79, 80, 135
    (+ n. 17)
  trills and, 129, 131
Pliny, 45
politics, musical, 226
Polybius, 45
Porpora, Nicola, 67 (n. 35), 72 (+ n. 47), 81,
    178–79
portamento, 86 (n. 71), 191 (n. 3), 223
    (+ n. 9), 234–35 (+ n. 5)
  in improvised variations, 232
  see also drag *and messa di voce crescente*
posture, 82
practice, 184
  and agility, 74–75
  injurious, 67
  in leaps, 66, 67
  mental, 184
  plan of, 84–86, 158
  suggestions for material, 169–70, 181
  time required for, 16, 85, 170, 186 (+ n. 5)
  timing of, 187
  see also exercises *and under* performance
Praetorius, Michael, 3
Pralltriller, 19–21, 130, 133 (n. 14), 140
pride, 219, 228
print size, 42
Printz, Wolfgang Caspar, 2 (n. 6), 162–63,
    169
Profe, Ambrosius, 8
pronunciation, 25, 63–64, 71, 85–86,
    161–63, 183–84
  register and, 77
  solmization and, 63–64
  Zarlino on, 47 (n. 3)
  see also vowels
pulse, 106 (+ n. 24)
  see also stress
punishment, 237
Puteanus, Erycius, 64
Pythagoras, 45

Quantz, Johann Joachim, 5, 42 (n. 10)
  and Affects, 94 (n. 15)
  Agricola and, 4, 12, 32, 41 (n. 6), 42, 66,
    169

and articulation, 152
and bass cadences, 29 (n. 174)
and cadenzas, 31, 212
and dynamics, 168–69
examples for improvised variations, 235
and ornamentation, 6, 13, 14 (+ n. 62),
    15, 21, 22 (n. 123), 131 (+ nn. 9, 11)
  appoggiaturas, 92 (n. 10), 93 (n. 11),
    101 (n. 18), 102 (n. 20)
  speed of trills, 18 (+ n. 94), 19
  and performance from memory, 174
    (n. 4)
  and rubato, 33, 193 (n. 12)
  and sicilianos, 158 (n. 10)
  on singers, 23, 75 (nn. 55, 56), 230
    (+ n. 11)
  terminology, 18 (n. 93), 88 (n. 1)
  and Tosi, 41 (n. 6)

Raaff, Anton, 42 (+ n. 17)
range, 67, 71–73, 77
  changes in, 67, 75, 80, 82–83
  physical basis, 70, 79–80
  register and, 74
  trills and, 18–19, 131
reading, 161, 162, 163, 183
  see also sight-singing
recitative, 25–26, 171–81
  cadences in, 25, 26, 174
  changing notes in, 174
  declamation and, 163, 177
  ornamentation in, 171, 172–73, 174–76
  practicing, 187
  rhythm in, 172, 173–74
  types, 171–72
recitativo accompagnato, 25 (+ n. 145), 26,
    173–74
reciting, 163, 177, 220
registers, vocal, 9–10, 67–68 (+ n. 39),
    73–77, 80
  agility and, 74–75
  breathing and, 74, 75
  transition between, 76, 77
  unification, 67–68
repeated notes, 152
  articulation, 160–61
  as ornament, 18 (n. 92)
rests, adding, after slides, 122–23
Reuther, Teresa de, 42 (+ n. 19)
rhetorical figures, 163
rhythm, 158–60, 169, 227
  in arias, 190, 192–94, 195
  in cadenzas, 205, 209, 210
  in divisions, 157
  dynamics and, 168
  in improvised variations, 232, 233
  in ornamentation, 15

in recitative, 172, 173–74
syncopated, 161
see also dotted rhythms *and* stress
ribattuta, 19
Riccoboni, François, 220 (+ n. 2)
Riccoboni, Luigi, 220 (+ n. 2)
Riemschneider, Johann Gottfried, 42
    (+ n. 15)
ripieno singing, 169
ritornellos, 180, 196
rivalry, 191–92 (+ n. 5), 219–20, 228
Rivani, 192–93, 194
"rockets," 225–26
Roger, Estienne, 194 (+ n. 14)
Rolli, Paolo Antonio, 42 (n. 15)
Roman pitch, 82, 83
Roman pronunciation, 81
Rosenblum, Sandra P., 33 (n. 197)
Rossini, Gioacchino, 36
rubato, 29 (n. 170), 32–34 (+ n. 188), 206,
    222–23, 227
    drag and, 23
    in improvised variations, 233
    terms for, 33, 222 (n. 6), 223 (n. 7)

Sainsbury, John, 42 (n. 18)
Sainte Albine, Rémond von, 220
Saletti, 72 (+ n. 51)
Salinbeni, Felice, 197 (+ n. 18)
Santini, *see* Stella, Santa Scarabelli
Santoni, Francesca Cuzzoni, 230 (+ n. 11)
Sauveur, Joseph, 10, 83
Scarlatti, Alessandro, 27
Schmeling, Gertrud Elisabeth, *see* Mara
Schneller, 130 (n. 6)
Schubart, Christian Friedrich Daniel, 42
    (n. 17)
science, 9, 10, 36–37, 41, 78–80
    see also physiology
scores, following, 189
semitones, major/minor, 65–66 (+ n. 31),
    88, 89–90
Senesino (Francesco Bernardi), 177–78
sgagateata, 22, 152, 153
shield-shaped cartilage, 79–80
sicilianos, 158
Siface (Giovanni Grossi), 193 (+ n. 8), 194
sight-singing, 53, 216
Simone, Pietro, *see* Agostini
Simonetti, 42 (+ nn. 20, 21)
singers
    employment prospects and situations, 3,
        4, 40 (n. 3)
    requirements in, 46, 183–87
singing
    books on, 2 (+ n. 6), 16, 21–22, 37–38,
        46–47

payment for, 3, 217, 218
teaching of, 2–3
    see also teachers
    see also voice(s) *and* voice production
Singspiel, 178 (+ n. 9)
slides, 15–16, 108, 119–25
    length, 120–23, 124
slurs/slurring, 22, 86, 153, 158, 161
    of appoggiaturas, 97, 161
    compound appoggiaturas, 119
    detached, 22 (+ n. 127), 26 (+ n. 155),
        160–61
    in divisions, 151, 153–54, 156
    drag and 23, 155, 235
    in improvised variations, 232, 233, 234
    notated, 14 (n. 65), 22
smiling, 82
snap, 130 (+ n. 6)
snapped turn, 148–49
soft hexachord, *see under* hexachords
softness, *see* dynamics
solfeggi, 65, 67 (n. 35)
solfeging, 62 (n. 24), 65, 85
    see also solmization
soliloquies, 173
solmization, 7–9, 38, 53–65, 85
Sorge, Georg Andreas, 66
sound production, 68–71, 78–79
    see also voice production
speakers, learning from, 163
speed
    developing, 155, 158
    see also under divisions *and under* trills
Sperling, Johann Peter Gabriel, 2 (n. 6)
Stella, Chiara, 193 (n. 12)
Stella, Santa Scarabelli (Signora Lotti), 193
    (+ n. 12), 195 (+ n. 16)
Stradella, Alessandro, 27, 198 (+ n. 23)
Strascino, *see* drag
stress, 104 (nn. 22, 23), 106 (+ n. 24)
    appoggiaturas and, 14, 15, 92–93
        (+ nn. 11, 12), 97, 101–02, 104, 106
    breathing and, 165
    in divisions, 155
    in dotted rhythms, 159
    ornamentation and, 14, 15–16, 20, 129
        see also appoggiaturas
    in slides, 120
    syncopation and, 161
    trills and, 20, 129
stringed instruments
    bowing, 22 (n. 127), 152, 153
    intonation in playing, 66
    vibrato, 149
strings, 69
    vocal cords and, 78
strong/weak beats, *see* stress

study, *see* learning
style, *see* "Ancient"/"Modern" style *and* taste
Suidas, 45
sustained noted, 84–86, 184 (+ n. 3)
swelling, *see messa di voce*
syncopation, 161, 234

taste, 5–6, 186, 195–203, 205–07, 212, 223–24
  imitation and, 185, 191–92
  in improvised variations, 232–33
  see also "Ancient"/"Modern" style
teachers
  number of, 224
  payment, 52–53 (+ n. 6), 170
  requirements in, 51–53, 170, 178, 181–82, 224–25, 230–31
Telemann, Georg Philipp, 24 (n. 140)
  Agricola and, 4, 34, 66 (n. 32)
  on singers, 42 (n. 20)
  and temperament, 66
  terminology, 12 (n. 54), 25 (n. 146)
temperament, *see* tuning
tempo, 151
  cadenzas and, 205, 209, 210
  in practicing, 155
  see also speed
tempo rubato, see rubato
terminations, 17, 19, 20 (+ n. 109), 110 (n. 26), 113–17, 129, 138–40, 143, 214
  breathing and, 166
  placing, 115
tessitura, 11, 74, 82–83
tetrachords, *see* solmization
theater, *see* acting *and* opera
theatrical recitative, 171, 173, 177
throat
  care of, 87
  defects of, 51–52, 67, 73, 187
thyroid cartilage, 79–80
time
  cadenzas and, 29
  in recitative, 25, 26
  see also rhythm, rubato, speed *and* tempo
Timotheus the Milesian, 45
tonalities, *see* keys
tongue, position of, 85, 86
Torelli, Giuseppe, 14 (n. 62)
Tosi, Pier Francesco, 1, 40, 41
  Agricola on, 40, 41, 42
  Opinioni, 1 (+ n. 2), 2–3
    translations of, 1–2 (+ n. 5)
    see also Agricola, *Anleitung*
  as singer, 41 (+ n. 6)
trachea, *see* windpipe
transposition, 11, 83

solmization and, 60–63
travel, 220
trilled turns, 147, 208
trillo, 18 (n. 92), 19, 152
trills, 16–21, 126–48
  and appoggiaturas, 19, 97, 110, 111–12, 129, 130, 135, 136, 138, 140, 141
  breathing and, 166
  and cadences, 207, 208, 214
  chains/rising/falling, 16–17 (+ n. 79), 130–31, 146
  consecutive, 136
  in divisions, 156
  double, 20, 131–33, 141, 142, 214
    in recitative, 25
  dynamics, 138
  ending, 136, 139
    see also terminations
  exercises for developing, 16, 17, 19, 38, 128–29, 135–36
  initial note, 17, 127 (+ n. 3), 129–30, 132, 134
  length, 139
  notation/symbols for, 130, 132, 133, 134, 141, 142
  physical aspects, 128–29, 135
  placement on/before beat, *see* stress
  placing, 20, 135, 136–38, 140, 141–42, 146
  preparation, 135
  in recitative, 172, 174
  register and, 68, 75
  rhythm, 138, 139
  rising/falling/chains, 16–17 (+ n. 79), 130–31, 146
  speed, 18–19, 129, 131, 135, 142
  and stress, 20, 129
  terminations, *see* terminations
  of a third, 75
  and turns, 146
  types, 16, 127–34, 140
triplets, 160
  breathing during, 165
truncated cadences, 26, 180–81 (+ nn. 11, 12), 204
tuning, 65–66 (+ n. 31), 89 (n. 4)
  see also intonation, pitch *and* semitones
Türk, Daniel Gottlob, 13 (+ n. 60), 15, 34–35, 120 (n. 29)
turns, 20, 140, 143–49
  appoggiaturas and, 113
  placing, 144–49
  in recitative, 25
  rhythm, 143, 144, 148–49
  and slides, 123
  trilled, 147
Tuscan pronunciation, 184

type size, 42

Ulrich, Bernhard, 35

Vanini (Boschi), Francesca, 193 (+ n. 11), 194
variations
    improvised, *see* improvised variations
    use of keyboard for inventing, 86
    writing out, 92
    see also ornamentation
Venetian pitch, 83
vibration, 68–69, 73, 78
vibrato, 21 (+ n. 115), 149, 184 (n. 3)
Vinci, Leonardo, 27
virtue, 183, 217, 219
vocal cords, 78–79
voice(s), 67, 71, 73
    age and, 75, 80, 82–83
    break between registers, 9, 11, 76
    breaking, 72, 80, 170
    care of, 85, 86–87, 158, 170, 183
    forcing, 158
    compared to instruments, 79, 149–50,
        161–62
    preference for high, 84
    see also range, registers *and* voice
        production
voice production, 9–10 (+ n. 32), 36–37, 41,
        68–71, 78–80, 165
    feeling, 79
    and trills, 17–18 (+ n. 89), 130, 135
        (+ n. 17)
    see also articulation, breathing *and*
        registers
Vorschlag, see appoggiaturas
vowels, 8, 37, 80–82, 85–86
    articulation during, 151–53, 157
    changing, 158
    comfort of singing, 73 (+ n. 53)

and detection of falsetto, 68
and divisions/cadenzas/improvised
    variations, 24, 27–28 (+ n. 156),
    157, 208 (+ n. 4), 233
and *messa di voce*, 84
physical aspects, 162
practicing on, 85–86
and registers, 10
successive, in Italian, 164

watering-can-shaped cartilage, 79–80
Wichmann, Kurt, 9, 38, 69 (n. 42), 72
    (n. 52)
wind instruments
    pitch, 83
    tonguing/articulation, 152, 153
    voice production and, 69, 70
windpipe, 69–71, 72, 73–74, 75, 77–78, 79
    and articulation, 152
    and trills, 130, 135
women/girls, 53 (+ n. 8)
    care of voices, 170
    and composition, 187
    and copying, 221
    transition between registers, 76
    voices not breaking, 73, 80
words, 161–62
    appoggiaturas and, 93, 107, 110
    breathing and, 24 (+ n. 136)
    ornamentation and, 208 (n. 4), 214
    place in practice plan, 86
    in recitative, 178–79
    and trills, 139
    see also reading *and* vowels
Wucherpfennig, Hermann, 36, 37

Zarlino, Gioseffo, 47 (+ n. 3)
Ziehen, 23, 151 (n. 2), 234 (n. 5)